The
Ultimate

IT Project Manager

A PLETHORA OF WISDOM IN ACHIEVING
EXECUTIVE LEVEL RECOGNITION & PERFORMANCE

DONATO PICCINNO

FIRST EDITION
FOREWORD BY RAYMOND AARON
NY Times Bestselling Author

For

Catherine, Luca, Nico & Rosa

Mum, Dad, Nat, Nay, V

Mia, Giovanni, Romano, Tony, Owen

Clara, Shauna, Connor

Kevin, Chris, Andy

Special Thanks to

Imran Siddiqui MD for www.ecomsoftware.co.uk

10-10-10 Programme

Saul Cozens

Martin Webster

James Randall

Richard Clarke

MC 2

The ITIL Mitchell Brothers. Ashley Ward & Jonathan Cooper

Rob Shoreson

Gavin Browett

Asaf Rashid

Cameron Gillian

The Circle of Trust

Scott Mason

Edward Day

Stuart Robson

Scott Cooper

Sarah Louise McGovern

TABLE OF CONTENTS

Table of Contents

FOREWORD

WITH THE VAST CHANGES IN technology currently affecting IT Project Management, Donato's book is very timely. It doesn't give you pretty pictures and templates; instead it makes you think and learn and solve problems before they happen. He provides a wealth of information about how to think differently, as well as practical advice on how to manage projects when the only certainty is uncertainty.

I met Donato in February 2013 when I showed him how to break an arrow with his throat! He learned from me that you can do whatever you put your mind to - you just have to change your way of thinking.

He has a high level of competence in his field, given his years of experience with several top companies. And he has applied his competence and thoroughness in his writing too. It shows in this book - it shows because the book is real and practical.

Laced throughout the book are anecdotes that expose Donato's experience and sense of humour. He tells you what can go right and what can go wrong. There are many IT Project Management books on the market but none match the honesty, realism, depth and usefulness of this one. I think it will be an invaluable resource for anyone involved in the world of IT Project Management and I thank Donato for the incredible amount of dedication and effort he has put into making this book available. He brings his vast real-world experiences and personality to life in this book. It's real and it's honest. It's a must-have.

I am honoured to be associated with this book and its author. I think it's a winner.

Raymond Aaron

INTRODUCTION

D O YOU LIKE THE BOOK cover? Don't worry - I'm not going to use my contacts back home to put a horse's head in your bed, if you don't like my book. *The Godfather*, by Mario Puzo, is the ultimate fable for anyone interested in redemption. *Redemption is an act of redeeming or atoning for a fault or mistake, or the state of being redeemed.* Redemption requires one to want to 'make a difference'.

My fate was a series of career moves culminating in becoming embroiled in a money-munching scheme that Martin Scorsese's *Goodfellas* would be proud of i.e. the delivery of IT projects. Just look at the statistics from Gartner, whose studies show 75% of IT projects fail. Every year I read the headlines from Standish. In the eternal words of Run DMC, it goes a little something like this:

- 32% of all projects succeeded: delivered on time, on budget, with required features.

- 44% were challenged: late, over budget, and/or with less than the required features.

- 24% failed: cancelled prior to completion or delivered and never used.

Looking at the Standish figures, the chances of delivering a successful IT project are 1 in 3. The Project Management Institute estimates that 70% of all projects fail, costing the global economy $6.2 trillion every year. Delivering IT projects is enterprise-wide knowledge work and it has become a bastion of irrationality.

Here is my opening gambit. We've become completely dependent on email to report on status. Most of our conversations about important work-related matters are done through text messaging - some instant and some not. Is that really the most effective norm for planning together, designing together, building together and testing together? Most people would answer 'No' but we continue doing it, knowing full well it is a suboptimal way of working. According to Attask, a leader in enterprise workflow management, using email in this manner consumes half our working day, and costs a company more than $19,000 per enterprise worker, per year. It is no wonder we do not have time to get the work done.

We are being overwhelmed with information to the point where I sense people feel incapacitated. How many other accepted ways of working are causing mis communication and latency on your average IT project? The answer is not quantifiable but the impact is. Look at the figures. A Forrester Research study identified a 66% project failure rate costing U.S. businesses at least $30 billion every year. Gartner uncovered that 40% of problems are found by users. And in 2007, a Dynamic Markets Ltd study concluded up to 80% of budgets are consumed fixing self-inflicted problems. In 1990, UK government wasted £1.5bn on a project to computerise benefit payments at post offices. Fast forward 10 plus years and exactly the same mistakes were made on the NHS NpFIT programme. It is like a blind-folded man bumping into a lamp post, then removing the blind fold only to continually bump into the same lamp post. These failures are not the result of one big mistake but the accumulation of many small acts of irrationality by managers, decision makers and teams during the project life cycle.

My book is an act of redemption, as it attempts to improve the odds of success, by imparting wisdom learned in the best way possible - by actually doing it and then seeing it work or not work, in practice. My book is 80% of what they don't teach you. The other 20% is what you do to make it better than what I've come up with. Alternatively, you could buy a book on silver bullet methodology; one of those painting by numbers books that makes you believe in following a few prescriptive flow charts to guarantee success. If that were true, Gartner, Standish and the myriad of authors on IT project failure, would not have much to write about.

Prescriptive methodology is only successful when it is fed with perfect information, followed by everyone involved in enacting the method, behaving perfectly rationally. Today's workplace is a hotbed of irrationality, politics, much ado about nothing, competing self-interests - all courtesy of globalisation, digitization, fewer people to do the work, disruptive technologies, multi-sourcing, overt political correctness, covert political correctness, junk food, pointless rules and austerity measures. The chances of one method delivering success in that kind of climate are zilch. The follow-me-I'm-right-behind-you-management consultants eulogising the single silver bullet method, have most definitely become purveyors of Hollywood science.

You may be one of those who subscribes to a school of thought that believes poor triple constraint management is the root cause of weak performance. To guarantee success, all you need to do is find a good project manager who can count, particularly those good at counting time, money and measures of quality. Measuring performance in terms of delivering a specific output to time, budget and quality works in the world of certainty. Maybe today's business environment is now so uncertain that the only certainty on an IT project is a constantly changing set of business requirements. In that kind of climate, anyone playing the role of an IT Project Manager, will need to think differently about how the work gets done. So the questions you need to ask yourself are: How do you measure the performance of an IT Project Manager when the requirements are constantly changing? How should an IT PM think and act? What do I need to learn and how can I learn it? What if the only measurement that matters is how much value a project manager delivered before the cash ran out and the resources ran out of the door? Have you been conditioned to think in a certain way that was designed for life before digitisation? Project Manager 2015+ will have less control and direct authority over budget and resources. They have all the responsibility and none of the authority; nothing less than an emphatic performance will be expected. IT Project Manager 2015+ not only needs to know how to manipulate and measure the triple constraints; they also need to know other qualitative performance traits known to lead to the creation of value. In a maelstrom of ever-changing business requirements: clarity; fun; unity; agility; confidence; well being; conflict; trust; communication enablement; and flow are more important than time, budget and quality.

The book is for anyone embarking on a career in IT Project Management or for those wanting to better themselves at what they currently do. The problem with text books on IT Project Management is that they are just not memorable enough. So I've made use of memorable mementos from popular culture in recent times, to get the messages across.

Andy Warhol made a tin of soup look interesting so I am going to do the same with the world of IT Project Management. You will find a few references to 'It is a hard knock life'. So what follows is a philosophical pretentious pastiche of metaphorical kitsch. Time to reject the loonfest ways of working that IT Project Management has become. Your next IT project does not need to be embryonic, statistical fodder for the next Gartner and Standish Report. Just don't follow rules designed for the change game in another age. Be the maverick artist and coat your IT project work of art with the sheen of certainty. You can give Standish and Gartner writer's block. I will go first.

The content in the book is geared towards the following themes: thinking differently; what to measure; how to measure; the environment; and guides to a number of different IT projects. Delivering those projects, coupled with measuring what matters most, along with greater mindfulness of the environment in which the project is being delivered, will give you an increased level of distinctive competence and the confidence to deliver any IT project within its acceptability threshold.

HAPPY MONDAYS?

'We wanna be free to do what we wanna do.'

Loaded

Primal Scream

HEARD THE NEWS TODAY - oh boy. And though the news was rather sad, well I just had to laugh. So what have I read that was sad, then made me laugh? I read the reasons why I want you to read this book! Don't know about you guys but as an IT Project Manager, I'm doing more chasing and having more arguments about getting work done than I did 5 years ago. Every day, I want to stand on the desk in the office space with a loud megaphone and a booming sound system behind me then shout, 'STOP, COLLABORATE AND LISTEN!' But I'm no Vanilla Ice turned scrum master. I'd also look stupid. Instead, I have trawled through the web to find some data on why I'm having more battles with middle management about getting things done, and why I'm having to play the game of phones, tracking down an engineer to do something that the engineer they gave me last time, could not do. The one before that had to go home early. His wife's cat died. I told him if he finished the job, I'd buy him two cats. He called me insensitive and hung up.

I have two options: explain to the client they cannot do their office move because a cat has died; or find another engineer at the 11th hour. But that's my story. Assuming everyone who will ever read this book is a Project Manager below is your story. Conclusion - your mellow is being twisted.

Over a third of you have been in IT Project Management for an average of 15 years; 50 per cent, 10 years or less; and the rest over 20 years.

90% of you will have a formal certification in Project Management. The rest need to go on a course after reading this book. Most of you will have concluded that the organisation paying for your training does not do what was taught on those courses.

50% of you will be stalked and harassed by a PMO for your timesheets, highlight reports and registers. The rest are lucky.

30% of you complain daily about important information for the project being all over the place. Within that 30%, there are a number of you who cannot answer queries from directors or executives about the project because you don't have the information instantly to hand. 10% will sit in meetings thinking why am I here? 20% will have constant concerns about poor collaboration across teams. 20% are frustrated and feel disempowered because requests for project work come in from all angles. 20% have no idea about the project team's workload or capacity because you just don't have the information.

Over a third of you will use email and spreadsheets as your favourite project management tool. 45% will use Microsoft Project. The rest use other tools because they hate using MS Project. Most of you will not be aware of the awesome new tools available as cloud services. Nor will the organisations you work for.

40% of you will use a waterfall approach most of the time.

More than 50% of you think your project team's workload has increased since last year.

70% of you will spend up to 40% of your time on status

update type activities. The rest of you aill spend between 40-50% of working time on this.

All of you cannot know at any one time what everyone expects you to know.

Most of you just want to deliver to time, budget and quality (2TB&Q) 100% of the time.

Up to 33% of the total project portfolio delivered by you guys will be delivered 2TB&Q.

Want to change the story? Live a working life less ordinary? Want to get off the plane?

'I'm not too sure where I've been; I've just got off a plane, mate. I think it was Spain or Norway or some mad place like that... I will ask Bez'

Shaun Ryder Happy Mondays

DON'T INADVERTENTLY SATISFICE, AIM TO BEAT THE PLAN

'I've been trying to impress that more is less and I'm repressed'

Getting Away With It

Electronic

As an IT Project Manager, you may have been inadvertently conditioned to 'satisfice? What does it take to realise this may be true - an epiphany? Generally, the term is used when an enlightening realization allows a problem or situation to be understood from a new and deeper perspective. What do you do? Try to carry on and solve the problem with the same thinking that created it? If Einstein was still around, he would not consider these people as rational.

When you constantly read about your trade failing, it gets to you. The fear of failure starts to become your best friend but being afraid to fail can make you over-cautious. I always have these weird dreams after reading stuff on IT project failure. The most vivid one is a dream where I am clay pigeon shooting with the worst project sponsor I have ever worked with. In the dream, I am asked about how I am going to make sure the project happens. I then ask the same question of the sponsor. The next thing I know, I'm a pigeon flying up very quickly.

The commentators talk a lot about the linkage between the fear of failure and poor performance. Are they really saying IT projects are scary clowns that live in the drains and we fail because we are afraid of what's involved? I have had a few dreams about running away from that guy but I would never describe an IT project as scary.

A more reasonable starting point for IT project failure would be the project was set up to fail and the problems were not spotted before it was too late. Alternatively, the project was set up to fail, the team knew this at the time but for some reason they did not do anything about it. Whatever way you look at it, there were flaws in the way the project was conceived, approached or implemented. Yet given the money involved and operational consequences, I find it hard to believe that anyone would deliberately set an IT project on the road to failure. Why do so many IT projects fail to perform in line with the expectations of the people paying the bill, then go on to make the same mistakes? The reasons for failure are well documented but it keeps happening. What if those delivering IT projects have become inadvertently conditioned to fail, in environments not conducive for IT project delivery?

It's a bit of a double whammy - like the day in the life of Louis Winthorpe III from the film Trading Places. However, Louis Winthorpe III was not conditioned to fail; he was set up to fail by two crafty old buggers. The rest of this book is about hidden dynamics setting us up to fail.

This chapter is about what we are classically taught to believe when it comes to measuring the performance of IT Project Management. We are taught to focus on measuring the triple constraints. We are taught that success is defined by delivering on time and on budget within preconceived constraints. Over the last 10 years I have attended many a must-do-better speech by a Director. I am grateful to some of them, as I have used the experience to perfect the technique of sleeping with my eyes open. The message is always the same - follow the method and deliver on plan. I tend to enter those meetings feeling like Bill Murray in the film Ground Hog day. When I come out of those sessions, I'm a Forrest Gump repeatedly muttering to myself, 'OK lieutenant Dang.'

Most of the definitions for Project Management and Churchillian speeches use the word 'on'. It is a word the experts and customers use all of the time when defining measures of success for a project. It is clear to me the language of Project Management is synonymous with the word satisfice i.e. an endeavor to meet an acceptability threshold. Satisfice is about just doing enough or the bare minimum to get away with it. That is exactly what a challenged delivery feels like i.e. it's merely about snatching victory from the jaws of defeat.

I'd never really thought about satisficing until I attended one of those boring must-do-better presentations from the headmaster. He stood up and spoke about the usual need-to-do-better and stated the reasons why. I started to sense that this presentation was different from all the others I'd been to, over the last 15 years. First, everyone was standing up and secondly, the Director giving the presentation was quite passionate and funny. Then the strangest thing happened; he told every project manager and programme manager not to deliver on plan! I thought he'd lost the plot. Then he said, 'I want you to beat the plan. I don't care how you do it - just do it.' I felt very uneasy about those words for a few days. The reason I felt uneasy was because I could not recall a single occasion in the last 5 years of my career where I challenged myself to beat the plan. Don't get me wrong; 99% of my projects were delivered within client expectation. But I can honestly say I never felt compelled to challenge either myself, or every single way of working I was expected to follow.

Therein lies the rub. Without a great booming driving internal voice challenging you, you become naturally inclined to accept that what worked last time will be just as optimal next time around. Organisations are deliberately designed to get us to behave in a certain way. So it is not unreasonable to assume the manager is being shaped by the organisation they work for. How many organisations do you know that are deliberately designed and governed for optimal IT Project Management performance?

If satisfice were a child, its parents would be 'satisfy' and 'sacrifice'. So the question is - what are we sacrificing when we satisfice? I have always wondered what my working day would be like if everyone around me had attitudes like Anthony Robbins, Usain Bolt, Serena Williams and Manny Pacquiao. These people do not do the language of satisifice. They are people who go beyond their perceived abilities. However, when we satisfice we sacrifice that possibility. I'm left wondering that if all those challenged deliveries were made up of people with an attitude found in highly focused individuals with total self belief in their abilities, would the success rate increase?

What does it mean to beat the plan? I could re-word the classical definitions found in Project Management, but those definitions were written for IT project delivery in less uncertain times. A controversial starting position would be the following statement: 'Whatever you will finally deliver, it won't be what you originally thought you would deliver.' Is this statement *that* controversial? Let's just accept the fact that all final IT solutions will have some variation from the original design. The greater the complexity of the solution delivered against a set of uncertain requirements, the greater the risk of variation. Now when you read the word variation, what was your immediate reaction as an IT Project Manager? Did you instantly assume that variation maybe healthy for the project? What if the variation resulted in value greater than what was promised? What if the variation increased the benefits in the business case? To beat the plan, you must deliver more value than what was originally promised. You won't do that if you have a satisfice mind-set. The implication here is that you have to measure your own acceptable performance threshold, then exceed it. How you do that is the subject of the rest of the book.

Japanese anime and contemporary comic books contain some of the most reluctant heroes you can ever imagine. Until circumstances dictate, they tend to have hidden abilities they don't want to use. Their ultimate nemesis is always a reflection of themselves. The reflection knows what the hero knows. How do you beat your reflection when your reflection can both move independently and do exactly what you do, at the exact same time? They become better than their reflection by doing stuff they thought they could never do. They do not accept the limitations imposed on them by others.

However, this is not enough to beat the plan. When you work on a challenged or impaired IT project, the environment is quite negative. Pointless politics, delusion and the avoidance of accountability are prevalent. Would it be unreasonable to assume that successful IT projects are more positive than negative? Being positive is a frequently used term in organisations today. I prefer the word 'happy'. When people are happy, they are positive. It's a cliché statement and a no-brainer. If the organisational structure, culture and ways of working do not lend themselves to the science behind happiness, then there will be less positivity. What if the psychology of happiness was more prevalent on the 33% of successful IT projects identified by Standish? Fundamentally, your chances of beating the plan are significantly reduced if you are not happy and your happiness is your responsibility. Today's large blue chip organisations are not exactly what I would describe as liberating organisational design; liberating in the sense the organisation is intentionally designed to get the best out of your average human being. Therein lies the paradox; sorting out less than ideal situations by design that cause negativity and cynicism, has to be a source of happiness for you. There is an excellent website (calleam. com/WTPF/?page_id=2338) that lists the 101 reasons why IT projects fail. Now go and read the list. To beat the plan, stopping the causal factors behind the 101 common causes has to make you happy. If the answer is yes, read on. If the answer is no, put the book down and think about a different career.

MEET YOUR NEW BEST FRIENDS. CLARITY, UNITY & AGILITY

'So don't become some background noise.'

Radio Ga Ga

Queen

T O BEAT THE PLAN YOU have to be swift. It's about you creating the most value; smarter and faster than anyone else thinks you can. Yet, even with all the controls and methodology in place and detailed graphs measuring the triple constraints, IT projects still fail. An exclusive focus on time, budget and quality appears only to lead to superficial swiftness; lots of activity, but little forward motion. There are three people-factors that can provide a powerful accelerator for performance: clarity (understanding the goal); unity (cross-company collaboration); and agility (adapting quickly). Maybe more of your time should be spent measuring the critical stuff you cannot see. Meet the critical friends you need in an uncertain world - Clarity, Unity and Agility.

'Sixth Sense' is a film about a boy who sees what everyone else around him cannot see. The film has a well known twist in the tale. The expert is not the expert he thinks he is. All the clues were around him yet he failed to realise the reality of the situation. The Sixth Sense was not the first film in this genre. The exact same thing happened to Donald Sutherland in 'Dont Look Now'. He instantly assumed the little person running around in the red coat was harmless. Both films teach us we should be wary of our perception filters. The child in the red coat is a classic cliché in Hollywood, designed to get our attention. I think the film makers all know we've been told the story of Little Red Riding Hood. Little people in red coats shrouded in mystery, means something bad might be about to happen. We've become accustomed to red indicating danger. Now that's OK if the danger is obvious but what if the warning signs are intangible and you are not consciously looking for them? You end up like the lead characters in films like Dont Look Now and the Sixth Sense.

Backtrack to May 2012 and despite my best efforts, I had a potentially impaired delivery on my hands. Those penny-dropping moments are always followed by a tsunami of hindsight. The root causes were so obvious; but the question on my mind was if they were so obvious, why were they not spotted before they became a problem? In the latter part of the film Jurrasic Park, an experienced big game hunter stalks a vicious raptor. He spots it and hones in on his target, then suddenly realises he has fallen into a trap he did not spot. That is exactly how I felt. The project was overloaded with experienced people and all the governance you could think of. I've read numerous books on the root cause of project failure. All the symptoms were present on my impaired delivery as it lay on the stretcher on its way to triage. On reflection, I was measuring all the traditional measures but was I measuring what matters most?

IT Project Managers are taught to focus performance measurement on time, budget and quality. Adept managers, innovators and leaders measure the ingredients that can lead to the creation of performance. I have seen some of the most sophisticated measures in excel to measure schedule and cost performance. If there were ever a cure for insomnia or premature ejaculation, working with and interpreting those spreadsheets would be it. However, if those spreados are having the same effect as Viagra, best to seek professional medical advice. So the question is, what matters most in IT project delivery and can you measure it? Maybe challenged projects were not measuring the universal ingredients that indicate the presence of a management environment with a propensity for successful performance or one with a propensity for poor performance.

What if there was a measurement system that could indicate a management environment's propensity for success? What would it measure? My starting point is that the performance of an IT project is inextricably linked to the performance of people. My next point would be that the nuts and bolts of IT Project Management is about getting value-adding work done within an acceptability threshold. So when the propensity to get the value-adding work done is high, the chances of success are high. My final point would be to design a generic measurement system that measures what matters most to get the work done. You would need to conceptually understand the factors that lead to high performance. I was taught 12 years ago that a person's performance is a function of ability, opportunity, motivation and expectation. It is simplistic and it is easy to understand.

Ability	The necessary skills and experience to complete the work.
Opportunity	The creation of the circumstances necessary to complete the work.
Motivation	The reasons why you do not need an alarm clock to remind you of the working day ahead.
Expectation	Clear articulation of what is expected of the individual completing the work.

Now imagine all those people working on your IT project and influencing its success. An unchecked accumulation of deficiency in any one of those variables, results in poor project performance. Now ask yourself this question. When was the last time, in your role as an IT Project Manager, that you paused for breath and measured ability, opportunity, motivation and expectation across your IT project? You probably didn't for three reasons: you did not know how to; this stuff is hard to measure; and it's not your job. After all, this people stuff is the job of line managers. Given that these variables are inextricably linked to the performance of your project, would it not be prudent to measure this stuff? Actually, I believe it is too difficult to focus on measuring ability, opportunity, motivation and expectation. It's all pretty intangible and no-one is going to openly admit to lack of ability or poor motivation. Just like in the cult film 'Office Space', Peter Gibbons, a disillusioned software developer at Initech, spends his days "staring at his desk" instead of working. The Vice President Bill Lumbergh prowls the floor. As soon as Peter sees him, he pretends to be interested in his work.

If ability, motivation, expectation and opportunity are like seeds, then what kind of climate stops them growing into John Wyndham's creation from his 1951 book, 'Day of the Triffids'? When you measure climate, you sample heat, light and humidity. Meet the gardeners nurturing performance in an uncertain and complex marketplace for FTSE 500 companies - The Forum Corporation. The Forum Corporation was founded by Harvard Business School graduates. In their book 'Strategic Speed', they identify why some organisations are quicker at transformation than others. The Forum Corporation has identified 3 core behaviours creating momentum towards success; clarity, unity and agility.

Clarity

Communicating a shared, clear understanding of the
transitional situation and direction.

Unity

Demonstrating a wholehearted agreement on the
merits of the direction and the need to work together
to move ahead.

Agility

A willingness to turn and adapt quickly while keeping
goals in mind.

Forum have taken it one step further. The Forum Corporation have come up with some easy-to-ask questions and ratios to measure clarity, unity and agility. The web is full of blogs on IT project failure and Amazon is full of books on the topic. If you look at the causes of poor IT project performance, they are symptomatic of poor unity, clarity and agility. I have reflected on the challenged and impaired IT project deliveries I have worked on. They were prevalent with examples of disunity, inflexibility and lack of clarity. The great thing about The Forum approach is simplicity. It is a quick temperature-check and a far more interesting use of time, than green shifting a highlight report. The problem with classical project management controls is that they point to the symptoms of the onset of failure and not underlying root cause. To beat the plan, you have to ask questions that leaders of the most successful organisations in the world ask of their project teams:

Would it not be to your advantage to understand whether
or not current organisational design and culture sets a
context which increases the chances of IT project failure?

Would it not be more insightful to understand whether or not the whole project team is empowered to deliver, before they commit to a delivery?

Would it not be more collaborative using measurement tools to encourage dialogue around the level of motivation, ability, opportunity and expectation within the project?

Why is everyone busy yet nothing is getting done?

The free to download app(available on iTunes June 2015) for my book gives you access to an application that will allow you to measure your IT project's level of clarity, agility and unity on a weekly basis. The application will provide you with a simple chart and pointers to improve these 3 behaviours. All you have to do is identify a small bunch of trusted positive sceptics involved in your delivery. Then invest 2 hours per week talking to them 1-2-1 around a set of core questions. By talking openly about what matters most to achieve project success, you will identify actions to improve relationships across the project. You will start to free your project from ambiguity. Give yourself the information to rapidly think and draw conclusions about what matters most. You will increase propensity to get value-added work done within the acceptability threshold.

LEARN A LITTLE. BRAG A LITTLE

'They want to know your secret. But you are
not telling'

Brilliant Mind

Furniture

E VERY IT PROJECT HAS A bit of everything. Feeling the
love in the room when an IT project plan comes together,
now means you have to know a bit about everything, thus
requiring a seismic shift from specialist to generalist, then back
again.

Management consultants come up with the most exotic
words to describe a transformational change in state, as the
result of newfound knowledge and the need to use it: seismic
shifter; paradigm shift; and the point of inflection; to name
a few. Given the pace of technical change, the bombardment
of technical information and the theory behind leveraging
technology, the task of staying in the know is akin to a scene
from the film *Inception*. The technical information that you
need, to be an effective IT Project Manager, is constantly
changing. Wouldn't it be great if you could plug yourself into a
machine, like Neo did in the film *The Matrix,* to fill your brain

with all the technical information you needed to do your job? I'm thankful such a device does not exist. Everyone would become an expert in everything, probably learn every martial art known to man, no one would agree, there would be lots of fights and nothing would get done. On a serious note, it is clear to me that a root cause of IT project failure is the allocation of inexperienced PMs. A cause of the inexperience can be lack of a basic technical understanding of the technology underlying the solution, coupled with a lack of appetite to learn about it.

Another reason why I felt compelled to write this chapter is to help anyone new to the world of ICT, considering a career in IT Project Management. I'm sure one of their aims is to identify the knowledge required to be effective IT Project Manager. It is a daunting task when you consider the vast array of topics and specialisms in the world of IT. Secondly, what you absorb as information, is not knowledge until you try to use it for a purpose.

In my experience as an IT Project Manager, you are expected to be an expert in whatever you are delivering. If not, your credibility takes a dive. The technical community will perceive you as a manager walking around with a banana stuck in each ear. They will say, "What do you call that guy with the bananas stuck in his ears?" "Anything you like - he cannot hear you!' There was this one project where I had to deliver resilient-wide area networking between an operational site and a data centre. I had heard on the grapevine that the network designer was not too happy about a PM with minimal technical understanding, leading the delivery. I'd never met the guy. So I did a bit of reading on the network solution, mainly because networking is three letter acronym over-load. He wanted a pre-meet 'to brief me on what I should say before meeting the client'. I knew it was not a meeting about that. He was going to tell me how concerned he was about the project being led by someone who was not as technically savvy as he was. Before he could say anything I said, "Circuit procurement lead-time on the MPLS is a bit of challenge. Hope there are no problems hooking it up to the POP. The client wants resilience. Hope we've got clarity on the need for diverse high. What about QOS?" He never questioned my technical experience ever again. I'm glad he didn't because for all I knew, multi-packet label switching was something shelf stackers did in supermarkets, QOS was a cheap packet of washing power and diverse high was a high energy hip hop dance crew!

Not knowing a bit about the technical domain of IT, accompanied by a lack of interest, is like running a garage without any knowledge of cars and being interested in hiking. There are two very important reasons why you should invest your own time in learning about what you are delivering. A significant part of an IT Project Manager's role is dealing with technicians and subject matter experts. Without technical knowledge, how would you know if they are telling the truth? How would you manage car mechanics and build a working relationship if you did not have an elementary knowledge of what they do and what they work with? The role of an IT project manager does contain an element of being a translator. In today's world, an IT Project Manager has to work across many business domains which span an organisation and its boundaries. These domains all have their own language: marketing speak; financial speak; HR speak; security speak; the language of logistics; the dialogue of distribution etc. The role of an IT Project Manager 2015+ involves being a bridge between these worlds and the world of IT. Project management has its own language full of words that many won't understand. Achieving clarity and engendering unity, requires an ability to translate for those who are not from the world of IT. There are those in the industry with a vested interested in making the role of IT Project Manager look complicated and full of mysticism.

I don't think anyone would disagree that an understanding of the technology behind the solution, the environment in which it operates and the theory to get value from it, is a prerequisite for the job. The challenge is working out what you need to know and knowing when you know enough to get you going. The secondary challenge is keeping the information bank topped up. This chapter describes a process that works for me and attempts to list the topics that you need an understanding of, to be a generalist IT Project Manager 2015+.

Knowing something about everything is to your advantage. Even the smallest IT projects I come across involve servers, networks, applications, security, service management, active directory and so on. As I write this chapter, I am witnessing the inception of a wifi and LAN device rollout for a well known UK company. The project has touch points with a tier 4 data centre, android end-user devices, a building site, the power supply and some pointy things that shoot hidden lasers across the rooftops. Think very carefully about this question: "What type of 'beat the plan' PM does the organisation, delivering this project, need?"

A specialist network PM?

A PM expert in everything except networks, with the ability to learn about network devices?

An IT PM with a passion for learning new things and with a track record of delivering projects they have never done before?

There is no obvious answer unless you ask the question, "Which one of these PMs is more likely to thrive in the current climate of economic uncertainty and constant technical change?" Under these circumstances I think you know the answer. If you want to be the latter type of PM, there are some critical things you have to do, like investing time wisely in your own learning, using all resources available to you. This is followed by surrounding yourself with critical friends whom you feel both compelled and comfortable to learn from. This is a topic I will explore in a later chapter. Before the internet, this was not possible. The internet holds everything you need to know but only if you are willing to go and look for it.

Imagine a big square in your head. Now split the square into 4 quadrants. Put a circle in the middle. The squares represent the macro level domains across the spectrum of IT delivery. The circle represents the management and theory required to get IT in a state where an organisation gains value from it.

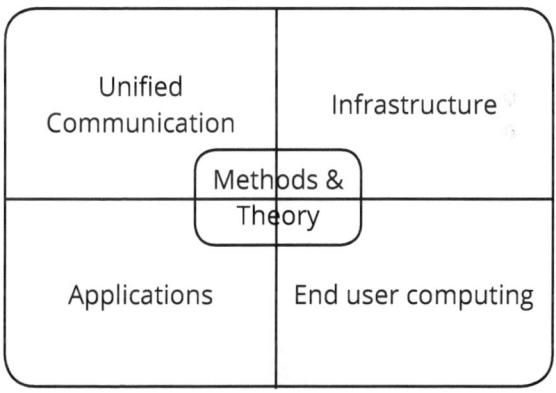

To get you used to the technique, spend 1 hour per month on each square researching the basics on the internet. Start with Google and youtube. It is a small investment of 48 hours across the whole year. Think about it in terms of making yourself more marketable by spending less time watching the news or soaps. When your next project comes along, write down the top 10 gaps in your knowledge - 5 from the 4 technical domains and 5 from the domain for methods and theory. Remember to write them down. Then identify 10 items of information you need, to get yourself in an informed position to experiment with this technique. Knowledge is acquired when you use information for a purpose. To illustrate the point, I have documented an example you could use. Now spend no more than 5 hours researching the basics on the internet. That is 30 minutes per topic. If something sparks your imagination, then buy a beginners' book on it. Do not buy a book and force yourself to read it. The information won't go in and if you are reading it on the train, you will get strange looks because everyone else is reading 50 Shades of Grey.

UNIFIED COMMUNICATONS

Lync, Avaya, CISCO, LAN, WAN, VOIP, FOIP, PSN, Call control, Multimodal communications, Presence, Instant messaging, Unified messaging, Speech, Conferencing, Collaboration tools, SIP, PSTN, Gateway, Router, Switch, WLAN, borderless networking, ubiquitous networking, MPLS, point of presence, firewall

INFRASTRUCTURE

Operating Systems, physical server, virtual server, P2P, V2V, P2V, platespin, VMWARE, IAAS, Tier 1 – 4 Data Centre, Fabric, Silicon Photonics, storage area network(SAN), virtualisation, image, workload, data centre consolidation, machine to machine communications

Methods & Theory

APPLICATIONS

ERP,CRM, EDRMS, Content Management, UX, Application Rationalisation, Application Remediation, Application Life-cycle Management, COTS, Database, Application Server, Middleware, Software Development, Workflow, Data Migration, MI/BI, Big Data, Open Source, J2EE, .NET, Sharepoint, SaaS, Paas, Docker

END USER COMPUTING

Converged computing, wearable computing, context awareness, phablet, tablet, active directory, desktop, MFD, mobility first, virtualised desktop interface, smartphone, Citirix, Active Directory.

Methods and theory is the glue that makes it happen. I have listed a starter for 10 below. The world of IT is methodology mad and given its complexity, following a repeatable and proven method statement is common sense. However, the aim is conformance and not compliance i.e. take what you need from the method and ensure the customer will see value in its use. Remember the aim of the exercise is not to become an expert but to acquire just enough information to be able to translate and converse in a language used by the subject matter experts and technicians.

Methods & Theory

Project Management (eg PRINCE2), Programme Management (eg MSP), TOGAF. ZACHAM. Enterprise Architecture, Transition, IT Outsourcing, Agile, Waterfall, six sigma, business analysis, requirements management, systems thinking, transformation, digitisations, MUSCOW, RUP, service orientated architecture, PAAS, SAAS, IAAS, utility based pricing, utility based computing, security, BYOD, ITIL, big data, data warehousing, analytics, systems thinking, organisational change management, bpr, performance management, social media

BE EMPHATIC

'Hello teacher. Tell me what's my lesson'
Mad World
Tears for Fears

T IS JULY 2011 AND I'm racking my brains trying to understand why getting a few servers built and some firewall changes completed, requires several call conferences and numerous emails. It is October 1998 and I'm trying to understand why getting a simple automatic FTP requirement installed, requires a room full of managers. My career to date is littered with these moments of reflection. It is a story I hear time and time again from others in the trade. The ability of human beings to turn the completion of the simplest of tasks, into a project in its own right, never fails to astound me. During those meetings, I'd go off into a daydream while the detail was endlessly debated. Nobody ever noticed I was not listening. It is even worse when you come to speak at those type of meetings. Nobody is really listening. Those meetings are full of people who just want to talk because there is no incentive to listen. People who make it their business to get noticed, live a different life. They are listened to, everyone goes out of their way to listen to them and they enjoy being listened to do. This process starts when they do something both positive and memorable. From that point onwards being noticed comes easy. It is these memorable and positive moments that interest me. They teach us about what it takes to really get noticed and when you get noticed people listen to you. I'm left wondering that if I was more like a 60s hell raiser such as Oliver Reed, Keith Moon or Richard Harris, then maybe those insomnia-curing meetings would not have happened.

It is the 1986 World Cup and England is playing Argentina. Maradona spends the next 90 minutes giving us a master class in two ways to get noticed; do something totally outrageous or something magical that leaves everyone in awe. Either way, he got noticed. Fast forward eight years to 1994 and he has taken the outrageous route again. But it was his second goal in 1986 that provides a metaphor for beat-the-plan IT project delivery. Maradona picked that ball up and was totally definite about scoring a wonder goal. He was a man without fear of failure. I have been looking for one word that summed up Maradona's goal and Keith Moon's antics, a word with an emphasis on being noticed, a word synonymous with clarity.

em·phat·ic

/em'fatik/Adjective

Showing or giving emphasis; expressing something forcibly and clearly.

Definite and clear.

My hypothesis is that the management of the successful IT projects identified by Standish, were more emphatic than those in the challenged or impaired category. Emphatic communication results in greater clarity. Being emphatic results in people making more of an effort to listen to you. Emphatic people exude referent power. So why is referent power important? In research conducted by psychologists, John R. P. French and Bertram Raven, they identified 6 distinct forms of power: coercive, reward, legitimate, referent, expert and informational. In the role of IT Project Manager, the use of coercive power is out of the question. You will end up on the HR department's naughty chair. I doubt in the modern day organisation that an IT project manager has the authority to grant a pay rise or pay a bonus - so that's reward power off the table. Legitimate power could have some mileage but IT Project Manager 2015+ has to work horizontally across the organisation and beyond its boundaries to get the work done. And what about delivering in matrix managed organisation? You have to negotiate access to resources via a manager who holds the legitimate power. That leaves you with expert, informational and referent. An IT Project Manager is a subject matter expert. They are inclined to rely on informational and expert power. However, without referent power traits such admiration or charm, you will be perceived as boring. You lose an ability to inculcate into another, a sense of personal acceptance or personal approval of you. Maradona did the opposite to millions of football fans when he scored those two goals against England in 1986. To beat the plan you need to exude referent power.

With the most innocuous everyday items you can be emphatic. Tommy Cooper was a genius at using everyday items to make people laugh; like the tea bag. In my experience, change managers are stalked and harassed by IT Project Managers. When faced with a tenacious and will-not-take-no-for-an-answer IT Project Manager, the Change Manager will work to rule. On one particular engagement, there would be a constant queue of PMs at the Change Manager's desk. I got to the point where I could predict the Change Manager's response to any attempt to either circumvent or expedite the process. I knew one day my turn would come - but I was armed with a tea bag. On the day, I introduced myself, explained my predicament, gave him a tea bag and said , "Just like that - have a drink on me". He smiled and laughed and said, 'That was a Tommy Cooper joke.' After that my changes got treated with a bit more TLC.

Back to Maradona's goal in 1986; it was so effortless. He went through the England players like a hot knife through butter. Would it not be great if you could feel the same when delivering an IT project? When Maradona scored those goals he was high on confidence, cheekiness and positivity. Keith Moon felt the same when he turned up at a Who gig in a ginger suit where Roger Daltrey gave him a chance on the drums. The rest is history. Ask yourself this...This. Sorry that was another Tommy Cooper joke! When was last time you picked up an IT project full of confidence, cheekiness and positivity? It's difficult to see how anyone can better the IT project's acceptability threshold without being full of positivity, confidence and cheekiness.

Emphatic people are always looking to improve on their last memorable moment. They are attention seekers. On his first appearance on American TV, Keith Moon was left alone with the pyrotechnic stuff. He kind of went beyond the 'cherry bomb acceptability' threshold. Keith Moon was a close friend of Oliver Reed. They were always trying to outdo each other. Oliver Reed was quoted as saying, "I'm the biggest star this country has got. Destroy me and you destroy the whole British film industry." It is a pretty emphatic attention-grabbing quote. Would it not be reasonable to assume that a cohort of projects in the Standish challenged or impaired category failed to grab attention? Is that surprising when it is the norm in large organisations not to rock the boat? Emphatic people have no qualms about rocking the boat and grabbing attention.

Emphatic people don't suffer fools gladly. It is not uncommon to hear from the project management community that traffic lights on their highlight reports mysteriously shifted towards green before being issued to the customer. The customer is being told what they want to hear. An emphatic person would not accept that. They stand by their position. They are prepared to be more honest than wise. Emphatic people are not afraid of people who get angry with them. Sometimes I wonder why IT projects, which are clearly not going to achieve what they set out to achieve, are not just stopped. Then there are the IT projects that are worth doing but the status quo sets them up to fail. I suspect no-one was prepared to be emphatic.

I GOT 99 PROBLEMS BUT A CARRY ON TEAM AINT ONE

'I never knew you. You never knew me.
Say hello, wave goodbye'

Say Hello Wave Goodbye

Soft Cell

TRADITIONALLY, IT PROJECT MANAGERS RELY on line managers in a matrix management organisation to address poor team performance. Cut out the middleman to accelerate your delivery. After all, you did say you were a people-person at the job interview. Jay-Z used to have 99+ problems; then he rapped about his woes. Ever since, he has definitely been a man on the up. He did not get to the top on his own. He had talented people around him. Every time I read about what Jay-Z has to say or when I watch him on the TV, it is blatantly obvious he has an effective team around him (not to mention the most beautiful woman in the world). IT projects involve dealing with 99 problems. To beat the plan, you have to be able to say on a daily basis, "I've got 99 problems on my project but a dysfunctional team aint one." Failed and challenged IT projects are the result of dysfunctional team behaviour. To reduce the risk of poor project performance, you have to be adept at addressing this behaviour. However, traditional project management methodology, combined with matrix managed organisation, removes line management of the project resources from the role of the IT Project Manager. We have been let off the hook! Line management is for general managers. If there's a problem with the performance of a project resource, escalate it to their line manager. It is mantra that I have encountered daily for the last 15 years and one I hear from peers on a regular basis. As a line manager myself, the call I dread most starts with, "Can I have a quiet word about..." I know what is coming next ; the 'infamy' conversation. The first reaction of anyone being told that the co-workers are not happy with their performance is a quote from Julius Caesar in the film Carry On Cleo (1964) "Infamy! Infamy! They've all got it infamy!" Fortunately, it is infrequent conversation. If the performance of a project is directly linked to the performance of the team, then being able to spot the signs of dysfunctional team behaviour and subsequently address it, is a pre-requisite IT Project Manager 2015+ skill.

It is actually quite easy to spot the signs of dysfunction in the project team. They carry on like the cast from the Carry On genre. However, the first thing you have to do is stop referring to people working on your project, as a resource. Resource is a word that implies an expendable inanimate thing. The second thing you have to do is watch every single Carry On film ever made. The Carry On genre is the ultimate metaphor for team dysfunction. To illustrate the different types of dysfunction that feeds IT project failure, I am going to use scenes from the greatest Carry On film ever made - Carry On Abroad. Hells Bells and Buenos Knockas, here we go. But before we get to the fun stuff, we need a framework to learn. I'm not one for reinventing the wheel. I have searched high and low for something simple and easy to understand. The best one by far is Patrick Lencioni's

Five Dysfunctions of a Team : A Leadership Fable (2002). The book caught my attention when I spotted a table where Patrick Lencioni described a team that avoided accountability. Those traits are absolutely what it feels like when working on a challenged or impaired IT project.

Creates resentment among team members who have different standards of performance.

Encourages mediocrity

Misses dead-lines and key deliverables

Places an undue burden on the team leader as the sole source of discipline

Patrick Lencioni's Five Dysfunctions of a Team : A Leadership Fable (2002:214)

Patrick Lencioni then goes on to describe the performance of a team that holds one another accountable. They are all beat the plan behaviours. I am of the opinion that Patrick Lencioni's books should be pre-requisite reading and study for any IT project manager.

Ensures that poor performers feel pressure to improve

Identifies potential problems quickly by questioning one another's approaches without hesitation.

Establishes respect among team members who are held to the same high standards.

Avoids excessive bureaucracy around performance management and corrective action.

Patrick Lencioni's Five Dysfunctions of a Team : A Leadership Fable (2002:214)

To beat the plan you need to be coached and mentored to manage people. Think about all your traditional IT project management training. Would I be correct in thinking most of it is of a technical nature based on engineering based approaches? To illustrate Patrick Lencioni's framework, I have taken each one of his themes and a scene from the Carry On Abroad film. Each one of these behaviours moves the team and yourself away from beating the plan. The greater the level of team dysfunction, the higher the propensity to breach the IT project's acceptability threshold.

Scene 1 : Fractional Assignment

In the film, Pepe runs the Hotel from hell. Pepe is the manager, waiter, concierge, chef and handyman all in one. The result is fractional assignment and, unsurprisingly, the hotel does not run properly.

Scene 2 : Inattention to Results

Kenneth Williams plays the tour guide, Stuart Farquar. Stuart Farqhuar has a huge ego and he is arrogant. He has taken his customers to the worst hotel in Spain, Hells Bells. He is an individual who will never suffer failure acutely. To be frank he is not that bothered. You can tell that Stuart Farqhuar has a huge ego by his reaction to Pepe, the hotel 'meet and greeter'. Upon Stuart Farqhuar introducing himself, Pepe gets his name wrong and calls him, "Stupid What, ah you are Mr Farquiarse." Pepe suffered from inattention to results as well. His guests were expecting an 'a la carte' selection of great Mediterranean cuisine. He definitely offered them a selection but it was not great.

Sausage, beans and chips

Beans, chips and sausage

Chips & beans (vegetarian)

A root cause of inattention to results is when an individual's goals are not congruent with the project's goals. The outcome manifests itself in terms of individuals concentrating on their needs, at the expense of the performance of other project team members. The other moral of this stuff is don't mispronounce anyone's name in your project team when you first meet them.

Scene 3 : Absence of Trust

There is a great scene in the film where Pepe rushes into the kitchen to confront Mama Pepe about the delays in serving up dinner. The cooker is not working. Mama Pepe is the expert with the cooker. Pepe questions her aptitude and ability, then proceeds to throw what he thinks is methylated spirits onto the cooker to get the heat going. It is cheapo vino. In the ensuing chaos, he smokes out the restaurant area and his patrons run for cover. Challenged IT projects are full of these moments. When a 'save the day - I know best' expert rushes in to save the day, they only make things worse. Normally, it is the end users on the receiving end. This happens because the expert does not trust the person they are trying to help. The 'save the day' expert has instantly assumed that the person he is trying to help is inept. However, the experts claim that sharing something about our lives outside of work with those inside work, is great way to build trust.

Scene 4 : Fear of Conflict

Sid James plays Vic Flange. He is a womaniser. His wife does not trust him; she won't let him out of her sight. When Vic introduces his wife he says, "This is the wife - don't laugh." I have tried this line as an icebreaker when I have taken my wife out. I have only ever done it once! In the film, Vic's wife just puts up with it. The longer she puts up with it, the further the relationship deteriorates with her husband. The same thing happens on a team, uncomfortable with or prevented from, engaging in ideological conflict. In this climate, discussing prickly matters crucial to the success of the project does not happen in an open, productive and transparent way. You cannot beat the plan without the team thriving on constructive ideological conflict over how to get the work done.

Scene 5 : Lack of Commitment

Stanley Blunt is a frustrated man. Physical relations with Mrs Blunt have not been performing against his KPIs for several years. To overcome his frustrations and assert his masculinity, he buys a bottle of the local 'Spanish Fly', a backstreet snake oil version of Viagra. He bursts into the hotel room in an assertive manner. Mrs Blunts likes the new Stanley. Unfortunately, Stanley has forgotten what do. He just gives up. A fear of failure has beaten him. He lacked confidence and tenacity to make it happen. According to Patrick Lencioni, a lack of commitment is caused by a desire for consensus and a team wanting a high degree of certainty before they commit. Having experienced impaired and challenged IT project delivery, I can say with certainty that there was a high prevalence of lack of commitment type behaviours as identified by Patrick Lencioni.

Ambiguity among the team about direction and priorities.

Windows of opportunity close due to paralysis of analysis.

Lack of confidence and fear of failure.

Repeated discussions and decisions again and again.

Patrick Lencioni's Five Dysfunctions of a Team : A Leadership Fable (2002:209)

For the last section, I have developed a quick assessment tool for Agile software development projects based on Patrick Lencioni's framework. This tool is not measuring production quality, time or budget. It is measuring the level of team dysfunction. My aim here is to use software development as an example but the idea is to get you to develop your own framework for different IT projects, by contextualising the questions for each type of IT project. The types are: data centre migration; package implementation; end user computing; wide area networking; and unified communications etc. However, Agile software projects that think they are Agile when, in fact, they are not, are notorious in the world of IT project failure. Below are 15 statements. For each statement, answer 3 for usually, 2 for sometimes and 1 for rarely.

1. Testers are open and honest in their discussion of software defects and bugs.

2. Developers call out one another's poor coding practises.

3. Everyone in the project team knows what backlog items eachother is working and how their work contributes to the overall project goal.

4. Infrastructure people, network people, support people and application people genuinely apologise to one another when they say or do something wrong.

5. Managers are willing to make sacrifices (such as budgets or reprioritisation) in their departments for the good of the project.

6. Software architects and lead developers are more honest than wise about their mistakes.

7. Scrum meetings and sprints are compelling and not boring.

8. Product owners leave meetings confident that the

development team are completely committed to the decisions that were agreed upon in the sprint.

9. Morale is significantly affected by the number of software defects and bugs identified during testing.

10. During scrum meetings issues are put on the board to be resolved.

11. Developers are deeply concerned about letting down the final users of their software.

12. The project team know a bit about each other's personal lives and are comfortable talking about it.

13. Discussion at scrums, sprint and inception-deck, end with clear and specific calls to action.

14. Developers challenge each other, the product owner and development manager about their plans and approaches.

15. Everyone in the development team is slow to seek credit for their own contribution but will point out those of others.

Now fill your scores in the table below.

8 & 9 indicates the dysfunction is not a problem for your agile software development project.

6 & 7 indicates that dysfunction is present and will be become a major problem.

3 to 5 indicates the dysfunction needs to be resolved immediately.

Dysfunction 1: Absence of Trust	Statement 4 : _____ Statement 6 : _____ Statement 12 : _____	Total _____
Dysfunction 2: Fear of Conflict	Statement 1 : _____ Statement 7 : _____ Statement 10 : _____	Total _____
Dysfunction 3: Lack of Commitment	Statement 3 : _____ Statement 8 : _____ Statement 13 : _____	Total _____
Dysfunction 4: Avoidance of Accountability	Statement 2 : _____ Statement 11 : _____ Statement 14 : _____	Total _____
Dysfunction 5: Inattention to Results	Statement 5 : _____ Statement 9 : _____ Statement 15 : _____	Total _____

Kenneth Williams

"People need to be peppered or even outraged occasionally. Our national comedy and drama is packed with earthy familiarity and honest vulgarity. Clean vulgarity can be very shocking and that, in my view, gives greater involvement."

LEARN FROM THE PUBLIC SECTOR

'And I'm wondering what I'm doing in a room
like this'.

Are friends electric

Tubeway Army

Y OU KNOW WHEN A MEETING is pointless because at the
end of it everyone is still talking about the same problems
that were discussed at the same meeting a week ago and a
week before that. The situation is symptomatic of a total lack of
clarity. Imagine 20 people in a room all giving a highlight report
for their work-stream after 2 o'clock in the afternoon. Within
10 minutes, the meeting starts to deteriorate when you notice
the proliferation of nodding. It is difficult to differentiate from
those who had too many carbohydrates at lunch-time, and the
victims of groupthink nodding in agreement. Yet behind the
scenes in a 1-2-1 situation, they express a completely different
point of view. I am always left wondering, why did you agree
with something you did not agree with? What do you do when
you find yourself continually attending pointless checkpoint

meetings? I tend to find myself in this situation feeling like Bill Murray from Groundhog Day, when working on public sector IT projects. The first film I ever saw in a business studies class back in the 1980s was 'Meetings Bloody Meetings' staring John Cleese. The school had purchased VCR2000 players. On the day, I remember getting into a fight, when an argument over betamax vs VHS, broke out. When the teacher was out of the classroom, Ferris Buellers Day off got an airing. Even today, I experience meetings that feel like the dysfunctional one at the start of the John Cleese film. I sit in those meetings thinking about doing a Ferris Bueller. I have the utmost respect for anyone working on the front line in the public sector trying to make a difference. Anyone who can deliver IT to improve social purpose and offer the council tax payer greater value for money, is doing society a great service. However, I have to say when compared to meetings in the private sector, meetings in the public sector about the delivery of IT projects tend to feel more dysfunctional. It is like there is a written code in the public sector, 'Thou shalt not upset each other '. The overriding cultural norm is to maintain an artificial harmony. Unfortunately, the avoidance of conflict reduces clarity and does not engender unity. I am not saying for one for moment that the private sector is an angel when it comes to avoidance of conflict but in my experience the problem feels more acute in the public sector. Yet when the 'space' is created for our public servants to engage in positive conflict, they actually welcome the opportunity and thrive on it. Therein lies the opportunity for any budding Ultimate IT Project Manager. If you can achieve 'beat the plan' level clarity in the public sector, you will be able to do it anywhere.

Given the strategic importance of IT and the increase in collaboration between the private sector, third sector and public sector, there is a good chance that during your career as an IT Project Manager you will work with the public sector. So it's probably a good idea to understand what kind of environment you are getting involved in and to recognise the opportunity you have been given. Delivering an IT project with a tangible business case in the public sector, is a lot harder than in the private sector. Inputting the search term 'UK government IT project failures', Google returned on average 29m results. The results show people care about IT project delivery in the public sector. The results also show the level of intense scrutiny our public servants are under. As I write this chapter, 49 major UK government IT projects are on the Major Project Authority hit-list. If you can beat the plan in this environment, great things happen. Firstly, you have protected the public purse and made a difference. Secondly, to deliver IT projects within the acceptability threshold in the public sector environment, you must be excellent at politics and communication.

I'm going to share with you some lessons I have learnt from working on IT Project Delivery in the public sector. Therefore, these lessons will help you improve project performance in the public sector. My first piece of advice is not to be too binary in your judgement about ways of working. You will initially perceive some ways of working as dysfunctional. The motivation behind the processes you will see is probity - the quality of having strong moral principles of honesty and decency. Probity is synonymous with honesty, integrity, rectitude, uprightness and sincerity. The public sector is a custodian of the public purse, the environment and the safety of the vulnerable. Hence, there will be caution about spending money or doing things too quickly. Sometimes the public sector get it wrong but in recent time times, they have never gotten it as wrong as the banks in terms of impact on society. The latter suffered from a severe lack of probity. You have to try and avoid being too cynical about the public sector to achieve beat the plan performance. My starting position is that the public sector does far more good than harm when compared to the private sector.

Appreciate why people work in the public sector. The end result should be project plans where no one has to work a 45 hour week, every week. Challenged and impaired IT projects suffer from unsustainable pace. You will create sustainable pace when you factor in, the reasons why people want to work in the public sector in the project plans. How great is that!

Within the public sector there is greater emphasis on achieving consensus before a decision is made. So mapping out your stakeholders is absolutely vital. In the text books, the budget holder is an individual. In the public sector, approval to spend tends to spread across many individuals. The text books on Project Management teach us that only one person can be accountable and many are responsible. As much as I would like it to be like that in the public sector, it's not. If you can organise a project along the 'one person accountable and many responsible', then great. I tend to view the roles that civil servants and their partners play in the following manner. Civil servants tend to take on many of these roles during an IT project while suppliers tend to keep roles distinct. The key point here is to avoid pigeon holing civil servants into one role. In the current economic climate, the public sector has to do more with less. So it is only natural to see civil servants taking on multiple roles. I have described the groups below. The most important thing to note is that they need to be externally motivated to talk to one another to ensure clarity and unity. I always work on the assumption that none of the other groups will find it comfortable telling each other like it is.

The Authorities

The authorities grant financial approval and formally approve key decisions. They tend to be directors, executives, members and commercial people. It will feel like management by committee.

The Solution Owners

Solution Owners represent the voice of two groups: the customer i.e. those who benefit from the project; and the end users i.e. those who will use the IT project's deliverables to deliver value . They are accountable for ensuring the builders build something of value for the council tax payer. There are essentially two groups of solution owners: a group who articulates requirements; and a group who produces the design. The first group are at their best when they articulate requirements in a customer centric manner. I find the best ones tell stories. The second group are at their best when they can understand and interpret descriptive customer centric requirements. Local government and system design speak have their own language and colloquiums. The key is to make sure some communications activities take place during the early part of the project to ensure everyone understands the language.

The Builders

The builders take the design and build the solution. Builders are at their best when the solution managers respond rapidly to their questions and their managers take the barriers out of their way. Builders on a public sector IT project tend to sit in distinct teams resulting in functional silos. These teams tend to have their own way of doing things. Because of the 'do more with less' mantra in the public sector, you will find that these teams are working on other projects or business-as-usual support work. This runs the risk of fractional assignment i.e. allocated to too many jobs. The end result tends to be low productivity, frustration and poor quality. This group know how long the work actually takes to do.

The Builders' Managers

The managers who manage the builders - nothing happens without their permission. They have all the middle management airs and graces. They will have an appreciation of what will work, what won't work and what is pragmatically possible, given departmental capacity and capability constraints.

The Change Agents

For an IT project to deliver, processes and what people do have to change. The change agents are responsible for business change. The IT project's business case will not perform in the event that business change is not thought through. It is the subject of many debate to say that an IT project delivered within the acceptability threshold but fails to achieve its benefits, is still considered a success. In my simple world, this kind of IT project is unsuccessful because the end result was wasted public money.

The Scrutinisers

These are the people who control the work environment. This group quality-assure how the delivery work is done. The public sector has lots of protocols and policy that need to be adhered to.

The Public Sector can be pretty hierarchical. I find it useful to think about the powerbases for each group in relation to one another. It will give you an indication on the propensity to get the work done, how to get decisions and where to go for help. I have outlined 3 examples below, illustrating environments where an IT project will find it difficult to perform. The assessment will be different depending on the organisational culture and you really need to get to know everyone involved before drawing a conclusion. Just place lo/hi in the boxes.

Command & Control

	Referent	Expert	Informational	Reward	Legitimate
Authorities				Hi	Hi
Solution Owners				Lo	Lo
Builders				Lo	Lo
Builder's Manager				Lo	Hi
Scrutinisers				Lo	Hi
Change Agents				Lo	Hi

Poor Communication

	Referent	Expert	Informational	Reward	Legitimate
Authorities	Lo		Hi		
Solution Owners	Lo		Hi		
Builders	Lo		Hi		
Builder's Manager	Lo		Hi		
Scrutinisers	Lo		Hi		
Change Agents	Lo		HI		

Poor Knowledge, Lack of Knowledge Transfer & Expertise

	Referent	Expert	Informational	Reward	Legitimate
Authorities		Lo	Lo		
Solution Owners	Lo	Lo	Lo		
Builders	Lo	Lo	Lo		
Builder's Manager		Lo	Lo		
Scrutinisers		Lo	Lo		
Change Agents		Lo	Lo		

Get to recognise the patterns which are less conducive to IT project delivery, during the early part of the project life-cycle. You have to test the waters to gauge the powerbases, sense the level of clarity and encourage it. It means you may have to work on your facilitation skills. If the groups cannot be collocated, then the best technique is to run regular workshops involving all of the above groups. It is the only proven way to get them talking to one another. You need to get yourself a big room and take out all the chairs. This will stop anyone going to sleep. Get a lead member of Director Level sponsor, to explain to the group why the project is important. A shared understanding of an important common goal increases unity. When everyone walks into the room, they will probably form cliques around their current team. Watch for outliers. Put them in a group with like-minded people. You have to facilitate the session in a way so that cliques are not formed. On a wall, plot the project's time-line. Using post cards, describe the project's products. Try and colour code the cards so there is one colour for each project stage. Issue some blank cards so each group can describe any missing products. You can use the questionaire available from itunes, (The Ultimate IT Project Manager, free to download, available June 2015). As the questions come in, plot the scores on the 'white noise' chart. At the end of the session, have 15 minutes to summarise what the numbers mean along with the action required to improve performance. Remember, the aim of the exercise is to gauge the powerbases, improve unity and understand the level of clarity at play on the project. The aim is not to resolve the underlying causes in the workshop. Get every group to plot their cards on the time-line. You are looking for people who are moving cards (placed by other groups) to the right or left on the time-line without any debate. The sign of a dysfunctional team is not considering the impact you have on others to get the work done. Anyone moving the cards without talking it through with their colleagues, is not being very 'teamy'. Look for Henry Fonda having a '12 Angry Men moment'. In the film 12 Angry Men, a jury of eleven instantly judge a man as guilty. The twelfth juror, Henry Fonda, has doubts and proceeds over the duration of the film to prove that his fellow jurors may have gotten it wrong. It is a master class in constructive positive conflict and how to deal with groupthink. Have a corner where members of the session can document the barriers that prevent the team from getting the work done. Now the one thing I've noticed about this type of session in the public sector, is the sense of trepidation when the first session starts. But if you can make it entertaining, you will start to feel a sense of liberation in the room. It is a we-are-here-to-make-a-difference kind of vibe. It is great to see. I don't get this vibe when working in the private sector. The techniques in the workshop are used as a matter of course by some of the world's most successful organisations. These companies implement innovative products and services we use on a daily basis. The overall impact is to create an accelerated solutions environment. There is greater visibility to all involved, of what needs to be done by when and the barriers everyone faces. This will not happen if the whole project team is not put together nor inspired to talk collectively about the work that needs to be done. The implication for you is the need to learn assertive facilitation and crowd control. If you can do this, your project will start to feel like a 'beat the plan' IT project.

Clarity

People communicating a shared, clear understanding
of the project situation and direction

Unity

People demonstrating a wholehearted agreement
on the merits of the direction and the need to work
together to move ahead

Agility

People with a willingness to turn and adapt quickly while keeping goals in mind.

USE THE POWER OF SOCIAL PURPOSE

'It shines like destruction. Comes in like the
flood. And it seems like religion'

Love Is A Stranger Lyrics

Eurythmics

O<small>N PAPER, THE PROJECT GOAL</small> looked impossible, causing many a sleepless night. Why then were a contract IT Project Manager, a management consultant and a new kid on the block, successful at doing something they had never done before? I was 15 years old when I watched Live Aid on the 13th July 1985. The event was attended by 170,000 people when you include the concert held at the same time in Philadelphia. Live Aid was the largest television of all time. The global audience was in the region of 1.9 billion, across 150 nations. It is estimated that Live Aid raised £150 million for famine relief. Bob Geldof and Midge Ure had zero experience in organising an event of the scale of Live Aid; yet they did it. If I were faced with such a challenge, I'd probably freeze like a rabbit in the headlights. I never really understood the power of what they felt until I became involved in a major transformation programme of services for the elderly, led by one of the largest local government authorities in Europe.

The public sector endures the greatest flak when it comes to failed IT project delivery. It is not because the public sector is less able than the private sector. The public sector has to be more transparent than the private sector. There are things both sectors can learn from each other. In my experience, the public sector has too much governance and consensus seeking around IT projects and the private sector, not enough. However, when it comes to using project management to deliver social purpose, the public sector is way ahead of the game. Social purpose delivers benefits to an individual, group of individuals or a community. Don't get me wrong: public sector IT project business cases are full of focus on saving money or making money but the emphasis is on social purpose. I've never thought of myself as a Mother Teresa type and I don't know that many people who work with the less fortunate. However, I have seen the unifying and motivating power of a business case communicated in the language of social purpose. I hold the view today that the programme would not have achieved what it did, had the team not put the effort into communicating the business case, namely a focus on communicating the social purpose of the programme.

Let me give you an example. The programme involved delivering commodity IT i.e. PCs and printers. The script for ordering this stuff is pretty straightforward in large organisations. You order it; your service order is placed in a queue; you chase the approver; unless you prod procurement from time to time, you get forgotten about; and when it turns up it tends to be wrong. The norm is to fill out a form stating what, where and when. Rarely you get to talk to a human being about your order. On the programme in question the opposite happened. This is because we filled out the forms and told people why the PCs were important i.e. how they were going to be used for services to improve the lives of the elderly. There were many examples of delays that went away as soon as we explained what it was we were trying to achieve with the required goods or services. Communicating the social purpose in what you are delivery in a compelling manner, results in greater unity. It is because there is a Bob Geldof in your average human being waiting to get out.

It is a no-brainer to conclude that if I don't do any communication to evangelise my IT project's business, my project will probably fail. We have been taught that our IT project has a greater propensity for success if we evangelise the business case in terms of return on investment. This is most definitely true if the aim is to secure the budget to deliver the project. However, this book is not about getting an investment decision. It is about getting the work done by increasing clarity, unity and agility. Delivering social purpose touches our buttons. Making a difference in people's lives unifies humanity. The language of social purpose is more unifying than the language of making or saving money. By emphasizing the project's social purpose, you will increase the propensity for success. In today's austere times, we are pretty bored to the teeth with the constant efficiency drives and cost cutting forced into our everyday lives. Saving money may get the juices of budget holders going but your average ICT project worker will be indifferent.

I'm not suggesting for one moment that any organization starts to ignore internal rate of return and makes investment decisions based on the delivery of social purpose. I am suggesting a greater focus on communicating the social purpose of the IT project to increase unity. People are more engaged and more motivated when the theme of the conversation is social purpose. One time, I got a call from a recruitment agent about an IT project management role, installing networks and PCs across a number of schools in the East Midlands. He did not sell it very well. The whole conversation was about this technology and that technology. In the end, I just told him to send my CV to the client just to stop him from stalking me. Anyway, I got a call from his client. He sold it to me a different way. The programme happened to be Building Schools for the Future (BSF). He spoke about the outcomes as a result of children using the technology. They ranged from reduced anti-social behaviour and greater social mobility. Following that conversation, I wanted that job so badly. Unfortunately, I never got that job.

It's 2007 and I am having a conversation with a social worker responsible for operationalising 4 x 64 bed state-of-the-art residential centres for the elderly. His challenge was to bring each centre alive. Building them was the easy part. Transitioning them into operational use was an entirely different ball game. He asked for my advice. I recommended that each centre had its own transition plan delivered by the staff who were going to run it. We spoke through the role of a transition manager in a business process outsource context. I suggested the role could be varied for the operational context of the residential centre. I never thought for one moment he would take the idea seriously! What did I know about residential centres for the elderly? However, he was not asking for an operational expert in the delivery of social care for the elderly. What he wanted was a method statement and plan for the transition. All the knowledge was there; it just needed a bit of structure and someone with a project management mindset to monitor progress against plan. My team consisted of three Project Managers, an articulate management consultant, your classical contract IT Project Manager, and a talented guy new to the company. They were all very capable individuals in the field of project management and they had gotten to know the client very well. However, I was worried about their possible reaction to news that I was changing their roles on the project to a Transition Project Manager. IT Project Managers like certainty. They are at their best when all the project bounds are defined and the quality plans are documented. Well, we had none of that for the sole reason that this kind of project had never been done before. I was confident we could use the tacit knowledge from across all public sector partners involved in the programme. Our advantage was we were not part of the politics and were comfortable operating horizontally across the various organizations involved. After all, I consider the ability to have a conversation with anyone about how the work should be done, to be a core project management competence. My team were very good at that. When I told them what they were going to be doing, the initial reaction was one of silence. They had seen how complex these centres were and were fully aware of the safeguarding context. I knew that they had seen the current arrangements for the residents. It is the clinical smell that stays with you. I said to my team, 'Do you think you will ever have another opportunity like this to be involved in the transformation of someone's life?' I will never forget that moment. There was no pushback, no trepidation and no anxiety. It was a sense of total clarity radiating an aura of 'we are going to the do this because it is important and we will make a difference'. In my 20 year career in IT across several sectors doing many roles, I have never felt that same feeling across a project team. So I'm sitting here today on a Sunday night in June 2013, thinking what if that same sense of surety, triggered by a belief in social purpose, were prevalent on all those IT projects in the 66% poor performing category? How many of us think about and consciously communicate how our IT project deliveries make a positive difference in the lives of those that use our solutions? The public sector teaches us that to beat the plan and deliver transformational change in people's lives, you need unity around social purpose. So the next time you want something doing, invest some time in explaining how their contribution to the delivery makes a difference - something I rarely see from IT project sponsors and IT Project Managers.

DITCH THE MCMURPHY HUBRIS

'Wound up, can't sleep, can't do anything right,
since I set my eyes on you.'

Fire Woman

The Cult

H UBRIS IS THE FIRST THING I look for when I listen to an
IT Project Manager bang on about the dire state of their
project. Hubris is a form of extreme self-confidence.
It indicates an overestimation of one's own competence,
accomplishments or capabilities, especially when the person
exhibiting it is in a position of power. It's an irrational state of
mind when you think every decision you make is the right one.
You feel you can get away with anything. It's no coincidence that
failing IT projects are full of people suffering from hubris. In
popular culture, hubris is rife. Talented and gifted people with
everything going for them, go and do the craziest things - Mike
Tyson taking a chunk out of Evander Holyfield's ear; Hugh
Grant's choice of location for dating; OJ Simpson's driving
technique; Maradona and his choice of stimulant; Eric Cantona
with his Bruce Lee impression. Popular culture is full of people
who have done the looniest things for no apparent rational

reason. It's like society wants to see them fail, then enjoy the fall from grace. Given what I've seen over the years, I have this sneaking suspicion that this influence has seeped into the psyche of the 21st century workplace. A lot of my working day is spent taking away the reasons to fail. You can call me paranoid but those reasons were put there long before I turned up on the scene. Hubris convinces you that you can deal with these problems, and have dealt with them, when in reality you cannot and have not. It's a form of delusion and confirmation bias that can get an IT project into a difficult situation. On an IT project, you have to be the only one not to suffer from hubris. To beat the plan, you have to burden yourself with the responsibility to stop everyone else suffering from it. Dealing with hubris is not something you can learn from a book. You have to experience it to be able to spot it. Unless you become adept at ridding yourself of hubris, it's hypocritical to point it out in others. This chapter is not about the psychology behind the latin phrase 'mea cupla' (it's my fault) or the hidden meaning behind Robert Plant singing 'Nobody's Fault But Mine'. The chapter is about both consequences and the symptoms of hubris, on a real life IT project. This stuff really happened. For those who don't know who Randle McMurphy is, he was the lead character from the book, 'One Flew Over the Cuckoo's Nest'. Jack Nicholson played the character in the film. Randle McMurphy suffered from hubris. The consequences to himself and those around him are plain to see. If there was ever a film that could be a metaphor for the project I'm about to tell you about, it would be One Flew Over the Cuckoo's Nest. I've started the chapter with a lyric from a George Michael song. George is one of those very talented people who have fallen from grace and then turned it around. As I write this chapter, he has just released his new album 'Symphonica'. It is pretty darn good. So I brought his Greatest Hits. Every time I hear his track 'Praying for Time', I remember that project I am about to tell you about. I've used the lyrics from the song as subtitles for the explanation of what went wobbly on this greek tragedy. The names have been changed to protect the innocent (mainly to stop them suing me!) The important thing to bear in mind is that unlike Randle McMurphy, nobody died. And with the benefit of hindsight it has a montypythonesque, Some Mothers Do Av Em, Only Fools & Horses feel to it.

The closing scene in the play can be summarised as a project £500k overspent (30%+ over budget), the most poorly built software solution I have ever seen, a phone call from someone who thinks I'm Damien from the film Omen. I've shared all this because these are consequences of poor management as a result of not tackling hubris. The themes are also prevalent on other challenged IT projects I hear about everyday. So if stopping hubris from happening does not float your boat, put the book down and change career.

These are the days of the open hand. They might just be the last.

Imagine an organisation with a team of very clever and passionate people who want to innovate with ICT. Now imagine that same group of people writing strategies and proposals year after year only for the organisation to reject them; word documents gathering dust or taking up disk space. Then one year the organisation says to those same people, "Here is 1.5m quid to spend on ICT. Please help us." This same organisation is over-burdened with constant change and has a poor record of conducting business change to achieve symbiosis with the introduction of ICT. An ICT function full of innovators is not going to say 'no' to 1.5m quid; but acknowledging the inconvenient truth might mean just that. Starved of the opportunity to innovate, saying 'no' to the £1.5m was never going to happen. On the verge of several years of austerity, the ICT function sees a diminishing opportunity to do all things it thinks it should be doing. That £1.5m looks like an oasis of running water to a thirsty seeker in a desert. It is hubris that leads you to believe an IT project, without the necessary business change to achieve the benefits, will be successful. When you do that, the project creates an irrational perception that just putting in the IT alone, will result in the realisation of the business case.

Look around now

Looking around to see if the project had been done before in the same organisation, is a great thing to do. Asking the question 'has this team got a track record in similar projects?' is a wise thing to do. It was hubris to assume the project could be delivered by a team with no track record in a similar delivery. No one on the core delivery team had a track record of doing something similar successfully, not even the lead supplier. It is hubris that leads you to believe that just because Microsoft had given these guys an award they knew what they were doing.

These are the days of the beggars and the chooser

An IT project flushed with cash in an environment where every other project isn't, is like a lamp attracting moths. Those people that the ICT function does not know what to do with, or who don't have any meaningful work, gravitate towards roles on exciting projects. When an important £1 million plus IT project needs to be done, you need to select people for the roles with the same rigor you would apply when recruiting for a new vacancy. It is hubris that leads you to believe that effective resource management is the process of allocating people who are available, without checking they have the right skills, temperament, relationship skills, technical experience and aptitude to deliver the project.

Ditch the McMurphy Hubris

This is the year of the hungry man

An indication that an IT project is failing to perform is when the team, trying to deliver it, constantly seek clarification on the requirements. An IT project starved of clarity, will fail. Constantly seeking clarification is OK as long as clarification is offered. But on this project it wasn't because there was no unity in the team. Lack of clarity manifests itself in meetings that go around in circles, where the participants engage in monologue duets. Monologue duets are two or more people talking at the same time without actually listening to each other. There is no unity. It was hubris to assume clarity can thrive when there is no unity. It was hubris to assume that just because someone is mega-intelligent, they have the ability to articulate requirements in a manner the average intelligent can understand. It is hubris that leads you to believe that just because the requirements are written down and signed off, that they will remain correct for the duration of the project.

Whose place is in the past. Hand in hand with ignorance

You only know what you know. But what if that's not enough? How do you recognise that the knowledge and experience you have learned won't help you? You cannot - unless someone points it out and you are humble enough to admit yourself that they are right. It is hubris that leads a person to believe that anyone can solve the right problem in the right way, without an incentive to do so or a consequence for not doing so.

And legitimate excuses

I knew the project was in trouble when a developer came up to me and said, "Only one person at a time can access the development environment to develop on." The first thing I did was send an email to the PM and technical designer asking why this was. I never got a response. A legitimate excuse was not forthcoming nor was an illegitimate one. It was the ultimate manifestation of avoidance of accountability combined with plausible denial. On attempting to discuss the matter several times face to face, I kind of got a Delboyesque riposte, "C'est la vie que sera sera mange toute." It was hubris that led the designer to believe they could design a fit-for-purpose environment for a development team when they lack the insight or experience to do so.

The rich declare themselves poor

The money ran out and the project carried on. The money the project did not have continued to run out but the project carried on. How can a project carry on when the money has run out? The Enron school of accounting is at work. In the world of business when the money runs out, bankruptcy is declared; the business ceases to operate. In the world of public sector IT projects, the laws of working capital management defy logic. It is because the money exists as numbers on XL spreadsheets. It is not real cash; you can't see the cash. The cash does not exist as a balance in a bank account. It is hubris that leads you to believe effective financial control exists when there is no reconciliation between the project accounts on XL and actuals on the corporate financial system.

And most of us are not sure. If we have too much. But we'll take our chances. Cause God's not keeping score.

How much are we authorised to spend? How much have we spent on the project? How much have we got left? How much will we need to spend to finish the project? And how much will we have left when the project is finished? An IT project that is in control can answer all these questions instantly. I knew the project was in trouble when I asked the questions. The only answer I got back was a list of actuals. Where was the budget vs actual vs forecast. It is hubris that leads you to believe one can be trusted to govern the finances of an IT project portfolio, when it is not ones money being spent.

I guess somewhere along the way. He must have let us all
out to play

Go forth and innovate. That is what was heard but it was not what the programme sponsor wanted. The programme sponsor wanted the operation to do more with less. ICT's response - take a load of duplicate people and place data from lots of different systems. Plonk it on an enterprise service bus. Get a master data management application to do some clever stuff with it like semantic translation and canonical schemas. To polish it off, use a fancy named algorithm to work out the most truthful item of people and place data. Then display it in a CRM system. I've always wondered what would happen if I presented a pitch for the solution in front of James Khan, Alan Sugar and Duncan Bannantyne. In return for one million pounds and zero return on investment, I will take a load of old out-of-date name and address data, work out the correct information and then display it in a CRM system. I don't think I'd hear, "I'm in - throw me the ball chief." I'd hear, "Please can you fetch Nurse Ratchett to escort our guest to a room for quiet reflection time." It is hubris that leads you to believe that delivering an IT project with a poor business case can be successful.

Crept out the back door

When an IT project goes off the rails, you have to spend money you don't have to fix it. It is not a place where suppliers want to be. Suppliers in the IT space have this knack of disengaging whilst keeping quiet about it. It's like they think if the customer does not make a fuss, they will forget about us. Why creep away if you have delivered a high quality product? Why not stay and fight to prove your product is not the root cause of the project's distress? Suppliers attempt to creep away when they know what they've delivered is poorly designed and built. Staying to redress the matter by self-funding the remediation effort is not healthy when you are about to get a bonus. It is hubris that leads you to believe that a supplier will do stuff free of charge because they like you. This particular supplier has some great 'Microsoft love us' marketing communications. The code they delivered never worked and they could never pin point why it did not work. The code they delivered was not easy to deploy. It broke stuff and required lots of manual intervention to deploy it. These are not the ways of working you'd expect from a supplier apparently adulated by Microsoft. It is hubris that leads you to believe your own hype when in reality, you just don't have the tools, expertise or understanding of the requirements to develop great software.

And it's hard to love, there's so much to hate. Hanging on to hope. When there is no hope to speak of

When you don't enjoy or love what you do, you will fail. The project team held onto people who hated working on that project. They did not particularly enjoy each other's company either. Coming in day after day and failing, is soul destroying. The team held onto people who were out of their depth. Some of them did not have the right attitude. I knew this was happening and I wanted to let them go but I didn't. Instead I tried to do things to make it easier for them. All I did was increase my own workload and not really tackle the real problems. In truth, I was not ruthless enough to tackle the root causes of everyone's angst which were mainly a dysfunctional team, poor requirements, poor design, naff suppliers and a project with a nonsensical business case. It was hubris-inspired delusion that leads us to believe everything will work itself out. What I should have done is suspend the project, stand down the team and get an independent assessment of the business case. In the long run, this course of action would have saved a significant amount of public money.

And the wounded skies above say it's much too much too late. Well maybe we should all be praying for time. These are the days of the empty hand....

A 12 month project forecast in month 2 to breach its baselines in month 6, is a project under control. A 12 month project forecast in month 10 to breach its baselines in month 12, is a project not under control. It is a runaway. It's hubris that leads you to believe you don't have to measure regularly and fail fast to successfully deliver a complex IT project.

Once you've been really bad in a movie, there's a certain kind of fearlessness you develop.

Jack Nicholson

SHOW ME THE MONEY

'I'm dirty cash, the one that you asked for'
Dirty Cash
Adventures of Stevie V

I N THE CURRENT ECONOMIC CLIMATE, IT Project Manager 2015+ has to be pretty darn good at asking for money. In the current economic climate, the last thing anyone wants to do is bet on a horse with little chance of winning if past form is anything to go by. So the question is, how do you ask for money? Successfully asking for money is akin to getting it from a bank manager or your wife! You'd better have a damn good justification, you'd better be able to pay it back, you'd better be transparent and you'd better know your numbers. Here are some hints and tips using metaphors from some great films, an illuminating moment from the world of business and a famous BBC children's programme from the 1970s.

Viva Las Vegas

Nicky Santoro, played by Joe Pesci, is the psychotic mobster from Martin Scorsese's 1995 film Casino. He makes the other character played by Joe Pesci in Goodfellas, look angelic. IT projects are like investments and some investors don't like to lose. The banker explains the risk to Nicky but Nicky is not listening. Nicky wants the banker to take his money and just come back with more. Unfortunately, for the banker, the investment does not work out. The banker explains to Nicky that he did make him aware of the risk. Nicky proceeds to explain in polite but gory detail what he will do to the banker unless the money is returned. The moral of the story is that a sponsor of an IT project looking for zero risk and high return, will be sorely disappointed if they think they can get that kind of performance in the world of IT project delivery. The statistics show IT projects are risky investments. There is one question you can ask a sponsor to see if they appreciate the level of risk. Would you bet the whole setup budget for the IT project on roulette, if there was a 33% chance of winning? As an IT Project Manager you do have responsibility to point out the viability of the sponsor's investment. Fortunately, sponsors are not characters from Scorcese films. They have employed you to deliver within a financial acceptability threshold. You will not beat the plan if you do not believe the IT project is achievable within the agreed budget. If it was your own money at stake, you would stop immediately for a rethink.

A Charlie Croker Cockney Murphy Moment

There is a scene in the 1969 British film The Italian Job where the whole truck explodes during heist training. An exasperated Michael Caine shouts at his crew, "You're only supposed to blow the bloody doors off!" It's the same reaction you get from a customer to a quote that they perceive as over-priced. If you take any commodity IT product, it is easy to shop around and get list prices. But similar information on software licensing, hosting and professional services to string it all together, is not so easy to come by. The answer is a simple one. You need to be able to explain why the price is the price, using benchmarks against your competitors. Going through this process reassures the customer you are not trying to rip them off. Remember, customers are a lot more aware as buyers of IT than they were 10 years ago. The statistics show the majority of their investments in IT have not performed in line with financial expectation. Customers have good reason to be suspicious. Taking on this responsibility puts you in the role of a purchaser. There is a body of knowledge available from the Chartered Institute of Purchasing & Supply available to learn from. Michael Caine's plan to steal the gold from a bank in Rome is perfection personified. Every angle is thought through to get the gold out of the city of Rome. The banana skin he did not see is at the point when he thought he was home and dry. As the coach hangs over a cliff edge with the loot edging towards the rear doors, the film ends with Michael Caine doing a no-win balancing act. IT projects are notorious for having a situation similar to the last scene in The Italian Job. When initiating an IT project, my starting point is that the only certainty at the outset of an IT project is that there will be some unforeseen last minute banana skin preventing payment, when you think you are home and dry. It is called Murphy's Law.

Bullet Time

The term 'bullet time' is a registered trademark of Warner Bros. It was first used to describe slow motion special effects in the 1999 film The Matrix. Bullet time is computer generated. The aim of the concept is to show imperceptible events. I have always wondered what I would see if we measured tasks on a T&M, with the same tasks on a fixed priced basis, using bullet time. By the way, this is just a theory. The T&M work would be slightly slower than the fixed priced work. If you analysed the film, there would be more going on in terms of events in the T&M situation than in the fixed priced situation. In my experience, work done on a T&M basis leads to higher quality than work done on a fixed priced basis. However, with T&M arrangements, the work tends to take longer than work done on a fixed price basis. In the current economic climate and before handing over the money, customers want certainty on time and certainty on cost. The end result is a greater propensity for a fixed price. However, fixed price only works well with well defined requirements and low complexity. Factored into the complexity level are two variables: the number of times you've delivered a similar solution before; and the maturity of the technology. The only reason Neo from the Matrix could dodge those bullets was because he practised for hours in the virtual simulator. So when determining the basis for pricing an IT project, I try to assess the level of certainty on the: 1) requirements; and 2) track record in terms of performance of similar IT projects in the organisational environment; against the complexity of the solution.

	Blue Pills	Red Pills
	Fixed Price	Capped Time & Materials
CERTAINTY	Fixed Price + contingency	Time & Materials
	COMPLEXITY	

It is probably a bit too binary a decision when you consider there has to be a point in an IT project where the requirements are highly certain. Use of the Cone of Uncertainty can help with understanding the point where requirements become more certain. In the cone of uncertainty, the risk of variation is lowest at the entry point on the funnel's stem. The approach requires a much more sophisticated type of negotiation, where T&M is used for uncertain and highly complex requirements whilst fixed price is applied for low complexity and highly certain requirements.

Gruel

There are ways of asking for money that will get you zilch. One such way is acting like Oliver Twist and begging for it. You have to be confident, polite, assertive and be able to paint a picture of future perfect. Future perfect is a view of all the positive things that will happen if the money is released for the project.

A Jerry Maguire Scene

Everybody hates a direct, pushy, over-confident salesman. Acting like Jerry Maguire and shouting, 'Show me the money' won't get you anywhere.

Gordon Gecko's Bank Account

Greed is definitely not good when it comes to funding an IT project. It instils mistrust. Being perceived as greedy reduces the likelihood of securing change control sign off and funds for future business. To secure the funds, the profit margin needs to be ethical.

Enron Accounting

In the late 90s, I used to walk from my employer on Baker Street to Victoria Station to get the train home. Every other day, I walked by Enron's headquarters. That place was 'reem', as they say in Essex. I must have applied 20+ times to get a job at Enron. The other company I wanted to work for was Arthur Anderson. I'd look at the Enron Victoria HQ and just assume they must be really slick at every conceivable process you could think of. But they were not slick. Enron were totally pants at good old fashioned honest basic accounting. Their system was so complex, nobody could figure it out. Once the scandal broke, no one was ever going to lend them money again. The Enron scandal also contributed to the dissolution of Arthur Anderson. Convincing a sponsor to part with their cash requires you to convince them that your process for tracking financial performance is robust and transparent. If you are going to fail using other people's money, then fail pretty darn fast and fail transparently.

Mr Benn

Decision-making styles of sponsors and decision makers who yay/nay about whether or not to release funds for an IT project, vary. The way the decision is made will indicate what type of management style will be applied throughout the delivery. IT project sponsors remind me of Mr Benn. Mr Benn is a famous BBC children's cartoon from the 1970s. He had many personas but whatever his persona at the time, his sole aim was to solve a problem for someone. I think there were 5 types:

The Teller

The sponsor will tell you what the budget is, there will be no negotiation and they will announce it to the world without consulting you. The decision is quick. In this scenario, just saying 'yes' will get you the money. But if there is no science behind the estimation, the delivery will either be at risk of being impaired or challenged.

The Seller

The sponsor will sell you the idea that the IT project is deliverable within the budget they have. On the face of it, this looks like consultation; but be wary of falling foul of idiot compassion.

The Consultant

The sponsor will invite feedback and input from everyone involved in the costing exercise. However, they will make it clear that the final decision is theirs. The final decision is normally a drawn-out affair.

The Yes Man

The sponsor will invite all contributors to the costing in a discussion as a group to reach consensus. Everyone's voice is equal. What tends to happen is that ensuring harmony over making an effective decision, becomes the deciding factor.

The Advisor

This is a mythical figure of a sponsor who will attempt to influence estimators by discussing their opinion. However, the sponsor leaves it up to the estimators to decide. This never happens so I don't even know why I am writing this!

One of the Smartest Guys In the Room
'Investors don't like uncertainty.'
Kenneth Lay Enron CEO

THE GOOD NAVIGATOR,
THE BAD AND THE UGLY

"I'm a man without conviction; I'm a man who
doesn't know. You come and go."

Karma Chameleon

Culture Club

AN IT PROJECT MANAGER CAN take on many personas. You are what you think. I'm on one of those company away days. We have a new Director who is going to give a welcome speech. I was expecting something along the lines of, "We need more process and governance." But it never happened. On one PowerPoint slide, he sums up what he wants and does not want from the programme and project management team, in the form of 3 sentences and four personas. It was the most no-nonsense, common sense slide I have ever seen.

Certainty on time

Certainty on cost

No surprises

Navigator

Critic

Victim

Bystander

Now, I've read hundreds of books and articles on IT project management. They all provoke howls of disapproval and cynicism. There must have been over 100 people in the room on that day and no one disagreed with the words or personas on those slides. The 'beat the plan' IT Project Manager is a navigator. I've never forgotten those slides. I have used those personas in many a conversation. On closer reflection, I have always wondered why he never used the word 'hero'. The most commonly used term to describe a poor performing PM has to be 'cowboy', a term that has transferred, I think, from the building trade into the world of IT project management. However, some of the greatest westerns contain characters with the traits required to beat the plan. And there are some westerns that represent how not to manage IT projects.

Sergio Leone probably produced two of the best westerns of the 20th century: The Good, the Bad and the Ugly (1966); and Once Upon Time In the West (1967). Both films were part of a genre known as the Spaghetti Western. Sergio Leone's lead characters were different from the stereotypical cowboys. On the face of it, their actions were pretty ruthless and self serving but their end goal was always ulterior. They did not suffer fools gladly. Nor did they suffer from idiot compassionate. They were lone wolf outlaws who were suspicious of the local law and government. A modern day IT project manager needs to be sceptical in a positive manner about imposed ways of working. I have always wondered who would win in a gun fight between Harmonica, played by Charles Bronson in Once Upon Time In the West, and The Man With No Name played by Clint Eastwood in The Good, the Bad and the Ugly. Both had lightening reflexes and they were cool under pressure. In both films, these guys took severe beatings but they always got up and came back fighting. They could anticipate the next move and they always collected on what they were owed. They are all 'beat the plan' behaviours.

Francis Ford Coppola was not the first to be asked to direct the Godfather trilogy. It was Sergio Leone. Sergio Leone turned it down to work on Once Upon Time in the West. Sergio Leone chose the project that interested him and not necessarily the one that would make him famous in the world of popular cinema. Sergio Leone did go on to make a gangster film Once Upon Time In America but it never matched The Godfather in terms of commercial success. To beat the plan, work on an IT project that floats your boat.

The most shown film on US television according to Wikipedia is the Wizard of Oz. In second place is The Magnificent Seven (1960). The Magnificent Seven is a film about leadership and winning against all the odds. Chris Adams, played by Yul Brynner, leads the posse. Even though they win the day, most of his team is killed. As far as Chris Adams is concerned, it is a hollow victory. To beat the plan, the team you start with probably won't be the same team at the end of the project.

There are some cowboys you shouldn't learn behaviours from, like the guys from the film The Alamo (1960). The Alamo is a metaphor for a condition found on impaired or challenged IT project delivery, with a great team up against impossible odds whose confidence is greater than their ability to win. The Alamo was about trying to snatch an impossible victory from the jaws of defeat. Then there was the Lone Ranger. On the face of it, the Lone Ranger was a pretty dynamic guy; a lone wolf rushing in to save the day, getting the glory and all that. The reality was that in nearly every episode of the Lone Ranger, Tonto saved the Lone Ranger from a sticky situation. If the Lone Ranger was an IT Project Manager, he would be an anonymous fool treading where wise men fear to tread. Butch Cassidy and the Sundance

Kid (1969) is among the 100 top grossing films of all time. There is a great quote from the film, which sums up a situation commonly encountered on impaired or challenged IT projects:

Butch Cassidy

Kid, there's something I ought to tell you. I never shot anybody before.

Sundance Kid

One hell of a time to tell me!

Below, I have edited the words to illustrate the point.

Techie

PM, there's something I ought to tell you. I have never done this before.

Project Manager

One hell of a time to tell me!

THE AESOP PLANNER OF PROJECTS

'When explanations make no sense. When
every answer's wrong'
Breakout
Swing out Sister

THE MOST TECHNICALLY BRILLIANT PROJECT plan is useless unless you communicate it with a performance that contains substance. Coming up with a plan that looks great is easy, with a tool like Microsoft Project. Making the plan a true reflection of reality, is where the challenge lies. It is 1976 on a school night and the rain is pouring down. I am bored. No going out as it is too dark. There are only three channels on the TV; not much to watch I'm afraid. I hate Crossroads - some kids at school keep reminding me I look like Benny. No internet or games consoles in those days. You either made up your own entertainment or read a book. The Ladybird books were great. The best low level designers I have ever worked with write their designs as 'Ladybird' guides. On those rainy days I always sought solace in a set of encyclopaedias. There was one volume in particular that got my attention. It was a book full of fables from around the world. I loved the ones written by Aesop, an ancient Greek slave. Every one of his fables has a lesson in its meaning. Some of those lessons can be applied to project planning. Picture the scene: a start date, an end date, a time box, a business case, a problem, a load of resources, people, a budget, methodology and a box full of project management tools. Throw the whole lot in a bucket, mix in a dollop of blue chip culture and watch common sense run for cover at 3000mph. So the next time you Gantt up your IT project, try planning it with the following fables in mind:

The Ant and the Grasshopper

Be the ant. The grasshopper spends the summer
months singing and relaxing while the ant is working
hard preparing for the winter. There will be quiet days
on your IT project delivery. Do not take it easy; use
the time to plan for harder times. Don't make your IT
project dependent on resources from managers who
behave like the grasshopper.

The Ass and his Masters

Don't be an ass who hates his job. In this story, the ass
is habitually dissatisfied with his master. He prays to
the gods for a new master. When the Ass is given his
third master, the gods tire of his moaning. The ass ends
up with a master who works him harder than the first
one. It's so easy to perceive the grass is greener when
times are challenging on an IT Project. There are only
two types of jobs: jobs you hate; and jobs you love.
Do IT projects that float your boat. Being habitually
dissatisfied will impact on your performance.

The Astrologer Who Fell into a Well

This fable is about an ancient and clever astrologer.
As he is walking along gazing at the heavens,
contemplating the secrets of the universe, he falls into
a well and kills himself. Project management
is all about forward planning and being clever
about it. Always keep an eye on what's right in
front of you.

The Bird Catcher and the Blackbird

A blackbird observes a man laying bait and asks the
man, 'What are you doing?' The man replies, 'Laying
the foundations for a great city' and walks off. The
blackbird takes the bait and is trapped in a snare. It
dies a slow lingering death. An IT project will fail to
perform if its business case pretends to be something
it's not.

The Bear and the Travellers

Two friends are walking down a lonely path in a
forest. Suddenly a bear appears. The first guy legs it
up a tree while the second guy plays dead on the floor.
The bear sniffs the guy on the floor, then wanders off
leaving him unharmed. His friend climbs down from
the tree and asks, 'What did the bear say to you?' 'He
told me never to trust anyone who runs off in your
time of need. ' All IT projects have downers and
you need people around you that you can trust to
help you.

The Belly and the Members

This is a fable where the hands are jealous of the stomach. The stomach gets all the tasty food. Out of jealously the hands stop putting the food into the mouth. The hands only see sense when they start to weaken. The moral is about the importance of team effort.

The Boy Who Cried Wolf

Everyone knows this story. Ever slightly spun the escalation to get what you want? Do it all the time and you will get found out.

The Crow and the Pitcher

A thirsty crow finds a pitcher of water. Unfortunately, the crow cannot reach the water with its beak. The crow uses all its strength to topple the pitcher but to no avail. The crow works out that putting stones in the pitcher one by one raises the water. The fable demonstrates the power of thoughtfulness over brute strength.

The Dog and Its Reflection

A dog carrying a bone sees its reflection in a pool of water. Mistaking the bone in the reflection for a better bone, the dog tries to grab it. The dog loses the bone and is left with nothing. The story is about the paradox of choice. This happens when you give customers too many options. They choose one but may be left with the feeling that some of those other choices may have been far better. The problem with too much choice is a risk of wondering if some of those other options may have been better. Give the customer too many options and they will prevaricate. Keep the options distinct and keep it simple.

The Fir and the Bramble

The arrogant fir tree brags about how useful he is. Fir tree wood is used in roofing, tables and just about everything that is made using wood. The bramble points out that men are on their way laden with axes and saws to cut the fir trees down. It is a fable about the virtue of being humble. Fill your project team with humble, hardworking people.

The Honest Woodcutter

Be the woodcutter. A woodcutter accidentally drops his axe in the river. Having lost the tool that was his livelihood, he sobs. The god, Hermes, appears and dives into the water. He retrieves a golden axe but the woodcutter refuses to take it. Hermes dives again. He retrieves a silver axe but the woodcutter refuses to take it. Hermes retrieves the woodcutter's ordinary looking, worn out axe. The woodcutter is overjoyed. So impressed is Hermes with the woodcutter's honesty, he gives the woodcutter the silver and gold axes as a reward. Honesty is the best policy.

So now you are a bastion of virtue but the virtuous can inadvertently stray. When you are asked for a plan are you really being asked for a Gantt chart? What the project needs is planning, more than it needs a plan. Planning is more important than a plan. A plan without planning is a work of fiction. So when you are asked for a plan, the most counterproductive thing you can do is get your head down on Microsoft Project and come up with a plan. The data you are using is arbitrary in nature. Arbitrary is a word that oozes command and control:

Based on random choice or personal whim, rather than any reason or system.

Unrestrained and autocratic in the use of authority.

Synonyms; high-handed

Being arbitrary has a high propensity to be wrong just like all losers who thought they were winners in Aesop's Fables. The plan needs to be less arbitrary and more data driven. So when someone asks you for a plan, don't write a plan; go and do the planning activities, preferably using data from people who have done it before and data from people you know you can trust. The most trustworthy people are like Aesop - they are comfortable telling you what you don't want to hear.

Project planning tools, like Microsoft Project, are software tools with the mental powers greater than a Jedi. These tools have the ability to convince a Project Manager that everything will be alright; tools that turn people into tools! It makes you think that things are under control when they are not. Worst of all, it makes people think they have predicted the future using the mythical man-day. These tools are the ultimate spin doctor playing on a Project Manager's perception filter. It tells you want you want to know. It feeds off one's confirmation bias. Those lovely lean blue lines make you think you've brought order to chaos. Finish-to-start planning only works if you are making stuff that has been made several zillion times before. Finish-to-start is a constraint that won't deliver 'version 1.new' of anything that does not involve making stuff. Human beings working in the knowledge economy, just don't do finish-to-start. Combine this with using pockets of free time from business as usual resources, and you've got yourself in a cat-and-mouse game with every other manager calling on the same resources. There are four dynamics that these tools cannot show you on a dashboard:

Parkinson's Law

The work always fits the time available.

Student Syndrome

People always leave important boring stuff to the last minute.

The Halo Effect

Time poor and bored people gravitate towards what they enjoy doing.

The Interpretation Principle

Of several possible interpretations of a plan, the least convenient is the correct one.

ARCHITECTS & DESIGNERS NEED TO THINK LIKE STEVE JOBS

'I'm looking for a partner, someone who gets things fixed'

Opportunities

Pet Shop Boys

ARCHITECTS AND DESIGNERS ARE CRITICAL to the success of a complex IT project. What can they learn from Steve Jobs? You can quickly make a lot of enemies by writing a story or publishing an article. Just ask Salman Rushdie or look at what has happened to numerous journalists and civil rights leaders. This chapter will probably infuriate a few architects and designers from the world of IT but I don't think they will issue a fatwa. It is June 2013, 6:15 in the morning and I am writing this chapter. I am on my way to a session with a client from the Health Sector. I have just bumped into my neighbour. He too is an IT Project Manager on his way to see a client from the Health Sector. Four miles away from my house is a fellow IT Programme Manager. We work for the same firm. He too is working with a client from the Health Sector. All of us are complaining about one thing - a lack of clarity in the design. What are the odds of three IT Project Managers from different companies, living within 4 square miles, working in the same sector complaining about the same problem? Kismet or what! The Health Sector has suffered from the most inept IT project and programme performance in the history of IT project delivery.

It is 1988 and I have just bought a Commodore Amiga. The operating system has a graphical environment manager (GEM) user interface. At the same time, I have just started my BTEC National Diploma in Computer Studies. The college PCs use Windows 1.0 and MSDOS. I take to those tools like a fish to water. Fast forward to October 1990 and it is my fourth week in my first year at university. I cannot remember the last 4 weeks probably because of the alcoholic haze. The University uses Apple Macs. For some reason I find them hard to get along with (although I do think the fonts are nice). For the next 20 years, I ignore anything with Apple in the title (apart from Cider and desserts with apple in). It is now 2011 and I am moaning about the number of naff MP3 players I have been through. So I decide to give the Apple iPod Touch a go. I stand in awe at its design. How the hell did Apple make that? The more I read about Steve Jobs, the more I find myself wishing why can't the designers on my IT projects think like Steve Jobs? But before I can complain about others, maybe I need to eat my own dog food. I have always come up with great ideas but gave up because I perceived I lacked the means to do it or the means to acquire the means. Steve Jobs never suffered from the same insecurity. As a manager, Steve Jobs would never have tolerated the inadvertently imposed nonsense that IT project teams come up against. From what I have seen of Steve Jobs, he is fearless. The designers I work with encounter several sorts of problems. To understand the nature of these problems, you have to think like Steve Jobs.

Steve Jobs must have gone through tens of thousands of

ideas for the iPhone, iPad and iPod. Can you imagine the wild and wacky ideas brainstormed behind the closed doors? It would have been amazing to be a fly on the wall. Which design did he pick? He picked the design he knew Apple and its manufacturing could produce within the limits of their current capacity and capability. I call this 'deliverability'. The designers I have worked with during my time employed by several organisations, for some reason tend to ignore architecture that prescribes deliverability. I can agree that it is a management issue to make it happen. But an excellent designer would not design anything that cannot be built given an organisation's capacity, organisation and capability constraints. An excellent designer factors these constraints into the solution design.

It is November 1998 and I am working for the UK's number 1 retailer. It's my first Project Manager role. The design has a requirement to get CSV file from a mainframe to a client server platform. This is a pretty fundamental requirement. I am in a room full of the experts. It has never been done before and no one knows how to do it. It is the first time VB6, active server pages and SQL have been used to develop a business critical application. I hire an SQL contractor. He cannot turn the logical design into physical design; the project spirals out of control. I did not spot the danger quick enough. My ass is booted off the project and I am told to be a business analyst instead.

Rewind to 1996 and the BSE crisis is in full swing. I have to design and build a computer programme to capture the data to process the payment. There are tens of thousands of bits of paper flying into Central Government from farmers who need the money; their livelihoods have been wrecked. My design will only work if the ID number for each cow is correct. The rule is: no correct ID number, no payment. The forms are completed by farmers who work in sheds up to their legs in mud and dead animals. Is it any wonder that 30% of the ID numbers are incorrect or ineligible?

It is 1994, my final year at uni. Human computer interaction project is a prototype touchscreen interface for catalogue companies like Argos and Littlewoods. Four years later, I notice the concept turned into reality. I kick myself for not following through on the idea after graduating.

16 years later and I am working with an agile evangelist in local government. We want to create a development capability to integrate back office with front office. His motivation is to give the frontline better information quicker so they can respond more effectively to customer service requests. We need a development platform. An army of architects meticulously plan the logical design. It goes through a robust architectural review process. The physical design specifies the build and application software in Lego building block detail. Its gets built. The application development team start to use it but firewall rules are blocking the biztalk application server from talking to the database server. Firewalls rules are also blocking the team foundation server from talking to the database server. All of the servers are in the same data-centre. Every firewall rule involves 10-15 people, 2 separate forms, lots of phone calls, 2 service management systems and an engineer who I believe may be related to Norman Bates. The application team are twiddling their thumbs in the makings of an abnormal sprint. Finally we fix the firewalls. The apps team complete the software install so they can start development. Note the 'team'. Team implies plural. The development environment contains an interesting feature; only one developer can develop on it at any one time. I send an email out to everyone involved in the design asking how and why this has happened. Only the PM responds; the designers and builders stay quiet.

Rewind 3 years and I am rolling out our voice-over ip solution to 20 home-workers. It is the first time this has been attempted and it does not work. The firmware on the corporate routers is incompatible with the session initiation protocols on the VOIP solution. The root cause is discovered accidentally. Once we get the phones going, we have to provide the users access to an early version of an externally hosted Microsoft Lync solution. It was called Office Communication Server (OCS). This does not work. I can access from my home PC. It works perfectly. Something to do with a proxy bypass, which I'd always thought was an incognito busy road that went around the outskirts of a village. That programme had 3 full-time voice and data technical design authorities. 4 years later and a fax over ip solution won't work. A server at a data centre in the south of the country won't talk to an exchange in the north of the country. It's my old friend session initiation protocol again. The supplier insists they have supplied all the firewall rules; we have reams and reams of them. I fall into the email tennis and trying-to-fix-a-problem-with-the-same-people-who-created-it trap. It is only when two sets of fresh eyes ask some eyes-of-a-child questions that the problem becomes apparent.

12 months after that, I am talking to a wiz of a Cisco designer and engineer. He tells me about a project to implement WiFi. During implementation the true requirement emerges. The agreed requirement is for data only across the airwaves. The true requirement is voice and data. He asked the question and played back the requirement during the design stage. The answer was data only.

Steve Jobs knew exactly what his customer requirements were. My 15 year career in IT project management is littered with these tales of woe; not following through on good ideas or uncovering unforeseen technical debt during build and implementation. I hear the same stories from many an IT Project Manager. The designers involved attribute the problems to 'inability to execute'. There is some truth in that statement but I am left with the feeling that if everyone involved thought like Steve Jobs during design activity, then maybe I would not hate firewalls and change management processes so much. I know when a design process is going to be flawed because I have this reoccurring dream. In the dream, I am walking along the beach on a desert island; I am stranded on the island. The sun is shining and it is warm. Sunlight reflecting off the calm surface of the sea creates the illusion there are diamonds just under the surface. In the distance a violent storm is brewing. There are horrible monsters in that storm. The storm represents what is going to happen on my IT project. It is my subconscious telling me I am not really happy about the way the designers are going about the design process. I notice a green washed up bottle and in the bottle is a magical leprechaun. He says he will give me one wish if I let him out. I let him out and he gives me the wish. Being the nice chap that I am, I wish for world peace and an end to child poverty. The little leprechaun says, "That is beyond my ability. Try something else and be selfish." So I wish for all the designs on my IT projects to be so good that they all work perfectly first time. The leprechaun asks me, "Which organisations are you working with and are going to work with?" I give him the list. The leprechaun says, "Let's have a go at that first wish!" The storm hits and all those Ray Harryhausen heebie jeebie stop-motion creations chase me around the Island. Steve Jobs did not rely on wishful thinking or magical fairy folk from the netherworld.

The definition of a challenged project is 'over estimated on time or budget and lacks important features when finally delivered'. IT projects slip a minute at a time. It is not hard to see the relationship between flaws in the thinking that went into the design process, and the symptoms of a challenged or impaired delivery. To beat the plan, it is the factors exacerbating the flaws in the thinking where the attention should go. I know many a technical designer and architect. They are deadly serious about what they do. Information Security Architects are the most serious. I think they carry around those pens with the red flashing lights that make you tell the truth, or forget stuff like the ones in the film Men In Black. They are good fun as well. I sent an email to an information and IT security guru. The email read along the lines, " I have a client in a sensitive business who has some concerns about the impact of bring-your-own-device

(BYOD). Can you help?" He called me back and I told him the client was a distributor of sex toys and the sales people, who ran the home parties, were getting more and more requests from the customers to BYOD. The client needed professional advice. My colleague was deadly serious about the matter. We need to do vulnerability assessment and architect out the information security management system (ISMS). Then there are logical and physical controls to consider. It took him a while to figure out he had been punk'd! The point is architects and designers are deadly serious about what they do. They want to see their creations work first time with the wow factor just as much as I do. But something is going on in our organisations today in the psyche of the IT project team which counters the influences that give us the performance we see from people like Steve Jobs and Mr Dyson. When I talk to these guys outside of the workplace about work in the context of what they do in their spare time, there are glimpses of Steve Jobs type thinking. In the workplace those traits disappear. My theory is that Steve Jobs had 'flow' and the business architecture around him, to make the design process exemplar. If an IT project can replicate the performance traits surrounding Steve Jobs, the climate starts to engender behaviours required to beat the plan.

My first observation is the structure of management found in the large organisations. The design is known as scientific management/command and control. It is the organisational structure behind the financial crash. Managed top down, the organisation is a triangle where the power and the high salaries are in the top of the triangle. Those at the bottom of the triangle don't have the power and have a significantly less salary than those at the top. Designers need to be in the top of the triangle sitting next to directors and executives who have the power to make things happen. If not, they will constantly seek alternative employers. Steve Jobs sat in the top of a triangle. His sphere of influence spanned all domains within the Apple organisation. The last place you should put a designer, responsible for designing IT that will change how the work is done, is in the IT function. They need to be part of the business world. Personally, I'm not bothered where I sit in an organisation. An IT Project Manager's powerbase is expert power, informational power and charisma. Maybe I've been shaped too much by the organisations I've worked for. Ok - we've sorted the power, status and money thing for our architects and designers. Their happiness levels will rise for a couple of months. But this alone is not enough to keep a technical designer's motivation levels off the Richter scale. They have to be part of a network that spans their employers' boundary. It is a network that feeds our designers with ideas, lessons learned and challenging feedback from peers about their performance. This network gives our designers access to positive sceptics and critical friends because: firstly, talented and clever designers don't listen to anyone with manager in their title; secondly, they are very happy when beating each other up with their metaphorical lightsabers, which represents the power of their knowledge; lastly, the network gives them access to coaching and mentoring. Designers love learning new stuff. Above anything else, they fear their skills becoming out of date. In my humble opinion they won't find this in their home organisation. It is because their employer recruited them to be the expert. So now they are paid loads, have loads of power and are hooked into the knowledge grid. But this is still not enough to get a designer, technical architect or any type of architect into a 'beat the plan' mindset. They have to love what they do. If not, they will make schoolboy errors. Lose the talented and gifted ones who don't love what they do; their designs will be mediocre. Steve Jobs loved his job. With all these ingredients, the results is Mihály Csíkszentmihályi,'s flow (Flow: The Psychology Optimal Experience by Csikszentmihalyi, Mihaly Jul-01-2008). Flow is an energised and positive emotional state where you will be at the top of your game. Steve Jobs radiates flow.

If you are part of an organisation that delivers many different kinds of complex IT projects, then maybe it would be a tad irrational to assume a single organisational structure could be designed to cater for all those different types of deliveries. Hence the reason why an IT project is a temporary management environment conducive to the scope of the delivery. So think about this. When was the last time you saw a complete method statement describing how the solution should be delivered within the documentation for a complex solution design? Surely the business architecture to build something, is an inherent part of the something that is to be built. My question is: Why is the architecture required to build the solution, (which in essence is critical business architecture), not seen as part of the solution design? Take any best of breed software product or commodity IT service. When you buy this stuff, there are reams and reams of information about how it is designed and what it does. Service orientated this, loosely coupled that etc. all based on a set of empirically proven and logical architectural principles. But where are the descriptions of the required business architecture processes, types of people and culture required to implement the product? When I buy anything from a shop, it comes with a set of instructions about how to put it together. Take fighter jets, for example. A fighter jet in terms of complexity surpasses any IT project. Fighter jets come with instructions about what you need to do to build one. I suspect Apple have documented to the nth degree the processes and culture required to build something like the iPad. The companies designing the products that IT Project Managers have to implement, do not think like Steve Jobs. The cynic in me believes these companies want to see failed IT projects so that their customers spend a fortune on professional services. Maybe IT projects have a high propensity to fail because the business architecture to deliver them was not as thought through as the technical architecture behind the product that IT Project Managers have to implement. In some ways, IT Project Manager 2015+ has to wear two hats: a business architect hat to specify the business architecture to deliver the project; and a leadership hat to make it happen within agreed acceptability threshold. The world of IT project delivery needs to think like Steve Jobs.

'A lot of people in our industry haven't had very diverse experiences. So they don't have enough dots to connect, and they end up with very linear solutions without a broad perspective on the problem. The broader one's understanding of the human experience, the better design we will have.'

Steve Jobs

GET A GREAT DESIGNER AND PUT THEM IN THE LIMELIGHT

'I don't wanna be hip and cool. I don't wanna
play by the rules. Not under the thumb of the
cynical few'

New Song

Howard Jones

THE TECHNICALLY GIFTED ARE PROUD folk. Like any proud
artisan, they don't want their peers to see mistakes or
failures. They want to work privately, in a cave, then spring
'perfect' product on their end users. Give them the X-Factor
and put them in the limelight.

It is 1977 and my parents pick me up from school. Instead
of walking home, we get on the bus into town. I'm like, "Oh
no. Walking around supermarket time." But we don't go to
the supermarket. Our destination is the cinema to watch Star
Wars. I will never forget that day. Mum and Dad bought me
a film programme guide that unfolds into a poster of C3PO
and R2D2. It is one of the most memorable partnerships in the
science fiction film genre. In the film, R2D2 is Luke Skywalker's

wingman in the X-wing. As they start their bombing run speed at the speed of light in the Deathstar's trench, I am in awe at the special effects. Then R2 gets blasted. It was a heart stopping moment. I was on the verge of crying. Skywalker loses his wingman. IT Project Manager 2015+ need many types of wingmen. Skywalker blew up the Deathstar without his wingman. Losing your wingman during a critical period of IT project delivery has a less exciting outcome.

This chapter is about a wingman you cannot do without; your lead techie guru. They come in all shapes and sizes depending on the needs of the project. Probably best to learn about what they do because these are the folk that design what you need to deliver. They guide the builders with the correct instructions. They come with the answers when it does not work, when the switch is flicked for the first time. If they don't do their thing well, the IT project will fail to perform. So you have to come up with the ingredients that will inspire them to come up with great designs, whilst they inspire the builders to build it.

Solution architect

Enterprise architect

Service architect

Functional consultant

Network technical design authority

Apps architect

Security consultant

Infrastructure technical design authority

Business design authority

Process architect

Integration lead

The problem is they can be prone to inadvertently succumbing to some clarity-killing, disunity-inducing ways of working. It is not their fault. There are many reasons. You have to be aware of the pitfalls they can fall foul of. If the design is wrong, flawed or beyond the capacity/capability of the organisation to build it, the IT project will fail to perform. Your project will end up as a statistic in the challenged or impaired category.

The first trap is designing a solution based on poorly defined requirements. In my world, the architect or designer does not see it as their role to validate requirements. So where do the requirements come from? From the customer, of course, and why not? After all, the customer is always right. Wrong. Firstly, the customer may know what they want but what they want may not necessarily be what the customer needs. Secondly, the customer may not be able to afford what they need or want. This is why it is considered common sense to run design and analysis activities in parallel with one another. The design will be deficient if the design stage is fed with information from the following climate:

Informal scope definition processes result in Shaun the Sheep woolly requirements aka vagueness.

Failure to address excessive scope volatility or uncontrolled scope creep (classic mistake award winner)

Open ended requirement statements. The wording tends to end in 'etc'.

Failure to control variations in scope or uncontrolled scope creep during the design stage

Poor understanding of the operational environment in which the solution is being delivered, needs to perform once the IT project is complete.

Requirements are defined by middle men who do not consult extensively with those who will eventually use the solution.

Lack of scrutinising the requirements against the IT project's objectives to ensure linkage with the business case.

Failure to broker agreement between stakeholders with differing perspectives or requirements

Failure to achieve a shared sense of understanding of the requirements across key stakeholders.

It is an acquired risk when a designer, in a lead role on an IT project, blindly accepts a set of requirements from a customer for the project. The designer has an obligation to ask a key question :

Are the requirements fit for design purposes?

All the world's greatest designers ask this question. That is why their products are great. The best CIOs I have seen in action ask this question. A designer that does not ask searching questions of the quality of the requirements, is a mediocre one. To beat the plan, you need excellent designers on the team. Your job is to execute the managerial actions necessary to create the climate so that your lead designer gets a set of exemplar defined requirements. Get yourself a business analyst. When solving a complex problem that involves enabling IT, a business analyst is not a nice-to-have; it is a must. They are trained to ensure requirements are properly defined. So let us assume you've got yourself an exemplar set of defined requirements for your designer to work from. Watch for their next set of actions. I have outlined below what to expect from a mediocre designer. To beat the plan, you need one that will do the exact opposite.

They will disappear for 4 weeks, not talk to anyone and a documented design will suddenly appear in your inbox asking you to chase customer sign-off.

They will have an expectation that the requirements won't change.

They will be surprised and a rabbit-in-the-headlights when the requirements change as they are writing the design.

These are behaviours that do not increase clarity and demonstrate a lack of agility. If we are what we think, then would it be unreasonable to assume designs inherit the traits in their creators? The disappearing act to write a design is known as 'going dark'. I think they do it for 2 reasons. The first is super ego. After all, they are the expert and they have a God given right to be right. All fine if they are right but how do you know they are right? The second reason is insecurity. They are afraid of their design being criticised. The 21st century has seen the birth of give-it-to-me-now celebrity status, all personified in reality shows like Big Brother and the X-Factor. These shows attract thousands upon thoisands of entrants seeking instant celebrity status. No matter how talented they are, they will put themselves in front of a highly critical panel of judges and a baying crowd. What the entrants get back is good advice from people with the experience and a 'wisdom of the crowd' vote of confidence. A 'beat the plan designer' craves celebrity status. They want the opportunity to share with the world, their design. They are fearless about putting it in front of the critics and sceptics. They are comfortable with taking constructive feedback on the chin. Your job as IT Project Manager is to help create the opportunity for this. So when I say 'share', I don't mean send it out on email or sharepoint for time poor managers to comment on. That is the worst thing a designer could do. These processes are not conducive for creating clarity and unity. Think about the recipient's average day: 50+ emails, 3-4 meetings, escalations and line management issues. When are they going to have the time to sit and read a complex design document with all those distractions around them? The most important reason why managers should not be solely responsible for signing off a design is because they are not the ones who are going to build it. Experienced builders generally know what will work and what won't work. A designer who is averse to involving the builders is a mediocre one. An insecure designer will ask you to take their design and walk it through with the builders. They are fearful of criticism. Do not do this. You are not the expert in the design. You will make mistakes. There will be questions you cannot answer. Attempting to answer those questions will reduce your credibility and worry the builders. Egotistical self-obsessed designers ask you questions for the following reason; talking to the engineers is beneath them. As far as they are concerned, it is a manager's job. When you act as a bridge between the designers and builders, clarity is reduced and latency is increased into the project communications process.

Once you've got yourself a design, the designer needs to put it through a 'dragons den'. This is a star chamber made up of people who have got to pay for the design, use it, test it, build it and support it. The designer needs to stand up in front of the audience and walk though their creation. The walkthrough has to be a memorable performance or nobody will listen. The audience needs to be encouraged to critique. One of the best techniques for a technical walkthrough is where the designer draws the solution on a white board. A great design is one that contains the substance communicated via an exciting performance. During a TED talk on fear, it was stated that death and public speaking where in the top 4 things people were afraid of. A great designer is proud of their creation and relishes the challenge of taking on the naysayers. You cannot beat the plan without a great designer. I once worked on a challenged IT programme for 2 years. Every IT project portfolio followed the governance process, yet we suffered from identifying some form of technical debt during implementation and testing. These were mainly, active directory integration, network latency, DNS and firewalls not being opened. The governance process relied on review by managers using email and share-point workflow. The process did not encourage involvement from the builders. The only delivery that did not suffer to the same extent as previous deliveries, was the one where I literally dragged the designer kicking and screaming to subject the design to a 'dragons den', i.e. to be scrutinised by everyone on the team.

The diagram below shows the elements of the design presented at the sessions, thus giving you an idea of the topics to be covered. Covering the right topics is important but making sure the right people attend, pitching at a level the audience understands, and making the session memorable, are equally important.

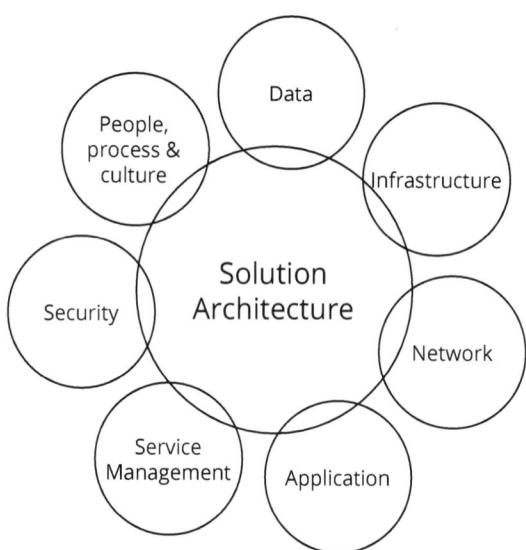

Designers are nurtured on a diet of methodology. Designers love following an engineering based approach, which is great.

After all, we do need them to be scientific and empirical. A great designer will seek conformance to a design method. They will use a method in a Tetris manner, using only what is needed from the method and where it makes common sense to do so. A mediocre designer will seek full compliance and adherence out of sheer bloody-mindedness.

To beat the plan, you need great designers who seek the limelight to show off their creations. They relish crossing lightsabers with those with the audacity to question their creations. A great designer is fearless when it comes to dealing with criticism. They want to talk to everyone who will be part of the journey to bring their creation to life. Get a great designer or make your designers great.

BUILD A VISION THEN BUILD RELATIONSHIPS

'What do we need to make our world come alive?'

Vision Thing

Sisters of Mercy

'DOMINION' IS A WORD THAT conjures up the picture of an unstoppable empire under control. Dominion is a word synonymous with sovereignty and control. Popular culture is filled with characters who have created dominion. They have full spectrum dominance over the domain they operate in. Evil geniuses in comic books; great football managers, like Alex Ferguson; Montegomary Burns from the Simpsons; business leaders like Jack Welch; all exude the qualities to achieve dominion. They all did a couple of things well. They took the time to sit in quiet contemplation. These guys had vision and were adept at surrounding themselves with the organisation to make their vision happen.

Synonyms for dominion:

supremacy, ascendancy, dominance, domination, superiority, predominance, pre-eminence, primacy, hegemony, authority, mastery, control, command, direction, power, sway, rule, government, jurisdiction, sovereignty, suzerainty, lordship, over-lordship, leadership, influence, the upper hand, the whip hand, the edge, advantage, hold, grasp, archaic-empire, rare-predomination.

I have worked side by side with some of the most productive IT Project and Programme Managers ever seen. They deliver projects while everyone else is thinking it cannot be done. Some of these guys were around doing this delivery stuff long before IT Project Management got 'the one true way' methodologised and robotomated. Most of them don't have an alphabet. They don't particularly specialise in one particular domain. They are just good at what they do. So the questions are: What are they doing? Why are they doing it? and How are they doing it? Before I answer, I will tell you what they are not doing. Now bear in mind they have a ridiculously dis-empowering low level of budgetary authority. They have no legitimate authority over resources. A lot of what they do is delivering in a multi organisation matrix managed environment, sometimes across different time zones. What they are not doing is playing golf with board members. They are not micro managing people to get things done. They are not constantly approval chasing. The project they are leading is not being de-prioritised. They are not waiting and waiting and waiting and waiting for decisions. The first thing they are not doing is writing a PID. The first thing they are not doing is writing a plan. The first thing they are not doing is all the project management stuff that goes in a temporary management environment, whose reason for existence is the delivery of a project. Here is the first clue.

Who creates the temporary management environment? You do - because if you don't your project will fail. Without first creating the management environment, your role as a project will just be one where you report performance against time, budget and quality along with the bad news because nothing is getting done. I can hear mumbles along the lines 'but it's the organisation's job to create the climate for my project to be successful'. Really? Think about your thinking here. Where does your way of thinking come from? Who told you this was way things are going to be? What if the managers are shaped by the organisation they work for? If you can write down the names of those both accountable and responsible for creating a temporary management environment in your organisation, for an IT project to be successful, and those names agree with you - great. If your organisation is one of those whose IT projects consistently exceed performance against original baseline, then there's o need to read this chapter. If not, read on and get Zen.

I love the way organisations talk about 'we have a culture of continuous improvement, empowerment and we will help you to live your dream and performance management.' That's all the climate you need for an IT project to thrive. So why does an organisation need a temporary management environment if the necessary climate is supposedly the norm? The way things are usually done are not the ways a 'beat the plan' IT project gets done. But there is some implicit small print from the status quo when attempting to do things differently. It reads, 'try not to be different in the way you do things to get things done.' Accepting this constraint results in your IT project only being able to move at the speed that the organisation usually moves at; which in my experience is not quick enough. For sales reasons, providers of ICT solutions, professional services, outsourcing and software are less than candid to their clients about how not-ready they are to gain value from what is being offered. It is just assumed that the customer has capacity and capability to do all the things they are not used to doing, to get the product in and adding value. Hence another reason for the creation of a temporary management environment. Let me give you an example. Take a very simple WiFi installation (couple of wireless controllers, 20-30 access points, 5 x access switches) at a new building that a customer is moving into. Here are 15 interfaces spread across several matrix managed organisations that need to be involved in the process of getting the solution up and running. Now I dare anyone to try and deliver the installation without thinking through the management environment to do so.

1. Security for physical access
2. The building contractor
3. The electrical sub contractor
4. The cabling sub contractor
5. The customer's network people
6. Reception people to put in the process for guest access
7. The supplier's network people
8. Various resource managers
9. The logistics people and couriers
10. Finance
11. Procurement
12. The team supplying the network engineers
13. The end users
14. The desktop people
15. Pest control. (Note on this project there were some creatures living in the server rooms!)

A primary action and critical role of the PM is to bring the parties together to achieve clarity, unity and agility. The environment to do so needs to be created. The masters of delivery I referred to at the beginning of the chapter have a couple of things in common. They create a vision of how the project needs to be delivered. They recognise their own limitations in delivering a 'beat the plan' vision of delivery. So their goal is to surround themselves with relationships and organisation to make it happen i.e. dominion over the delivery space. It requires a healthy disrespect of and a Fleetwood Mac you-can-go-your-own-way attitude to, how things are normally done around here. They recognise that organisation exists only through action. They know organisation never pre-exists action. They take the action because they know what it is they need, to beat the plan. You will never hear these guys say, 'What do you want me to do?' You will hardly ever hear the people who work for them, and with them, ask the same question.

So the rest of this chapter is an attempt to bottle what these masters of delivery do with a few simple tools and a bit of science. The first tool demonstrates how to use the Campbell Ashridge Mission Model to frame your project's mission statement. This will help you instil a sense of self-empowered direction and purpose. The second tool is the Auguste Rodin's Thinking Man's IT Project Delivery Target Operating Model. This will help you define and then implement the relationships and organisation necessary, to achieve dominion over the delivery space. The third tool is the clarity-o-meter; a simple set of questions designed to help you understand the level of clarity present in your project team. Please bear in mind that these are not documents you produce for some committee to approve and then implement. These tools are about helping you get clarity on the mission you want to execute and the organisation you feel the need to surround yourself with. It's about articulating what your gut instinct is telling you i.e what you feel you need. Then, and only then, can you have the conversations necessary to put in place. That will depend on the strength of your argument, what you can offer in terms of an incentive to engage, and whether they like you or not. These are the behaviours of a successful 'beat the plan' IT Project Manager.

The Campbell Ashridge Mission Model from Andrew Campbell is a paradigm that is both easy to understand and use, to create a sense of mission. Outlined below is a picture of the original framework:

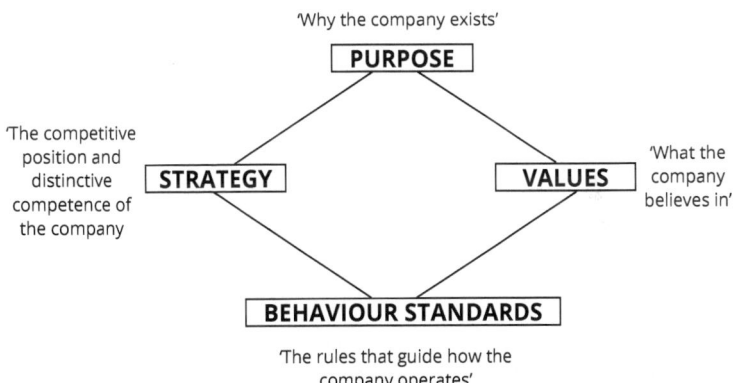

The key to the exercise is to define a mission statement for the project's temporary management environment. There are 11 rules. Rule number 1: Don't write it down yet. Shut your eyes and picture the mission model in your head. Turn yourself into Rodin. Rule number 2: Change the word 'company' to 'project team'. Rule number 3: The project's mission model cannot inherit any dysfunctionality from your organisation's or delivery partner's general management culture. Rule number 5: The project's mission model must inherit the what's-great-about-your-organisation's-or-delivery-partner's -general-management culture. Rule number 6: Think about the organisation you most admire and why. Now pick some performance traits and add them to your mission statement that you feel will give your project greater clarity, unity and agility. Rule number 7: Think of strategy as the means to achieve the project team's purpose. Rule number 8: When it feels great write it down. Rule number 9: Ask yourself some searching questions before you write it down. Is the project's mission inspirational? Is the project's mission ulterior? Does the mission model paint an attractive portrait of the project's business case? Does the project's mission model articulate the competitive advantage as a result of the business using the project's deliverables i.e. the ICT solution? Rule number 10: Focus your communication efforts on achieving a shared sense of understanding of the project's mission model across everyone you need on board, to get the work done.

Le Penseur (The Thinker) is a sculpture by Auguste Rodin. The sculpture is a nude male figure greater than life-size, sitting with his chin resting on one hand as though deep in contemplation. The image is often used to signify philosophy and intellect. Some say the figurine depicts Dante at the gates of hell pondering his great poem. The sculpture reminds me of the those guys that make IT project delivery look like a walk in the park. They don't want to walk through fire and brimstone to get things done. They want an easy life where promises are kept. They know they cannot do it on their own. They also know that micro management, accompanied by prescriptive granular task level project plans developed by the person who is not going to do the work, is a time-stealing daily tsunami of emails and a recipe for failure. I know that most of them disappear off the grid for a while to think through who they need around them, before rushing headlong into a delivery. Surrounding yourself with the organisation to get an IT project delivered is synonymous with structure, process and governance. This way of thinking comes from the way we are taught and experience management in large organisations. But doing this effectively requires the Project Manager to think in terms of creating a network of relationships motivated by positive and negative reinforcement to: a) ensure everyone gets what they want; and b) everyone is working towards a common goal. It is a society or community of collective interest. There are scientists who have tried to come up with frameworks, which describe how a society is constituted. Most notably (and outlined in the diagram below) is Anthony Giddens in his piece, 'The constitution of society: Outline of the theory of structuration', (1984 Cambridge: Polity Press. ISBN 0-520-05728-7). I've included the Giddens framework to show there is science from people with alphabets after their name, who have sought to identify the building blocks behind a social group. Traditional IT project management and development methodologies are process centric; that is do this, and then this followed by that. This is fine if: everyone involved in the delivery is an engineer; the requirements are crystal clear; the requirements never change; and the solution has been implemented a million times before. But modern day IT projects are not like that other than the zen aspects behind agile IT project management.

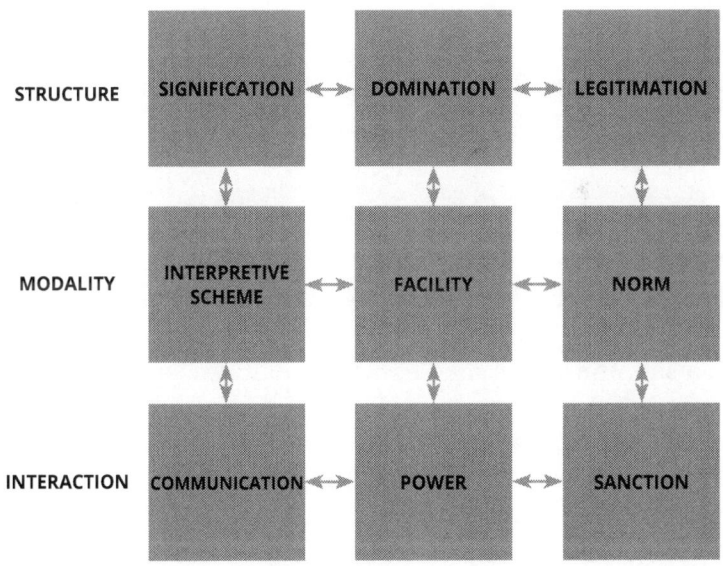

A colleague of mine is in the business of turnaround or delivering large technology-enabled transformation. During my dealings with him, he made lots of references to the words 'Dung Beetle'. Initially, I was taken aback as I thought the reference had a very negative connotation. Then I read this on Wikipedia: "The American Institute of Biological Sciences reports that dung beetles save the United States' cattle industry an estimated US$380 million annually." The dung represents all the vitally important managerial, political, financial, people and quality management stuff that a technically focused left-brained IT Project Manager finds completely boring. Thus, an inadvertent tendency to gravitate towards the stuff that floats our boat, whilst ignoring the 'dung', will significantly reduce your chances of success. The 'dung' is all the really important non-technical management leadership stuff you have to do on an IT project that you don't want to do. You probably don't have time to do it and you might not be very good at it. But what you have to be good at is recognising the limits in your limitations and having the get-up-and-go to surround yourself with people who can either deliver the necessary ways of working tthat they don't teach you on a project management course, or make up for your weaknesses. Here is my attempt to articulate the gaps in the ability of IT Project Managers that I've experienced on challenged programmes, being conducted in a multi-vendor and matrix managed environment.

Every piece of software, management process or hardware you will deliver will have a method for implementing it. You need people around you who not only know about what the hardware and software can do, but also the technical sequence in which it should be built and serviced. Every technical component in a technical solution will talk to another technical component. Servers cannot communicate unless they are networked. Applications on servers cannot talk to eachother unless they are interfaced. Therefore, understanding the technical critical path and it's critical path is more important than just having a macro understanding of the critical path. However, it will be impossible for you to understand every technical intricacy and how each solution component's method statement fits with every other solution component's method statement. Surround yourself with clever people who understand the sequence in which technical solutions need to be built.

The next pieces in the puzzle are the delivery principles. Live by these principles whilst delivering an IT project. To beat the plan, everyone involved in the project must live by these principles.

Predictable outcomes

Fiscally prudent

Operationally stable

Satisfied stakeholders

Easier said than done if you try to do this on your own. Surround yourself with people who will keep everyone around you satisfied. Surround yourself with people who can empathically measure satisfaction and sense dissatisfaction. Unless you enjoy being King Solomon, surround yourself with people who will tell eachother when they are not satisfied with eachother. Surround yourself with people who will proactively redress dissatisfaction without being told to do so.

Every IT Project Manager needs a Captain Scott from the Starship Enterprise. Captain Scott is the guy who make the point in an excitable manner, "Carry on like that and IT is gonna blow." Operational stability tends to mean one thing to an IT Project Manager; in the rush to get the solution live, functionally it does what it says it should do in the build documentation. Achieving operational stability is much more than that. It is delivering the solution in a manner that is not disruptive to business-as-usual. It's about thinking about how the solution will be supported and serviced post go-live. Transition into operational support starts at the beginning of the project and carries on long after the project has been closed. Surround yourself with operational people to help you do this. Work with them to achieve clarity on the service design before the service design is implemented. During the design stage, walk them through the solution. Listen to them when they say they can't support part of the solution. The only people who truly know the absolute meaning of operationally stable are operations people. It's one of their key goals every working day, thus leaving you to focus on getting things done.

There are 3 types of IT Project Manager - ones that can count and ones that cannot. Did you know that 70% of spreadsheets used to report financial information contain errors? How do you know you are being fiscally prudent? Are you black and white when it comes to reporting the financials or are you 50 shades of grey? Getting to the financial truth is not easy. You are dealing with actuals from invoices, accurals from purchase orders yet to be invoiced and money you need to spend in the future. Surround yourself with accountancy types whose expertise is the visibility of the financial truth. Surround yourself with a financial dragon's den of characters, like the ones Alan Sugar surrounds himself with, to scrutinise what you've spent, how you've spent, how you buy, who you buy from and what you are going to spend. When was the last time you thought about supplier stratification? In plain English, do you truly know how dependent your IT project is on a supplier and could they be easily substituted if their performance became unsatisfactory? Procurement and vendor management are integral processes in the world of project management but sometimes generalist knowledge and just doing the basics may not be enough. Make sure you have access to people who know about how to buy and how not to buy.

How do you predict an outcome if you are neither psychic nor a clairvoyant? The truth is you will have a far better chance of predicting the future if lots of people, who have done and measured a similar delivery, are involved in the process of prediction. You need to surround yourself with people who get a buzz out of measuring performance. The more complex the project, the more things you need to measure. The themes are quality, volume, clarity, unity, capacity, expectation, motivation, opportunity, value for money, and ability. They are probably measures you are not used to measuring. Surround yourself with people who know to measure important things you are not used to measuring. An outcome is easier to predict if people, with experience of delivering the outcome, are involved in both the measurement and the delivery. The world of IT changes constantly so it's likely that part of your delivery will involve delivering something you've never delivered before. You have to be comfortable with the feeling of not knowing everything, seeking advice from those who can fill gaps in your knowledge and you have to be comfortable living with uncertainty. To do this, you will need to create a network of experience you can dip into. It literally means being able to pick up the phone and ask someone a question about anything you are not sure about.

When it comes to allocating work packages, the text book reads like this: Document a work package; give it to a team manager; off the work package goes into a black box; the work gets done. Should you care about what goes on in the black box? You probably do care but only at the point when you hear things have not gone to plan. What if you had a choice of 2 black boxes for a complex and important piece of technical work? The first box is made up of processes that, when followed, results in the work you want doing, getting done. The second box contains a team manager who is a great coach, team lead, mentor, passionate about their team's performance and a big fan of reward and recognition. If IT projects are an assembly line of complex work packages, which black box would you want to feed your work package into? Welcome to the 'process over people' box. That's the box your instincts are telling you to feed complex work into. It's a world populated by smart and wise people. Smart people learn from their mistakes. Wise people learn from the mistakes of others. Smart and wise people work for great managers who understand the power of continually developing and rewarding their teams. Surround yourself with great people-centric managers who lead teams that love to learn. They will never ask you 'what do you want me to do?'

IT projects tend to be conducted in a multi vendor environment involving matrix managed organisations. If that's the case, which one of the following words is the most important: joint, partner, delivery or governance? Can you deliver or govern effectively when collaboration with your partners is weak? Project management methods tend to encourage governance models around customer-supplier type relationships. 'Joint' means candour and honesty in conversations with your partners. 'Joint' means giving your partners and suppliers the chance to redress when they get it wrong. 'Joint' means encouraging your suppliers and partners to be more honest than wise. 'Joint' means pushing the internal organisation to make the necessary things ready, so your partners and suppliers can thrive. In my experience, the higher up you go in an organisation the more times you will hear reasons for poor IT project performance attributed to external factors; the big one being supplier performance. As you move down the organisation, the reasons become attributed to internal ways of working. Partner and supplier performance is not immune to the impact of poor internal ways of working that plague the modern day IT project. So it never fails to amaze me the amount of money organisations pay on IT suppliers, then go out their way to avoid removing the internal barriers, which results in poor supplier performance. Joint delivery partnership governance is a management bingo buzzword that means each partner or supplier is looking inwards to remove barriers that prevents eachother from performing. Surround yourself with governance that is not afraid to look at its own internal machinery and challenge inept ways of working. Work at relationships so there is comfort when you have to point out naff internal ways of working, which compromises IT project performance.

'The first method for estimating the intelligence of a ruler is to look at the men he has around him.'

Niccolo Machiavelli

BECOME THE LORD OF
THE 7 RINGS

'Much communication in a motion. Without
conversation or a notion.'

Avalon

Roxy Music

'I' PROJECTS ARE MADE UP of five iterative interlocking types
of processes, resulting in distinct multiple catalytic teams.
Understand the pattern to achieve greater agility, clarity and
unity.

'One ring to rule them all' is a phrase that anyone, who
knows anything about elves and dwarves, will immediately
recognise. It is taken from the inscription inside the ring from
J.R.R. Tolkien's fantasy epic, The Lord of the Rings. According to
Wikipedia, Tolkien's Lord of the Rings is the second bestselling
novel ever to be written. In 1978, I remember sneaking into the
local cinema to watch the first animated film. But it was not
until 1992 that I actually read the whole book. Two years later,
I've got my first role on an IT project. As the years pass by, I
am left with a feeling that the Lord of the Rings metaphorically

maps to the more successful IT projects I have worked on. Secondly, the ring metaphor is a much more accurate way of conceptualising a successful IT project team structure than any hierarchical diagram.

Successful IT projects flow like Tolkien's trilogy. The first book in the trilogy is called Fellowship of the Ring. It is about the team coming together but it comes together as a result of going through, and overcoming, adversity. The battles, trials and tribulations faced by the fellowship in the first book are hard but they become progressively harder as the trilogy progresses. The Mines of Moria came before the battle at Helms Deep. IT projects are the same. Analysis is hard but it is not as hard as design. Design is harder than analysis but not as difficult as turning the design into reality. Build may be harder than design but not as hard as achieving production capability. Achieving production capability is challenging but not as challenging as both proving and sustaining service utility and warranty, to a post go-live support team. If the critical path or critical chain is sequenced to take account of team dynamics and learning curves, then the team has a greater propensity for success. Every delivery challenge on the critical path has to be seen as an opportunity to prepare the team for the next challenge. The second book in the trilogy, The Two Towers, tells the story of the first decisive battle between the free people of Middle Earth and Lord Sauron. The Wizard Sauramon joins forces with the dark Lord Sauron. Sauramon creates an army to exterminate the race of men. On an IT project, Sauramon's army represents the years of cynicism and scepticism faced by an IT project team, as a result of the end user experience of IT project delivery over the last 15 years. It's the 'here we go again heard it all before' vibe you get from the users when an organisation announces to great fanfare, that it is going to implement a new system. Welcome to the battle for hearts and minds. You cannot beat the plan without winning the battle for hearts and minds. The team's fortitude has to be as strong and timeless as the fortifications at Helms Deep. Just like Sauramon's Uruk Hai throwing themselves at the fortified walls of Helms Deep, cynicism and scepticism comes in constant waves. The project team needs to have dedicated resources challenging scepticism and cynicism by communicating and permission marketing the logic behind the project. Demonstrations, showcases, Q&A sessions, extensive involvement of end users throughout the project and adequate investment in training, are your weapons. The last book in the trilogy is The Return of the King. Aragorn is the mysterious ranger. He is the rightful heir to the throne of men but years of infighting, tribalism and politics prevents Aragorn from taking his rightful place. But times have changed; the hordes at the gates of Gondor necessitates the need for a king to unify the race of men. Aragorn seizes his chance with the help of Lord Elrond. So is there a king or the queen equivalent when it comes to delivering a successful IT project? I don't think there is one but there is a certain type of leadership that will make or break the delivery. You cannot beat the plan without this form of leadership. It is the leadership required to take the outputs from an IT project, then gain the acceptance required to embed the deliverables for operational use. For an IT project to be successful, this type of leadership has to come from the stakeholders, who are ultimately responsible for using the solution as a tool to gain the value promised in the business case. The leadership in Return of the King is a metaphor for the ultimate beneficiaries of the solution. They provide the leadership to transition the solution into operational use. In the first two books, you kind of sense Aragorn is an important player in the background. But in reality, most of the first two books is not really about him. Impaired or challenged IT projects contain Aragorn-type senior end users representing the operational world who will put to use whatever the IT project has been tasked with delivering, but with one difference; they never provided the leadership synonymous with Aragorn's return as the king. Why does this happen? I have outlined the main reasons below. To beat the plan, the underlying causes have to be identified and addressed from the outset of the delivery.

Not knowing the role they had to play in terms of requirements management, design, testing and transition of the solution into operational use.

Lack of power to onboard their home organisation during transition.

Poor interest in getting involved in the project.

Being overburdened between business-as-usual responsibilities and other IT project work.

Individual confidence is greater than ability, to play the role they need to play to get the project live.

I spend 25% of my working life talking about, and writing about, how an IT project or programme should be organised. There is an obsession with conceptualising these structures using hierarchy. The problem I find with hierarchies is that their primary purpose in life is to show accountability, escalation paths and the pecking order for making a decision. What we should be more interested in, from a 'beat the plan' perspective, is to logically conceptualise IT project team organisation to get the work done, encourage communication and facilitate collaboration. The use of interconnected rings, (seven to be exact) frames the logical organisation of an IT project centric delivery. Not one ring to rule them all bound by darkness but a fellowship of seven rings, creating a precious-precious-must-have-the-precious radiance that is more radiant than each individual ring. (That's what Gollum would say.) To beat the plan you need to be Lord of the seven rings.

THE ULTIMATE IT PROJECT MANAGER

One Ring to Analyse

A ring to represent the team and the tools for capturing and prioritising the requirements.

The ring bearer is called a Business Analyst.

The Business Analyst is all-knowing in the problem domain.

The ring represents a continuous process of reviewing, communicating and validating the requirements throughout the IT project.

One Ring to Design

A ring to represent the team and the tools for designing the solution.

The ring bearer is called an Architect but they each have specialism.

An Architect is all-knowing in one or more solution domains.

Data

Information

Infrastructure

Networks

Applications

Security

Property

Integration

Process

Culture

Organisation

ICT Service Management

The ring represents a continuous process of reviewing, communicating and refactoring the design as the requirements change.

One Ring to Build

A ring to represent the team and the tools for building the solution.

The ring bearer is a master craftsman with an army of clever engineers.

All builders do is build and hangout with the architects when they are not building

One Ring to Test

A ring to represent the team and tools that will test the solution.

The ring bearer is a master of all types of testing.

Automated

Unit

Factory acceptance testing

System and integration testing

Functional testing

Performance testing

User acceptance testing

THE ULTIMATE IT PROJECT MANAGER

One Ring for Operational Acceptance

A ring to represent the team and tools that will transition the solution into formal support.

The ring bearer is a master of service strategy, service design, transition, lean, automation and the following ICT process scope.

Incident and Problem Management

Request Fulfilment

Asset and Configuration Management

Change Management

Release and Deployment Management

Service Catalogue Management

Service Level Management

Availability Management

Business Relationship Management

Supplier Management

Financial Management

IT Service Continuity Management

Service Asset and Configuration Management

Information Security Management

Service Portfolio Management

Procurement

Application Life-cycle Management

Testing to prove service utility and warranty

Become the Lord of the 7 Rings

One Ring for Business Change Management

A ring to represent the team and tools who will ensure the end users are ready to gain value from the IT project's outputs.

The ring bearer is a master of business architecture, business process change and business change management.

The ring bearer creates the incentive for using the solution or a consequence for not doing so.

One Ring to Bind them All

A ring to bind all rings.

The ring bearer institutes managerial, architectural and technical governance.

The ring bearer is the holder of all knowledge of standards, measures of the desired future, measures of what has gone before and measures what is yet to come.

The ring bearer wears a wizard hat.

Gandalf: The Lord of the Rings: The Fellowship of the Ring (2001)

'A wizard is never late, Frodo Baggins. Nor is he early. He arrives precisely when he means to'

MOMENTARY LAPSES OF MUSICAL REASONING

'Music revelation rock and roll and soul'

Tribute

The Pasadenas

926 E. McLemore Ave. Memphis, TN 38106 is the address for the home of Stax Records. There is a huge neon sign with the words 'Soulsville USA' on the front. Stax Records gave us Otis Reading, Issac Hayes, Sam and Dave. Soulsville is the home of soul music. When listening to those who founded Stax records and worked with the artists, they will say music is the sentiment from a man's soul. Sentiment is a thought influenced by or proceeding from feeling or emotion. I find music a source of inspiration. Lyrics in songs can provide metaphors to help you raise your game. Take a 10 minute break and think about how you feel about your IT project. Then try to relate those feelings to your favourite songs. If Bat Out of Hell is a metaphor for your IT project, it is probably going off the rails. You seriously need to re-plan or you will end up feeling like a big bloke who has just crashed his motorbike into a big spikey cactus. The most memorable answer I had from someone was, "I

can hear Cliff Richard We Don't Talk Anymore." That is exactly why his project was not performing. He definitely was not a Cliff Richard fan. It turns out his mum used to the play the song quite a lot when he was a kid. Clearing your head and looking for meaning in your favourite music can help you achieve greater clarity, agility and unity. I know when a design stage is going to be problematic and the odour of over-engineering hangs heavy when I keep hearing Avril Lavigne's 'Complicated', after talking to the technical architects.

For me, Pink Floyd offers some great lyrics to look for meaning and inspiration to beat the plan. In 1987, Pink Floyd released an album A Momentary Lapse of Reason. Impaired or challenged deliveries are the result of cumulative lapses in reason. Every time there is a small dose of lapse in reason, project performance suffers. Your aim as a 'beat the plan' IT Project Manager, is to stop the momentary lapses of reason.

In September 1975, Pink Floyd released the album Wish You Were Here. 'Wish You Were Here' is a great quote as it represents what it feels like to work on an IT project that performs in a manner that will beat the plan. There is a saying that quality finds a home. Quality people and high performers are attracted to people with a track record of delivering successful IT projects. The laws of attraction are at work. Your mobile phone will be full of quality people who will want to work with you. Have you noticed that when your IT project is struggling, you spend a lot of time tracking people down? The people you really need are probably already taken. If your project is performing, you won't have this problem. On the same album is a track called Shine On You Crazy Diamond. Here is the lyric that stands out the most:

'Remember when you were young, you shone like the sun. Now there's a look in your eyes, like black holes in the sky'

When I delivered my first IT project 15 years ago, I just went for it. Failure never crossed my mind. I didn't know enough to know whether or not what I was doing, was risky. 15 years later, I'm a lot wiser and cautious before pressing ahead. As we become older and wiser, we tend to take less risks. In my experience, Project Managers are at their most risk averse at the beginning of the project. Experienced IT Project Managers are creatures who crave certainty before doing anything. The ones new to the trade are eager to please. They see the deficiency in some of the collaboration tools that the more seasoned veterans have come to rely on. Graduates today want to use Google apps and social media to communicate. They look at Outlook email like its something from the stone age. Shine On You Crazy Diamond is about keeping that devil-may-care spark and willingness to try new ideas we all had at the start of our careers. It is an impetus to get things going without overly worrying about the end game. Nowadays, IT projects are complex and the requirements constantly change. The only certainty is that the requirements will change when you start the project. The only sure fire way of dealing with this situation is by moving at speed in a climate of clarity, agility and unity. Alternatively, you could plan and plan and plan until you have a fine grained task list, scripting everything that needs to be done. Behold your creation - a perfect predication of the future. If it were that easy you'd be in the Casinos making millions. In the current economic climate and constant technical change, by the time you've got your fortified painting-by-numbers project plan, the requirements will have changed.

Comfortably Numb is a track from Pink Floyd's 1979 album, The Wall. Delivering an IT project invariably means dealing with brick walls. When you see that wall coming your way, what do you feel? Do you feel down and lacklustre? Do you curse those who put a wall in your way? Do you feel a sense of injustice, after you probably had nothing to do with creating the barrier but you are put in a position to deal with it? To beat the plan, you need to think differently. The wall was put in your way to make you stronger, faster and more resilient on future IT projects. Love the walls.

In the song, Comfortably Numb, there is a lyric 'Is there anybody in there? Just nod if you can hear me. Is there anyone home?' For me, the lyric is about people not listening. The worst thing you can do on an IT project is not dealing with people who don't listen. Not listening destroys agility, reduces clarity and prevents the formation of effective working relationships. Not listening kills the performance of an IT project. Do not tolerate anyone who does not listen - including yourself. Having reflected on my time in the world of IT project delivery, here are my top 6 not-listening behaviours on challenged and impaired IT projects. I'm sure the management psychologists have many more:

Confirmation bias

Lots of distractions

Short attention span

No incentive to listen

Sensitive to being told what to do

Fear of criticism

To beat the plan, learn to spot how prevalent the behaviour of not listening is on your IT project.

Comfortably Numb has a verse that goes 'I'll need some information first. Just the basic facts. Can you show me where it hurts?' You could consult the Gantt Chart. It is a good place to get your facts about when it is going to hurt financially. However, that assumes your Gantt Chart is data driven. Is your Gantt truly data driven? Ask yourself this: Where did the data come from? If it came from you and you alone, then your plan is a collection of unchecked assumptions and mythical man-days. You missed out the 'I need some information first' bit of the planning process. It is the part of the process where you go to someone who knows how the work is done and the reality of getting it done. Challenged or impaired IT projects start with plans full of unchecked assumptions and project plans put together by no one else other than the IT Project Manager.

Dark Side of the Moon, released in 1973, is one of the most commercially successful albums of all time. If a 'beat the plan' IT project was a music album, it would be Dark Side of the Moon. How very apt then that it has some things in common with project management. Firstly, there is a distinct triangle on the front cover of the album. The triangle is used commonly in project management to represent the triple constraints; time, money and quality. Secondly, there are two songs on the album entitled: Time; and Money. Every course and book on project management I have every experienced (and there have been a few) always teaches the triple constraint using the triangle. Project management, in terms of performance measurement, is so much more than that. When I teach people about performance measurement in project management, I show them four triangles with different measures that merges into a dodecagram. To beat the plan, exemplar performance in each of these measures is the aim of the game.

'Ticking away the moments that make up a dull day. Fritter and waste the hours. In an off-hand way.' – Time.. If that is what the day feels like on your IT delivery then just stop, get the team together and have an honest conversation about why the project is comfortably numb. You never have enough time so best not waste what time you have. More importantly, best not to perceive the presence of time that you don't have. Believing that although the project is behind schedule, the team can somehow magically catch up later, is irrational.

'Money, it's a gas. Grab that cash with both hands. And make a stash.' – Money. IT project delivery has become reliant on the use of contractors. In my line of work, the day rates range from £350-900+ per day. Large scale ERP rollouts stand out as distinct in the challenged project category. Those rollouts tend to rely on highly skilled contractors. When you get a constant churn of contractors on your critical path, the plan acquires both schedule and quality risk. So you need to avoid recruiting the do-as-little-as-possible-and-take-the-money-and-run ones. Their favourite song is Little Green Bag by The George Baker Selection. It's the theme tune to Tarantino's Reservoir Dogs, which is a film about robbing banks and trying to get away with it. So how do you spot Mr Black? (Nobody wants to be Mr Pink). They have a CV that shows job-hopping, like a butterfly fluttering from flower to flower on a hot summer day. When you recruit a contractor with an in-demand skill, you need to look for the clues. Are you being used in a bidding war by their agent? The agent is only interested in getting the best deal for themselves and their client. Has the applicant's CV got a string of engagements lasting no more than 3 months with different clients? The best contractors get extensions after their initial engagements or have repeat business with a particular client. References that are not from their last gig could indicate that their last engagement may not have gone so well. Follow through on references. Look on their CV for personal investment in technical training. It shows they are serious about keeping their skills up to date so they remain competitive.

High Hopes is a track from Pink Floyd's 1994 album, Division

Bell. Challenged and impaired IT projects suffer from divisions caused by: politics; creative differences about achieving the same outcomes; and turf wars. In these situations there is a temptation to keep the factions apart, succumb to dealing with unilateral escalations and let sleeping dogs lie. Unilateral escalation is a situation where one team escalates to a manager and expects the manager to deal with the problem on the disgruntled party's behalf. Their immediate aim is to get you on their side. Out will come the email audit trail, documentation and quotes from the local process bible. As soon as you show empathy for that stuff, your objectivity goes out the window. It is not a healthy way to do deal with things, mainly due to Chinese whispers. Toleration is not advisable if the divisions are reducing clarity, creating disunity and engendering rigidity. You won't beat the plan in an avoidance-of-conflict kind of climate. There is a great line in High Hopes, which says it all: 'Looking beyond the embers of bridges glowing behind us.' This is exactly what you've got to do. I have listed below what I try to do.

Establish clear expectations face to face

Get to know what I am dealing with

Be known and recognised for direct and open communication

Initiate a discussion with both parties

Make them aware of the impact they are having on everyone outside the conflict

Set up consequences for those who are not co-operative

Recognise that not all conflict is bad.

Challenged and impaired IT project deliveries reach a point when the IT Project Manager is a passenger on Guns and Roses' Night Train, 'Well I got one chance left. In a nine live cat.' You will find that track on the album Appetite for Destruction. To beat the plan, you need to be a shooting star leaping through the skies. Like a tiger defying the laws of gravity. (And stay away from Studio 54).

LEARN TIN & WIRES: PART 1 AND IT'S A LEAN NETWORK SOLUTION DELIVERY FROM HIM AND AN INTELLIGENT WORKSPACE FROM HIM

'How can you say I go about things the wrong way?'

How Soon is Now?

The Smiths

THERE ARE 2 WORLDS IN the spectrum of IT project delivery such that if you get the delivery wrong nothing works and nothing can be supported. The first is network solution delivery and the second is transition of an IT solution into support. This chapter is about delivering a local area network solution. I find commentators on the subject tend to focus on the technical nuances of the delivery with a bias towards waterfall methodology. I think it is because only someone with 'engineer' in the job title at some point in their career, digs network projects. I'm left with the impression that delivering a network solution should be the most logical and rational IT project experience one could ever had. But in my experience they are not. I can recall on several occasions the 'how soon is now' question being put to engineers along the lines of 'how long will it take?' Some come across as having an accurate answer but I know they are guessing. These guys are proud folk and know that not knowing an answer reduces their credibility. Some (the more honest than wise ones) offer a totally unpalatable rational and logical answer from an estimating point of view, 'We will know when it is done.' Then the 'how can you say I go about things the wrong way and no one is listening to me' conversations ensue.

I have a theory. Network techies and dudes are engineers by nature. They see the world in a scientific, logical and empirical manner. However, they deliver what they do in a world that is the total opposite of the climate they want to see in place. That is when the comedy ensues. The comedy is miscommunication and inefficiency - primary sources of project risk. I've always been fascinated by the question, 'How does one get these two worlds to catalytically and symbiotically exist?' What follows is my attempt to answer the question.

There is a comedy sketch that makes the top 10 in any survey of great British TV comedy moments. Created by the Two Ronnies, Ronnie Barker and Ronnie Corbett, The Hardware Shop is a showpiece in the art of people saying one thing and hearing another. On youtube, the clip has pulled in 600k views. That's not bad for a comedy scene written 38 years ago. Life as any manager is spent dealing with consequences as a result of people who don't listen, won't listen or hear what they want to hear. Yet there are people who have turned up on the shores of America who could not speak a word of English and have gone on to become multi-millionaire great communicators and listeners in their field. You cannot do that without mastering the art of communicating. They have mastered the meaning of active listening and they know the barriers to active listening. On a failing or challenged IT project, you will find a common gripe across all teams is the feeling of not being listened to. Unrealistic expectations get set when everyone is talking but no-one is listening or thinking. I'd never really thought about the theory behind 'people not listening' because as long as I was confident the course of action I'd set a project on would pay off, then I was not really bothered if the team or I felt listened to. But that approach only works when you can control everything to get things done. Chaos, coupled with those responsible for reducing the level of chaos failing to listen to one another, has to be the ultimate catalyst for IT project failure. My first experience of this situation was an engagement on failed data-warehouse migration. Nowadays they call it BI/MI/Big Data. One's initial instinct was to focus on the technical and process centric root causes of the chaos behind the failure of the project to perform. You see, in my naivety I'd always thought the chaos fed the propensity not to listen and the inclination not to listen created more chaos. What I had not counted on was a behaviour known as 'agenda anxiety'. A detailed recovery plan was documented and presented informally at Director Level. The crux of the root cause was the solution design and a general failure to adhere to the basic principles and method statement for a data migration. In a nutshell, the target solution was primarily designed to be an Online Transaction Processing system whilst the source data-warehouse solution was an Online Application Processing system. I'd always been taught that for performance, flexibility and operational stability reasons, keeping OLAP and OLTP systems separate was generally the rule of thumb. To the lay person, the project was trying to ram a square peg into a round hole. In the main, everyone agreed with the technical steps but the period of performance was not acceptable. The constraints were such that the time-line was the time-line. When I explained the constraints, the feedback was along the lines of, 'It will be pretty moronic to pitch that time-line as the expectation on time.' My response was, 'Have you any suggestions in terms of de-scoping to shorten the time-line?' which was usually met with an awkward silence and a parting response, 'I have to go and I hope this conversation has been useful.' To keep the peace, I'd usually respond, 'Yeah great, you've been very helpful' when what I wanted to say was, 'You've been as much use as a chocolate teapot and massaging your ego is like running my nails across a blackboard.' For an easy life, we told the powers that be what they wanted to hear in terms of timescales. I'd succumbed to the dreaded groupthink. This resulted in the project that looked like a graceful swan gliding in a controlled manner on the river when, in fact, it was paddling like Speedy Gonzales high on copious amounts of speed and going nowhere. In the end, I had to come clean and do a grovelling reset of expectations to the Director in question. When I told him he responded, 'I play golf with the CEO and he will get to hear about this.' That was the end of my role on that project along with a feeling I'd achieved top score in the art of getting the most number of CLIM points (career limiting move) in a 10 min conversation. Ultimately, the project played out in line with the time-line I had predicated. Despite numerous investigations, I could never ascertain whether or not there was a conversation with one of the UK's top CEOs where my name was linked to a failed data warehouse migration project. Many years later, I was told by an expert in golfing with the rich, famous and powerful that the top subjects discussed during golf were making more money, women, hunting, sport and business domain type stuff. Apparently, there is a protocol and etiquette about what gets discussed. Discussing a failing IT project during a game of c-level golf was a big no no and would likely result in being missed off the next invite list. The experience left me with no doubt that I needed to learn to play golf and, even though, whatever you are proposing is common sense, tastes like common sense, smells like common sense and reads like common sense, there are factors at play that block the process of accepting that common sense is common sense.

So here are some common reasons why people don't listen: monologue duets i.e. a number of people talking at the same time without listening to one another; agenda anxiety - a term author, consultant, motivational speaker Nido Qubein uses to describe "the feeling that what we want to say to others is more important than what they might want to say to us." Lots of noise in the environment is another. The Two Ronnies Fork Candles sketch has all these ingredients. There are other things about the sketch: a very inefficient stock control and fulfillment process, which is symptomatic of an inefficient supply chain aka an 'un-lean' supply chain. A combination of poor active listening and inefficient project process is a guaranteed route towards becoming a challenged project. I call this pairing 'The Two Ronnies'. Projects that seem simple on paper during the definition stage will move in to recovery mode as a result of letting the Rons run amok. Kill off the Two Ronnies 'fork handles school of communication' whilst ensuring project processes are lean, and you will rid the project of latency i.e. wasted time. Latency feeds schedule risk which in turn results in rushed jobs to catch-up, which in turn generates quality risk.

Installing 2 x cisco virtual switch solutions (VSS), 39 access switches and wi-fi into a 24/7 365 operation moving into a new building - sounds easy? This chapter is about how to deliver a local area network (LAN) and WLAN solution in a lean manner, and the pitfalls that will befall your delivery if a) you don't actively listen, b) you are not actively listened to and c) the delivery approach does not conform to the principles of lean. These projects are won in the prep, planning and design stage. So the chapter focuses on those stages. There are 2 ways of looking at a network project. The first is with a pair of reductionist tinted glasses on. What you will see is essentially a series of activities to configure some network switches and then plug them into a network. The problem with seeing the delivery in this light is it make the project boring. And when your project is boring, the inclination on the part of others to engage in it is reduced. People want to work on exciting things that make a difference. Making people's lives easier and more productive is what network solutions do. LAN, borderless network and wi-fi solutions enable the creation of the smart workspace. Smart workspaces drive innovation and improve customer service. People love to work in them and when people love where they work, staff retention is high. See your network project in a transformational light and brand your network project in this light when talking about it. People are always interested in talking about and getting involved in anything that is transformational.

Lean is a practice that considers the expenditure of resources for any goal other than the creation of value for the customer to be wasteful, and thus a target for elimination. Lean is a culture embraced by Toyota. Being lean results in deliveries that get close to 'now' when you ask what the dead-line is and the customer replies, 'How soon is now?' According to Wikipedia in 1999, Spear and Bowen identified four rules which characterize the 'Toyota DNA':

Rule 1: All work shall be highly specified as to content, sequence, timing, and outcome.

Rule 2: Every customer-supplier connection must be direct, and there must be an unambiguous yes or no way to send requests and receive responses.

Rule 3: The pathway for every product and service must be simple and direct.

Rule 4: Any improvement must be made in accordance with the scientific method, under the guidance of a teacher, at the lowest possible level in the organization.

Now bear in mind that the network project team and customer interface consisted of many experienced network technicians, engineers and project managers. But collectively there was a failure to be great at the a-b-c. The upshot of the project was a 25-30% budget over-run and the solution lacking some features that were promised at the beginning - all classic hallmarks of a challenged project. So my lessons learned on future network deliveries consisting of technically competent people, is do whatever is necessary to get everyone to actively listen, be actively listened to and follow the principles of lean.

Let us start with an overview of a typical boilerplate for a network project. The technical stage plan for the delivery of a network solution can be summarized as follows:

Prepare. The typical deliverables from this phase include:

- Target operating environment : High-level design (HLD)
- Requirements Documents
- Bill of Materials
- Current state assessment Survey and Results (CSAS) Site Survey Forms (SSF)
- Source operating environment due diligence : Sites impacted, network hosts, devices & services
- Impact Assessment : Current network and service design
- Impact on customer peak business activity (PBA)

Plan. The typical deliverables from this phase include:

- Solution Test Strategy (STP)
- Schedule
- Resource profile
- Synchronisation with customer change management

- Governance established
- Communications plan
- Migration plan

Design. The typical deliverables from this phase include:

- Design & specification of pre migration remediation
- Low Level Design (LLD)
- Service design & procedures revised
- Network operating centre design & procedures revised

Implement. The typical deliverables from this phase include:

- Prestage
- Build
- Network Ready For Use (NRFU) Test
- NRFU Test Report
- Rehearsal
- Implementation Log
- Cutover and transition into service

Operate & Optimize. The Optimize phase can happen at any time after a network solution is operational; typically it happens either when there has been a minor or major change in the business or technical requirements of the network or is scheduled as a 'check-up'. During this stage, the current business and technical requirements will be compared to those used when the network was initially designed. If any changes are recommended, then the phases start again from the beginning to ensure consistency and an ongoing good design.

Technical stages can overlap depending on complexity and the approach to transition iterative. This is particularly if the solution is incremental migration and not a big bang cutover. For governance purposes, the rule of thumb is to overlay the management stages from a method such as PRINCE2. Just make sure the level of governance is appropriate for the level of risk. The stage plan needs to be further complemented with the use of ITILv3 to ensure the network solution can be properly supported post go-live. The chapter will take you through each technical stage and enrich with processes, ways of working and ways of thinking to make the delivery lean. The name of the game is to ensure all project processes and how the work gets done, aligns to the 4 principles of lean. You and your delivery team must communicate in a manner that avoids behaviours associated with 'not listening'. The theory developed by Earl Nightingale (March 12, 1921 – March 28, 1989) one of America's earliest and greatest motivational speakers, is 'our attitude towards others determines their attitude towards us and we become what we think about'. In terms of listening this means receive, appreciate, ask and summarise but do it without any of the following behaviours:

Gossip
Being judgmental
Asserting opinions in an arrogant manner
Negative outlook
Lies

The second set of factors you need to be mindful of, is that the delivery of a successful stage plan contains 10 instrumental success factors that must always hold true. If each project stage exhibits performance against these factors then the subsequent stage is de-risked.

1. Everyone will behave rationally throughout the project.

2. The project will have perfect information.

3. Physical access will be unfettered and granted immediately.

4. There will be no issues with structured cabling and power.

5. All the equipment you need will be available when you need it.

6. All network, firewall and active directory changes will be actioned immediately when you ask for them.

7. No animals or big hairy insects will live in the communications rooms.

8. Everyone on the project is an expert in networks and the OSI model.

9. All engineers and designers will have the necessary skill to configure the solution.

10. All engineers and designers live in close proximity to the campus.

The only logical way these 10 assumed instrumental success factors (ISF) can hold true is if the project's delivery DNA becomes the Toyota DNA. To illustrate the point for each ISF, I have described a potential source of latency that, if left to fester, will create an accumulation of schedule and quality risk.

Future Perfection	Source of Latency / Non Value Add Activity
Everyone will behave rationally throughout the project.	Unless you are network expert, network projects are boring. To counter the boredom the non network person on which the project's success depends will find other things to do.

The project will have perfect information.	Accurate designs of the legacy network do not exist on paper. The design exists in a variety of people's heads. Some will have left the organisation.
Physical access will be unfettered and granted immediately.	Unless you've got authorisation signed in duplicate, blood and triplicate, the security guard will turn into ED209 from Robocop and ask you to leave premises. Note you get longer than 20 seconds.
There will be no issues with structured cabling and power.	The plugs in a comms room and the juice in an office building is not the same as the plugs and the way your juice works in your home. Buying network equipment is not like buying electronic consumer products. Electronic consumer products tend to come with everything you need, connection wise, to get it to work. To the unfamiliar, understanding harness links and patch cabling is like asking a sloth to solve the Rubik's cube.
All the equipment you need will be available when you need it.	The thing you need last will be available for delivery first. The thing you need first will be the thing that will be delivered last. You won't know what the thing is you need most until you really need it. Space in an office block is at a premium. No one makes money from using lots of space to store network kit and uninterruptable power supplies. If the cost centre owner is not your best mate, you wont get what you need delivered in less than 5 working days.

All network, firewall and active directory changes will be actioned immediately when you ask for them.	Project changes are normally rated priority 3 or 4 i.e. 5 – 7 working days. Everyone before you has used every excuse possible to raise the priority including, 'I play golf with the CEO'.
No animals or big hairy insects will live in the communications rooms.	Animals and insects love warm secluded places. Pest control people generally don't venture into comms rooms. Next time you meet one, ask the question.
Everyone on the project is an expert in networks and the OSI model.	If you know what a VPL is, the chances of you being interested in a VPN are zero percent. You need to be a mathematician to understand IP address schemas. You will be embarrassed to ask a technical person for an explanation of what all the TLAs mean. You will not be able to resist the urge to pretend you know what these guys are talking about.
All engineers and designers will have the necessary skill to configure the solution.	Your average engineer and designer is an expert in one thing and has general knowledge of other network things. Designing and configuring a network device requires input from many different experts. No two Cisco Certified Network Associates (CCNA) or Internetwork Experts (CCIE) are the same. Just because they have Cisco after their name does not mean they are experts in everything Cisco has to offer.

All engineers and designers will live in close proximity to the campus.	There are not enough designers and engineers to do all of the network work at any one time. They are like police officers. In austere times, organisations do not carry a bench of experts waiting for work. The best ones are always taken.

Preparing for a LAN/WLAN Project

Beware of the Two Ronnies (1984) : The Sheikh In The Grocery Store

A very rich Sheikh walks into a quaint English village grocery store waving around a big wad of money. The Sheikh's English is not that good. The shopkeeper listens to him and suggests what he is asking for is not what he needs. The Sheikh waves the money around and threatens to leave the shop. The shopkeeper proceeds to agree with the Sheikh. Don't be the shopkeeper.

Normally, a LAN/WLAN project starts with a set of documented customer requirements. The PM passes them to the designer and commands with great bombast, thou shalt do a high level design (HLD). The designer asks a few questions and bingo - a HLD is produced. Tally ho off we go into low level design. Rein in cowboy; you've just put yourself on a path to breaking rules 1, 2 & 3. How can one possibly plan for rules 1-3 without first understanding the environment in which the project is being delivered? So before embarking on a complex LAN/WLAN project, the two most important things that the Project Manager and designer need to understand are:

16. The physical and technical environment in which the network delivery is being conducted;

17. The target operating model (TOM) in which the network solution acts as a core capability. i.e. the operations that take place in the Campus.

Here are some 'Gemba' type discovery activities that are a must. The total duration for the delivery on which this chapter is based would be about 5 days. Go and see the location of the server rooms and comms rooms. Understand how and where the core network layer is hosted and its proximity to the access layer. Sit with the resident network expert and go on a safari through all the legacy documentation. Gain a basic understanding of the following themes in the source operating environment (SOE):

Themes	Meaning
Core Layer	The set of equipment in a network that provides the connections for the distribution layers and access layers of the network
Distribution Layer	The set of equipment in a network that provides the connections to the access, server or application layers of the network.
Access Layer	The set of equipment in a network that provides the connections for end user devices, such as PCs.
Access Stack	A set of connected network devices in the Access Layer that operate as a single entity for management purposes.
Digital Media	Video, audio and other related media assets encoded in such a way as to enable storage, manipulation and replay by computing devices.

Themes	Meaning
Domain Name System	A distributed hierarchical naming system for computers, services, or any resource connected to the Internet or a private network. See also http://en.wikipedia.org/wiki/Domain_Name_System
Dynamic Host Configuration Protocol	An auto configuration protocol used on IP networks. See also http://en.wikipedia.org/wiki/Dhcp
Differentiated Services Code Point	Also known as Diffserv is 6 bits in the IP Header (TOS field) that is used to differentiate classes of services. See also http://en.wikipedia.org/wiki/Differentiated_services
First Hop Redundancy Protocol	A networking protocol which is designed to protect the default gateway used on a sub network by allowing two or more routers to provide backup for that address.
Internetwork Operating System	The operating software used within the vast majority of Cisco Systems routers and current Cisco network switches.
Intelligent Resilient Framework	The ability to connect two or more switches together into a single managed entity. This may also be known as clustering of switches.

TLA	Definition
DC	Data Centre
IP	Internet Protocol
QoS	Quality of Service
TCP	Transmission Control Protocol
UC&C	Unified Communications and Collaboration
UPS	"Uninterruptible" power supply
URL	Universal Resource Locator
VLAN	Virtual Local Area Network
WAN	Wide Area Network

Get the customer to run a series of walk-the-floor, day-in-the-life workshops either in the new campus or if not on campus, then using a model. The workshops are about what goes on operationally in the campus. Grab a load of operational people who are responsible for the workplace design in the campus. Get them to talk through, and walk through, how the occupants will work, communicate and collaborate. Rich pictures are a great way of envisioning how people will work, communicate and collaborate in a new campus. Use these sessions to elaborate transactional volumes and types of transactions flowing across the network.

So now we have all the information to complete our preparation stage products and move into planning. You've just risked breaking rule number two. The preparation stage is the most optimal time to identify key stakeholders who can make the project happen. What I'm talking about here are people who can help you get into the physical and technical environment quickly and people who can make decisions quickly about what needs to be done to meet the requirements. The Gemba activities increase clarity for the planning stage but the working relationships to enable agility, need to be thought through and established as well. Outlined below are all the key critical chain activities in the LAN/WLAN delivery. For every one of them, 'make it happen' (MIH) engagement points are needed into the customer and supplier organisation to get the work done. In the project initiation document(PID), get the names agreed and make the time to talk them through what you will be asking of them over the coming months. The working relationship and level of collaboration must work in a manner that results in conformance to lean, rule 2.

Process Role	Why you need this
Requirements Management	Agreeing and signing off a set of prioritised business requirements. Initially, there will be many expectations of the solution. Not all of them will be met. The requirements will change and prompt discussion is required to reset expectations.
Business Change Management	The services using the new network will need to be user acceptance tested. The implementation of WLAN I.e. the Cisco Identity Service Engine (ISE) or Mobility Services Engine (MSE) will requires changes in business process. They are solutions used for introducing bring-your-own-device (BYOD) ways of working. New workflows need to be defined, introducing the necessity for a business process reengineering stage plan into the plan. The purpose of this is to introduce the revised business process.

Process Role	Why you need this
Technical Governance	Reviewing designs whilst ensuring architectural alignment, compliance to technical standards and recognising historical technical constraints. The introduction of a new solution introduces discontinuity into the legacy network. Both solutions have to co-exist and integrate seamlessly. Otherwise, the project will risk business operational stability.
Financial Management	These type of projects start off with an initial bill of materials (BOM). It is unlikely the BOM will be a complete list of what you need. There are always surprises such as additional GBICS, variation in power cords, different types of cage nuts, fibre cables and patch leads etc. Most of these items can be delivered within 24-48 hours. The last thing you need on the critical path, is a lead time of 5 + working days to get approval to purchase a couple of 100 pounds worth of additional items at the point you need it. In a lean project, the aim is zero latency between asking for it and getting the financial approval. In a lean project, the aim is zero approval chasing. Projects that do not operate in this manner are breaking lean rule 4.

Process Role	Why you need this
Facilities Management	This gets you, your team and your suppliers physical access. Also provides storage space for all equipment. There is quite an amount of space required to store 2 x Core switches, 39 access switches, 100 or so access points, 2 x wireless LAN controllers and required uninterruptable power supply (UPS) units. For that kind of volume, you will need a couple of vans and a lorry. You will need somewhere to store all the equipment prior to installation. If you cannot get unfettered access quickly to the Campus, your project will burn money. If the logistical processes and physical access processes are not lean, then the project breaks lean rule 3. The end result is latency and schedule risk.
Access Management	Getting your technical team remote access into the network and end points required by the new solution. E.g. integration into network performance management such as Solarwinds and Radius. Integration of the ISE into Active Directory. Frequent and constant repeat visits to site are a drain financially and are inefficient if the project's engineers do not live locally. If the project can configure everything on site and get it right first time, then great but that will only happen if the design contains a perfect description of the configuration. For this level of complexity, such an outcome is considered unrealistic. Remote access, combined with automating the rollout of configuration, is the most efficient way of configuring a large volume of network switches.

Process Role	Why you need this
Procurement Management	Processing purchase orders, liaising with vendors and keeping track of deliveries.

So we have understood the environment, done some discovery to both illicit and elaborate requirements. We have identified and warmed up our make it happen (MIH) engagement points. The project is now in a good position to close off the delivery of the products that come out of the preparation stage. The aim here is to be agile - deliver just enough preparation so that detailed planning can start. Outlined below is a summary description of the deliverables and contents. Make sure the team has a central repository available to them e.g. Sharepoint, so they can readily access this documentation and keep it up to date.

Deliverable	Contents & Purpose
Requirement Definitions	A prioritised list of requirements described what the solution needs to do in terms of functional and non- functional requirements. For governance purposes and aligning to lean rule 4, (the reasons will become clear later in the chapter), the list needs to be prioritised into Must Have, Should Have, Could Have and Won't Have.

Deliverable	Contents & Purpose
High Level Design (HLD)	The high level design is a first cut high level overview of the solution. Its contents include: Target network architecture diagram; Purpose of the solution; High level summaries and principles stating how the following will be done to meet the requirements • IP addressing; • Open shortest path first(OSPF); • Quality of service(QOS); • Authentication; • Network performance management; • Routing; • Security; • Failover; • Availability; • Interfaces; • Software versions; • Technical constraints; • Standards and naming conventions. The high level design needs to state any required technical prerequisites or subsequents: • Electrical power • Racking and environmental control • Structure cabling and cross connect from WAN network termination equipment (NTE) to core network switches • Patch panels • Patch cabling

Deliverable	Contents & Purpose
Bill of Materials (BOM)	The BOM is the initial list of all the hardware (switches, racking, controllers, cables, GBICs etc), software (licences) and services required to install the solution. Hardware and software-wise its contents include: • Product code • Product title and description • Unit of measure • Quantity required • Unit cost • Total cost • Lead-time • Special handling instructions Services-wise, the BOM should detail the initial estimates for the direct & indirect labour (project management, project support, designers, network engineers, electricians, installers, logistics, patch cabling etc) chargeable to the project. • Role title • Role description • Role category (Management, design, engineering, specialist, 3rd party etc) • Estimated number of man days • Daily rate • Source

Deliverable	Contents & Purpose
Current state assessment Survey and Results (CSAS), Source operating environment due diligence : Sites impacted, network hosts, devices & services	A body knowledge and documentation describing OSI layers 1 -7 of the current legacy network solution. An RF survey of the current environment in which the WLAN solution operates should be conducted.
Impact Assessment: Current network and service design	An assessment of the technical and operational impact of introducing the new solution within the current network architecture. The assessment needs to identify all risks to the delivery and the operation as a result of changing the legacy network. Particularly, attention needs to be given to current IT service management arrangements and how they will have to change so the operation of the new solution can be sustained.
Impact Assessment: Planned business activity (PBA)	An organisation's network is the 4th utility. There are going to be times during the project delivery where the operation needs the network undergoing enhancement to be left alone. These periods of time are constraints on the time-line that need to be understood early, so any unavoidable right shift across the plan is deemed acceptable.

Plan

Beware of the Two Ronnies (1980) : Nothing is Too Much Trouble

Ronnie Barker is a shopkeeper in an old fashioned sweet shop. His first customer is an old lady. He points to a sign on the wall. It says, "Nothing is too much trouble" in his establishment. The old lady leaves and Robbie Corbett walks in. His intent is to test Barker's slogan. Among other things, Corbett wants him to sort out liquorice sweets because he only likes the pink ones. He also asks the shopkeeper to unroll liquorice rolls because he wants to know their length. Barker shows some signs of frustration when he claims that "nothing is too much trouble, not even you." Eventually, Barker goes completely berserk when asked to count out an exact figure of hundreds and thousands and pours two whole jars of them on Corbett's head. Don't be the shopkeeper.

Having built up a sufficient body of knowledge about the project's purpose, climates and outcomes, thought needs to go into the project approach before the planning deliverables can be determined or produced. What I'm talking about here is whether the approach needs be waterfall centric or Agile centric. There is no right or wrong answer as the answer depends on the features of the project environment. Here are some quick pointers:

Case for Agile	Case for Waterfall
Hi complexity	Lo complexity
Fixed time, budget & quality Willingness on part of the customer to constantly re-evaluate scope	Fixed time, budget, quality and scope Fixed scope and no room for flexibility or concession

Case for Agile	Case for Waterfall
New and unfamiliar technologies	Mature and proven technologies
New challenge for the team	Delivery team have a track record of delivering similar projects

Either way, the DNA in plan needs to lead to conformance to one key principle, to be considered lean.

Every activity in the plan and every transaction leads to the creation of value in the eyes of the customer.

Let's start with a look at the content in the schedule that will have the most influence on the time-line. The length of the critical path will be most sensitive to activities with long procurement lead-times. These items will be procurement lead-times for CISCO kit, which can range from 2-4 weeks from the point of order. And commissioning lead-times for any wide area network (WAN) links into the campus, can range from 40 to 120 working days from the point of order. So order them as soon as the BOM in IILD Is baselined. The leanest plan will demonstrate the following future perfect performance:

As soon as the network kit is delivered, it is pre-staged and configured to a point where it is ready for installation on the Campus.

- As soon as any WAN links are commissioned, core layer, access layer and distribution layer network devices are installed and immediately ready to be connected for an integration test of the whole network solution.

- Skilled resources are readily available at the above points to install, test and optimise.

So the immediate priority is to order the bill of materials, following completion of high level design. The length of the critical path will be most sensitive to external dependencies outside your responsibility. These dependencies will most likely be the completion of any mechanical and engineering (M&E) works delivering structured cabling, electricity, server/comms rooms, environmental controls and any fixtures for mounting wireless access points.

Within the plan, overlay business activity periods where you will not be able to impact the production network. This will start to give you visibility of potential periods of non-working time during cutover to production or integration with legacy network.

Logistical activities will soak up a portion of the project management activity. These activities are both critical path and critical chain so need to be shown on the plan.

- Delivery and secure storage for inbound equipment into pre-staging and configuration;
- Pick and delivery to site for installation;
- Preparation of notifications and approvals to deliver and unload equipment on the campus.

In the leanest delivery, the customer will want a readily available resource to turn up on site, plug the network switch in, test it, tune it and leave it in a production-ready state. Achieving this aim will involve an expert carrying out the majority of the complex configuration, and testing it offsite so that a lower skilled engineer can just plug it in and patch cable it on campus. So what you need to secure is a working area i.e. a secure network device garage workshop where switches can be racked and tested. In particular, attention needs to be paid to proving operational capability and resilience between a pair of core layer physical CISCO switches that make up a virtual switch solution. Connectivity between the core layer device, access switch and wireless access point can then be tested. So you may need 3- 5 days of activity on the plan to set this working area up, in preparation for the delivery.

Clearly, the design stage on the schedule will make or break the project's success. When I look at these plans, there are about 3-5 summary activities that read like, "Run a workshop where the customer will tell us the technical requirements using semantics and language we can use for a detailed design." The CCIE will then write a low level design document, send it to the customer and the customer will sign it off. Really? In reality, compilation of low level design products require constant and frequent review. For the complexity for the reference project in question, the most optimal approach for each programme phase would have been a low level design stage over a 3 week time-box. The start of each week would involve a half working day workshop, then 1-2 hours of review. The main reason is that as more design detail emerged as the team moved up the layers, it would have a bearing on design detail in the lower part of the stack. I can hear sighs of disbelief. So think about this: a network solution in a new building, which is being delivered as part of a transformation programme or major workforce location needs to support the following network hosts:

- CCTV;
- Secure access and swipe systems;
- Unified communications i.e. data, voice and video;
- Analogue to digital conversion i.e. fax and telephony;
- Blue light services;
- Intelligent building services;
- Bring your own device;
- Audio, visual and multimedia;
- Voiceover IP and contact centre type telephony.

Think about the potential number of VLANs, DHCP and

IP addressing implications. Get this stuff wrong and important communication processes just won't work. The design products not only describe how the solution needs to be built; the quality of the content instils a level of confidence that states that when a network host is plugged into the new network solution, it will do what it is designed to without any reconfiguration. This ensures adherence to lean rule 2. Imagine a building with 400 phones and 40 CCTV cameras that each need to be configured with some change local setting so that the device works. Discovering this issue during implementation and testing is symptomatic of the 'going dark' i.e. lack of frequent collaboration and communication during low level design. Complex local area network projects are won or lost in the design stage. The schedule should demonstrate a healthy amount of time for just enough up-front, low level design, and the design activities need to be prescribed in a manner that encourages frequent communication and collaboration.

Resource availability and continuity will have a major influence on the schedule. The rule of thumb here is: the closest you get to the point where you need a resource without having asked for it, the less chance you have of getting it when you need it. Nowadays, organisations just don't have excellent people sitting around waiting for work. Remember when you were a kid playing a team game on the local green? Remember having two captains and each captain picking a team? Always the same 3 people left at the end for a reason. The same thing happens in organisations that provide resources for IT projects. Quality finds a home and anyone technically savvy in what they do, does not have to ask for work. So you have to request them several weeks in advance, and having a reputation for being great to work with, helps. (Laws of attraction and all that.) The instrumental success factors at play are upfront requests and keeping the same technical team throughout the implementation. Discipline yourself to show and track in the plan activities to schedule, mobilise and retain the technical delivery team. Those unfamiliar with the demands placed on IT delivery teams, just assume resources are readily available. Mobilisation lead-times and resource availability levels are constraints on the critical path that should be understood by everyone involved.

The overall duration of the delivery is sensitive to the proliferation of finish to start (FS) relationships between the activities i.e. activity x must be finished before activity y can start. Finish to start relationships between activities are the result of resource availability and technical constraints i.e. completing the commissioning of the access layer is technically dependent on commissioning the core layer. There are a couple of things to be aware of while producing a GANTT using a tool like MS Project. The default setting for linking activities is finish to start. Ask yourself this question: how many times on previous IT projects have you disciplined yourself to go through the detailed plan with the team and challenge the assumption that all links are finish to start? If you do this-great. But if not, you may have inadvertently pulled together an inefficient plan. By going through this process, you will identify opportunities to compress the time-line and you could be creating buffer between the activities and finish-no-later-than or must-finish-on, delivery dates. Discipline yourself to challenge the assumption that every link between activities is a finish i.e. 100% completion required to start the next activity relationship.

A different way of looking at the delivery plan for a network project from an agile and lean perspective would be to view it as a factory, consisting of interacting work centres and processes. In a lean delivery, these work centres are instantiated when needed and not burning cash on idle time, waiting for inputs when not needed. Sounds strange does it not? Agile delivery has a number of key principles that have to be enacted to achieve greater certainty in a complex technical delivery in dynamic environment. Installing 2 x cisco virtual switch solutions (VSS),

39 access switches and wi-fi into a 24/7 365 operation moving into a new building at the point it completes its construction phase is complex, uncertain and being done in a dynamic environment. No GANTT in terms of initial baseline content at the start of the delivery will be the same picture at the end of the delivery. The reasons for the variation are twofold. Firstly, the foundations for the project were not firmed up i.e. deliverables from the preparation stage. Secondly, the complexity is such that the natural consequence will be a necessity to build incrementally and develop iteratively. These are two key principles behind agile delivery. As the project moves from high level to low level design and build activity implicit, assumptions behind the requirements may be proved incorrect, which in turn means the requirements will have to be both reviewed and reprioritized. Procurement in a network project is not a one-off process. Initially you will buy most of the big ticket capex items and then, as the project evolves, there will be a need to buy additional items. Based on an assumption that the prepare stage starts with the mobilisation of a Project Manager and lead CCIE/network technical designer authority, the work centres that make your plan happen could look like the diagram below:

Interdependence between work-centres to achieve lean outcomes

Planning

High Level & Low Level Design

Testing

Procurement & Logistics

Pre-stage, RF Survey

Installation & Engineering

Requirements Mgt

Resource & Multi-skilled Team Management

The Project Context

We don't quite know what we need

High volume of complicated hardware

Installed in a new building while the building is being built

Middle of a capital city

Engineers want to know exactly what the customer wants before doing anything

Culture of big design up front

Big spiders live in the comms rooms

Fixed delivery date

Now go and do a search on the web for vendor recommended standard blueprint plans. Most are linear in nature. These type of plans tend to work in a climate of certainty, low variation in the original requirements and low complexity network solution. You need to ask yourself how confident you are that a linear approach will work in the project context described in the diagram above.

What we are taught

Prepare ➡ Plan ➡ Design ➡ Implement ➡ Operate ➡ Optimise

The plan needs to contain testing products; namely, a testing strategy, test management setup, test planning and test scripting. I kind of get weird looks from the network world when I start recommending a testing regime with the same level of rigour found in application deliveries. There is a big difference between IT professionals that work in the application space, and IT professionals that work in the network space. Those that work in the applications space don't expect just built software to work first time. Contrast that with the look of shock and utter surprise on the faces of their network colleagues, when issues are found during testing. Don't get me wrong; I love working with the network engineers. They are the most down-to-earth nuts and bolts IT professionals you will ever work with. They have this expectation of themselves and the technical hardware, that it will all work perfectly first time it gets turned on, configured and plugged in. And why shouldn't it? After all, CISCO and Hewlett Packard network devices go through manufacturing process on a par with mass produced consumer electronics. We programme those devices and they all tend to work first time. Maybe such a belief is leading to a view that somehow testing on these kind of network projects can be less rigorous than the regime found on application projects. Nowadays, configuring a network switch is akin to writing a computer programme.

Cisco internetwork operating system (IOS) is referred to as a scripting language; whereas a development language like C#, Scala or Java are referred to as software development kit (SDK). If I said to you, here are two technical words,: software development kit; and scripting language; which do you think is the most complicated? IOS is a programming language for network switches and it is as complicated as any SDK. In fact, I would say it is far more complicated. Application development languages are more natural language centric than the script on a network switch. The challenges in terms of guaranteeing interoperability between a changed application, legacy hardware and software are exactly the same when adding an extensively configured network switch to a production environment. Hence why the planning stage needs to deliver a suite of testing products. A best in class method to employ is the ISEB Testing Methodology. The framework is known as the V-model. Don't use it prescriptively. Just take what you need and nothing more. In the following table I have described the content found in a test strategy. All you have to do is take what you need, create a word doc localised for your project and get the sections filled in, preferably using output from a 90 minute workshop involving the technical delivery time and anyone involved in testing. You are more likely to build consensus on the need for a robust testing strategy, by exploring its content with all possible participants in a workshop. A successful test execution requires adherence to lean rule 4. That's where you will find people who understand the operational environment. An understanding of the operational environment is an instrumental success factor during testing.

Deliverable	Composition	
Test Strategy	1	Glossary
	2	Table of Contents
	3	List of Tables
	4	List of Figures
	5	Executive Summary
	6	Introduction
	6.1	Purpose
	6.2	Test Strategy Audience and Responsibilities
	6.3	Referenced Documents
	6.4	Summary of Acceptance Criteria
	7	Test Summary
	8	Scope
	8.1	Project Background
	8.2	In Scope Activities
	8.3	Out of Scope Testing Activities
	9	Test Strategy
	9.1	Overview
	9.2	Testing Principles
	9.3	High Level Requirements Traceability Matrix
	10	Testing Organisation & Governance
	10.1	Testing Delivery Roles and Responsibilities
	10.2	Testing Governance
	10.3	Test Communication, Reporting & Meetings
	10.4	Project Test Deliverables
	10.5	Defect Management

Deliverable	Composition
	10.6 Retest and Regression approach
	10.7 Project Test Traceability
	10.8 Environment and Code Configuration management
	11 Test Execution
	11.1 Pre-stage: Unit Testing, POST and DOA
	11.2 Application Testing
	11.3 Network & Security
	11.4 Authentication
	11.5 Monitoring & Management Toolsets
	11.6 Failover
	11.7 Entry/Exit Criteria
	11.8 System Integration Test (SIT)
	11.9 Performance
	11.10 User and operational acceptance testing
	12 Test Environments
	13 Planning
	14 Test Tools
	15 Risks and Issues
	Appendices Table 1 Glossary, Table 2 Referenced Documents Table 3 Requirements Traceability Matrix, Table 4 Allocation of Testing Responsibilities, Table 5 Roles & Responsibilities Table 6 Project Test Deliverables, Table 7 Defect Severity, Defect Priority

A project manager is as much use as a chocolate teapot without a capable team. I'm probably teaching some of you to suck eggs but I think a constant reminder of how badly a network project can go because the team was dysfunctional, is healthy.

Late delivery

Cost over-run caused by poor technical work

Micro management increasing management time

Elevated risk of major incidents during service operation

Poor estimating due to lack of experience

So the question is, what kind of functional and technical people do you need and how do you want them to behave? There are 4 skill groups required for a project of this nature. Prior to any onsite working, the project needs to ensure all resources have necessary security clearance and certifications to work on a building site.

Skill Group	What they do	Qualifications
Design	Capturing and a validating requirements Running technical workshops Producing designs & bill of materials Root cause analysis when things go wrong Training and coaching for technical support staff	Cisco Certified Internetwork Expert (CCIE) or equivalent Voice solutions : Cisco Certified Voice Professional (CCVP) or equivalent.

Skill Group	What they do	Qualifications
Engineering	Configuring network devices Configuring network performance management Rack and stacking network devices Testing & troubleshoot Conducting RF survey Patching hosts to network switches Training and coaching for technical support staff	Cisco Certified Network Associate (CCNA), Network Professional (CCNP) or equivalent Voice solutions : Cisco Certified Voice Professional (CCVP) or equivalent.
Installation	Patch cabling Electrical works Rack and stacking network devices Installing uninterruptible power supply (UPS) Installing and commissioning racking Mounting wireless access points and network points.	
Project Support	Procurement & logistics Resource scheduling Organising physical and logical access.	

Now for things to think about. When delivering a borderless network capability into an organisation, implementing a core LAN is technically interdependent with implementing a wireless solution. After all, a connected workspace allows anyone, anywhere, anytime, and on any device, to connect securely to an organisation's network. So what you don't want is the wireless solution being developed in isolation to the network solution. At the end of that road is a user experience, whereby the user wanders around the campus with a wireless device, be it smartphone or tablet, and the experience is interrupted because the device has to re-register to the network. It's an outcome as a result of poor communication during the design stage; poor communication across the technical team; and organising the technical team into a 2 distinct functional teams - one that designs and builds the network and one that designs and builds the wireless solution. The answer is to have a lead CCIE owning the whole design and multi-skilled network engineers (CCNA). In my experience, network engineers don't see installation type of activities as part of their job description. They also find it mundane. Yet the installation activities are just as important and just as complicated as configuring a network switch. So it does make sense to have separate resources for installation available to work with the network engineers, particularly where patch cabling is concerned. Patch cabling is a pretty time intensive role and nothing works unless it's right. Get it wrong and the result is a maintenance headache. To the uninitiated, think in terms of electrical sockets and a plug with 3 pins. Perfectly reasonable given most electrical devices we come across have 3 pin plugs. Racking for network devices and power connections for network devices in those racks, use different types of connections for hooking up to the juice. They are the kind you would find on equipment used in manufacturing. For some strange reason, network designers and engineers just assume all the power requirements will be as they need to be. Wrong! The electrical supply requirements and how network devices are powered, need as much validation as the network configuration. Nothing works without the juice, so assuming it will all be there or the electrics are something that can be sorted at the time of implementation, is leaving something important to chance. There is nothing more demoralising for a network engineer than turning up to site to configure a network solution, only to find they cannot power anything up or they have to spend their time snagging the patch cabling. Hence why it is prudent to mobilise an experienced electrician and a patch cabling guru, with experience of working in data centres and communications rooms.

Design

Beware of the Two Ronnies (1980) : The Confusing Shopping List

A shopkeeper and a customer try to decipher the customer's wife's shopping list. Needless to say they did not end up getting her what she asked for. In a lean network project, design information and the designer need to be available to anyone who needs them anywhere, anytime and anyhow.

How can you build something in a lean manner if there is not a single body of codified body of knowledge (BOK), created by people passionate about it describing how to build it? The answer is you cannot. The wording of this question is deliberate. Notice how I have not used the words 'design document'. The design is a package of information. It is a solution design package (SDP) mainly consisting of method statements. I have used the word 'codified'. Moreso now than before, there are far more effective ways of holding easily accessible codified information than just writing it all down in a word document: on-line visual requirements management tools; social media; content management systems; and wikis to name a few. The last thing on anyone's mind nowadays is putting two hours aside to read a design document. It's boring, there are far more interesting things to do and we are all time poor. What we are interested in is what is important to us and we want to home in it on quickly. We want someone to explain it to us and help us understand it quickly. The last thing we want to do is read everything there is to know about a network solution design. We also want to know that everyone who needs to review it has reviewed it.

Our solution design package needs to demonstrate four qualities. It is a cocktail of focus, simplicity, balance and 'Martini': focus to ensure it only contains content pertinent and relevant; simplicity so the content is understand; balance so we only do just enough design; and lastly, Martini i.e. the content is available to anyone who needs it anywhere, anytime and anyhow. So what is in our solution design package? :

The power supply specification describes how racks are powered, including uninterruptible power supply (UPS) and the specification for racking power distribution units (PDU). Nothing wastes time like going to power-up a network device, only to find the PDU is not powered, the power lead connector is not long enough or the connectors don't fit. The juice is one of those things that engineers just expect to be in place.

The datacentre layout is a computer aided design (CAD) plan showing where everything is and how everything is laid out. Nothing wastes time and money like discovering there is no room to install a network device during its implementation.

The patch cabling schematic shows how everything is to be patch cabled, including patch panels. It should detail types of cables (UTP, LC-LC, LC-ST), lengths, attenuation (OM1-4), GBIC/SFP endpoint specification and quantities. We don't want to waste time finding out, during implementation, that the GBICs are short haul when they need to be long haul and the engineer does not have the correct cables.

The low level design describes the configuration of each network device. Compiling a low level design is about dropping down into build level of detail, for everything in the high level design. The following needs to be described:

- Remote access solution
- IP schema and addressing
- VLANs
- Firmware
- Ports and interfaces
- Scaleability
- Integration with network performance monitoring eg Solarwinds and N-Able
- In service software upgrade (ISSU) capability, automated upgrading features and constraints
- Routing
- DHCP scopes
- Requirement firewall changes
- Integration with Active Directory
- Open shortest path first (OSPF)
- Quality of service (QOS)
- Authentication
- Security
- Failover
- Availability
- Software versions
- Technical constraints
- Standards and naming conventions

The aim is to install once, configure once, and test once. If the complexity is such that several iterations are required, then remote access and ISSU become critical tools to keep the implementation agile. A bad design is one which incurs latency, where powering off a switch results in an outage of the production services using the switch. So any capability that allows the technical team to rapidly access the network device anytime, automate an enhancement to the config on 5+ switches whilst productions services are protected, should be considered a necessity and not a nice-to-have. If not, then the project acquires schedule risk as a result of change management approvals, managerial time to get resources rescheduled and time taken for repeat onsite site visits.

Implementing WLAN and Wi-fi requires some design products that are distinct from core network. The design is driven by how the solution will be used. Use-cases collected and review via workshop, are advisable. These use-cases describe who will use the solution and how they will use it i.e. voice, data and video. The intelligent workspace has all kinds of people from in and outside the organisation doing all kinds of things on the corporate network, using all kinds of devices e.g. smartphone, VOIP, e-fax, video, CCTV, desktops, laptops and tablets etc. The list grows week by week! We should not be surprised bythis given that we are living in the internet of everything. Implementing WLAN requires the installation of access points (AP) and a check to see the signal from these APs has sufficient coverage. So the plan needs to contain an RF survey, followed by an exercise to use the results to plot on a floor/CAD plan the points where access points need to be mounted and installed. Assumptions are the root of all evil if you are a Project Manager. They are neither lies nor truths waiting to become truth or a lie. The most evil of assumptions are the ones which look like common sense so you don't bother validating them. Always make sure the network points are shown on a CAD plan with the proposed location of the access points. You'd think the process of connecting a device to a wireless network would be simple. In fact, it is pretty complicated and needs to be thought through. This is particularly the case if the current process involves handing out bits of paper with passwords on and if the lean aim is to automatically connect anyone using the network before they know they need to use the network. There is a process that goes on before your device connects. That process in the intelligent workspace needs mapping so the WLAN solution can be configured. This mapping contains all the information needed to configure CISCO ISE, active directory and WLAN hardware. The process mapping shows the steps so the following key questions can be answered before access is granted. Is the user allowed to use their device on this network? Is the user who they say they are?

So there you have it - a lean blueprint to improve the chances of a successful local area network project, in the context of a transformation programme delivering the intelligent workspace. Win it in the prep, planning and design.

"All we are doing is looking at the time line, from the moment the customer gives us an order, to the point when we collect the cash. And we are reducing the time line by reducing the non-value adding wastes."

Taiichi Ohno

LEARN TIN & WIRES PART 2: MONKEY MAGIC'S & MURDOCH'S DATA CENTRE MIGRATION MASTER CLASS

'That ain't working, that's the way you do it'

Money for Nothing

Dire Straits

DCM IS A THREE LETTER acronym that strikes fear into the hearts of the most hardened IT Project Manager. A DCM is probably the most complex IT infrastructure project in the world. Everyone's doing it all the time, so best to learn all you need to know about the basics. Get it wrong and it's money for nothing. However, upon closer examination, the business drivers behind migration of legacy services to next generation hosting services, feel synonymous with performance traits expected from a beat-the-plan IT Project Manager.

Masaaki Sakai is probably a name you don't recognise. If you were a child in the late 70s and early 80s you will have seen him on TV. He played a character called Monkey, from the

Japanese series of the same name. Monkey battled all kinds of enemies in the air by flying about on a magic cloud. Whenever he needed his magic cloud all he would have to do is whistle - his cloud would instantly appear. During this era, the same could not be said for commissioning servers to host software. It was a long and tedious business. Provisioning servers or mainframes took time. The customer purchased capacity they did not immediately need.

Monkey Episode 3: A Great Journey Begins

Fast forward 30 years and adoption of cloud solutions, such as SaaS, PaaS and IaaS, continues to gather pace. Gartner predicts that by 2014, 75% of UK business will be leveraging cloud. Users of cloud solutions only pay for what they use. The process for commissioning servers or scaling up is very quick. A reduction in operating expenditure, accompanied by increased agility for the digital future, whilst reducing organisational rigidity in a time of constant merger and acquisitions, is an attractive proposition. The reality hits, when an organisation realises the enormity of the challenge, of moving their data and applications from old world to cloud world. Old world can normally be found in a tier 1-4 data centre or in disparate tier 2 server rooms spread across an organisation's property portfolio.

For anyone wanting a career in IT project management, DCM is an excellent experience to have under your belt. All IT projects have 2 things in common; the need for network, and the need for servers. Nothing happens on an IT project without servers (aka tin) and networks (aka wires). DCM is much deeper than moving tin and connecting wires. The business drivers behind migration to cloud are exactly the same performance traits that organisations want from IT Project Manager 2014+.

Increase growth

Deliver results & tangible value

Reducing operating expenditure & total cost of
ownership

Rapidity

Elastic and flexible approach

Control

Improve IT apps and infrastructure

Reduce the carbon foot print

In today's digital times, DCM is risky business for any organisation. Organisations rely on their servers for business-critical operations. There is a rule of thumb in the trade that states that 70% of pre-cloud IT budget is spent on keeping the lights on i.e. maintaining current IT estate. That's money not spent on value-add activities leading to greater competitiveness and agility in uncertain times. Take an ERP system as an example. What If, as a result of a new product launch, the B2C traffic and transactional volume increased by 33%? How long would it take the pre-cloud IT department to scale up the infrastructure? Could it be done easily and cheaply in less than 2 weeks? What if the organisation mobilises an uber array of geographically dispersed techie talent to develop the next greatest app to drive sales? How long would it take a pre-cloud IT department to provide the tooling for the team? The answers all depend on how unwieldy the organisation's infrastructure is. Infrastructure as a service offers: a reduction in risk; an increase in predictability; quicker time to market; reduced operational expenditure; turnkey environments; end-to- end support; proven interoperability; less management; and repeatable deployment.

In all likelihood, the Target Operating Environment (TOE)

within the scope of a DCM will be a cloud platform. There are 4 types; private cloud, public cloud, hybrid and community cloud. These cloud solutions are becoming a daily staple in the buffet of technologies you will encounter on an IT programme. When the Target Operating Environment is cloud, you need to view the cloud solution as a key capability for delivering the DCM business case.

Monkey Episode 16: The Most Monstrous Monster

The starting point for any DCM is to liken the migration to changing an aeroplane's engine whilst in mid flight. Your aim is to change the engine without anyone realising you have changed the engine. There are many types of DCM. Understanding the types of migration, will influence the shape and approach to the project.

Data Centre Relocation(DCR)	Relocation of services from one data centre to another
Data Centre Consolidation(DCC)	Relocation of services host at many locations to fewer locations.
Data Centre Transformation(DCT)	Using DCM as a means to radically improve efficiency and effectives.

Monkey Episode 7 : The Beginning of Wisdom

Data centre migration is not a data migration. DCM involves data migration but it is only 1 constituent part of the programme. DCM is not a purely technical project - many stakeholder groups are impacted across the organisation. A purely technical focus will just bore them. There is a plethora of documentation on DCM. For ease of understanding, I have tried to take all of those approaches and represent what is common between all of them. Dealing with anything complex requires a model to abstract and conceptualise an approach. I will start with a simple view of the organisational architecture impacted by the DCM. For planning purposes, you have to place the organisation into 4 distinct domains.

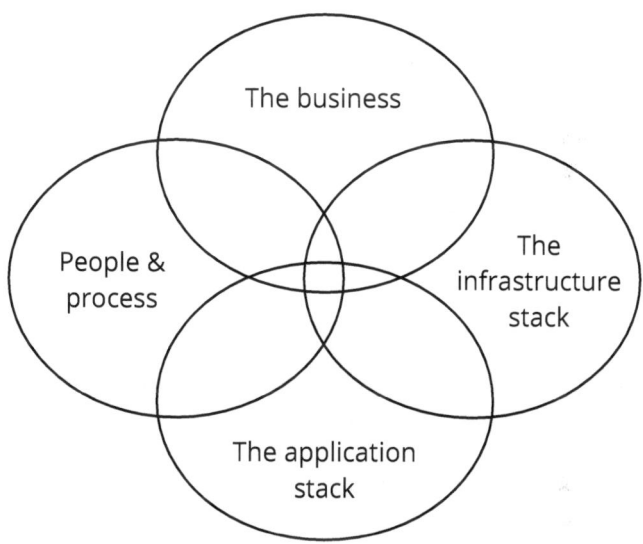

A DCM is a programme of iterative activities that spans each of the domains. Impaired DCMs have a common theme. The phasing on the plan was very 'waterfall', and the activities on the plan were finish- to-start over long durations. The more successful DCMs have the same phasing but the phasing is iterative across the domains, which makes absolute sense when dealing with complexity and uncertainty. In the diagram below I have indicated the extent of the involvement of stakeholders from each of the domains to deliver a successful DCM.

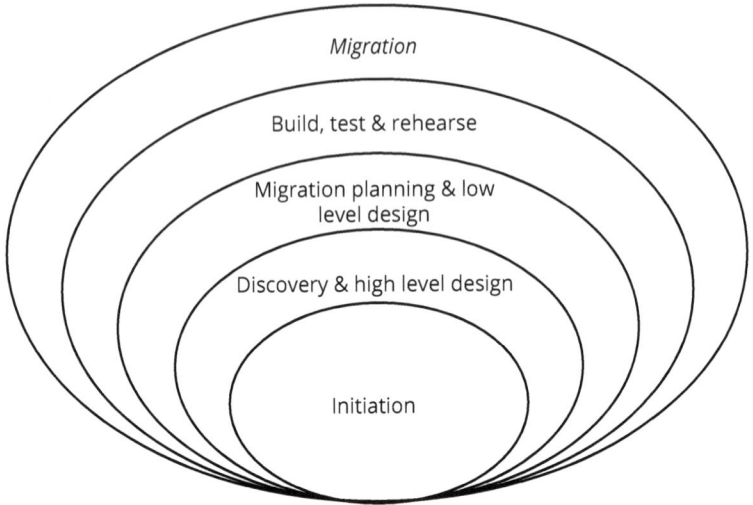

Prior to initiation, the questions on everyone's lips will be: How long will it take to complete the migration? How much will it cost? How do we resource the delivery? And within the technical ranks of the IT department, what will happen to my job? Embarking on a DCM without first achieving clarity on these matters is a recipe for failure. The first critical success factor in a DCM, is the whole organisation having a shared and common understanding of why, how much and when. Achieving this aim requires execution of communications plan, to ensure transparency and a candid conversation about the impact.

Timing all depends on how much time you have to migrate from the Source Operating Environment (SOE). Migration of the SOE followed by optimisation on the Target Operating Environment, gets you out of the legacy data centre quicker than optimising the SOE, prior to migration to the Target Operating Environment. The more time you have, the greater opportunity you have to optimise both the source and Target Operating Environment.

So the 'how much time do we have' question is about ascertaining when & why the organisation needs to get its applications and data out of the Source Operating Environment.

The 'why' question should be answered in a dreaded future context i.e. what is the commercial impact on the organisation, if the migration is not achieved by the dates requested by the business? Using this approach identifies unreasonable time-is-of-the-essence delivery dates. It is unreasonable because when there is no reasoning behind why the delivery date is the delivery date, it is just a date plucked from the air with a propensity to become an expectation. This kind of planning risks an organisation's business operational stability.

How much? It all depends on the return on investment in the business case and the ease of access to funding. The best advice I can give here is to invest time in understanding the actual cost of similar migrations with all the hall marks of success. I would urge caution when using cost models based on unproven assumption, sensitive to volume of servers, whether they are physical or virtual.

All DCMs are unique because of the interdependency between applications, network, OS and data. It's the complexity in this relationship that drives the effort required to achieve a smooth DCM. That knowledge exists in 2 places: performance and configuration data in the Source Operating Environment; and in technicians' heads as tacit knowledge. Addressing the HR question is critical. Without addressing concerns from technical staff who maintain the Source Operating Environment (SOE), they will be less than enthusiastic about getting involved. A critical success factor in any DCM is having access to information about the make-up of the Source Operating Environment. There are some key messages that must be understood by technical staff and IT managers impacted by the change. There is a way of getting these messages across. The key message is that less maintenance and management activity frees up budget to invest and innovate in IT for business advantage. It's difficult to see how any technician or IT manager could disagree. How engineers are led, managed or motivated will make or break a DCM. A DCM involves processes and tools that extract, transform and configure workloads on 3 environments - source, interim and target. A workload consists of application, data and OS, migrated from one environment to the other. In all likelihood multiple teams of different engineers will have to be engaged given the differing environments, OS, data tiers and application stacks. The aim of the game is to get them all working as a team. It means pre migration acquires a focus on team building for the main event. There is nothing more detrimental to a DCM than a dysfunctional cohort of engineering teams finding it hard to collaborate. After all, these are the guys who know about the environments and how to make the tools sing. It's the engineers you will need onside to figure out why something that works on paper does not work in practise. Because of these reasons, your relationship with the engineers and technicians is more important than your relationship with anyone else involved in the migration. Designers, testers, managers, sponsors, security consultants may be more vocal but they are not the ones pushing the buttons and looking at technical stuff in the middle of the night figuring out how to make stuff work when it doesn't work.

So as a PM, you have to build a certain type of relationship with them. In practise, this means demonstrating a healthy respect for them. The moment you treat them like robots by spoon feeding instructions, their productivity will go south. You have to include them in key decisions about how the migration will be technically delivered. Ask them for ideas on how to optimise the migration or simplify the migration design. The feeling of being involved in the design leads to improved quality and less unforeseen technical debt suddenly manifesting itself during migration. Understand what motivates them. For some it will be money. For others it will be gaining new knowledge. Adopting a policy of transparency is paramount. Don't hide anything from them that may dis-empower them. Be selective with the engineers who engage on the migration. Look for positive attitude, team players and the proactive kind. If they can't offer this, do not let them near your migration. Lose the negativity addicts or the ones that will only work from painting-by-numbers prescriptive method statements. They are real time stealers. Engineers are grounded types so your plans have to realistic or they will see the holes.

Monkey Episode 25 : The Country of Nightmares

So we are at a point where I have touched on some key macro level themes, that start to inform the key variables behind shaping a DCM for a successful outcome. The main driver behind cost will be resources. The lowest cost approach is to utilise in-house resources. It is an approach that should come with a health warning. In the current climate of austerity and challenge on IT budgets, it is unlikely that the IT function will have people just sitting around with the pre-requisite skills. In reality, under these circumstances, project activities are added to the day job. In my humble experience, this approach (combined with matrix-managed or tower-structured IT functions), results in fractional assignment. This takes the delivery down the path towards a project with the issues encountered on a challenge delivery. There will be a temptation to consider the use of contractors to rapidly acquire the skills needed. The challenge with filling the delivery with freelancers is two-fold. Firstly, they will lack local knowledge of the Source Operating Environment. Secondly, there will be a constant debate and creative differences over migration methodology. Overcoming these challenges requires consideration to creating a Differentiated Delivery Organisation (DDO).Here are the options. Option 1 involves pulling the in-house resources from BAU into a dedicated team, then backfilling for BAU. The logic here is BAU work is less complex than migration work. Backfilling for BAU work is easier to recruit for, than sourcing freelancers for extensive migration work. Option 2 involves partnering, normally with a systems integrator. Option 3 is a hybrid approach.

Central to the success of option 2 is choosing the right partner, coupled with flexible contractual arrangements that empower both organisations to play to their strengths. The buyer and its incumbents tend to have access to all the knowledge about the Source Operating Environment while the integrator can bring method, experience and expertise in the Target Operating Environment. A flexible contractual arrangement is paramount. The optimal points where accurate estimates can be made are on completion of the 3 phases that form a migration project or programme, pre- migration, migration and post migration. To reduce the propensity for contract frustration, it makes sense to have breakpoints at the end of the pre-migration phase and 25% completion into the migration phase. At these points in the migration, the most informed insight to firm up estimates will surface.

An old hat at DCM will spot a buyer trying to transfer all the risk, by fixing a price too early in the discovery and design process. The savvy integrators will walk away. No commercially astute integrator takes on 'merde' business. The ones desperate for business will say anything and agree to anything to get the deal, then bog down the delivery with change-control overload. The old adage 'you pay peanuts, you get monkeys' holds true on many a challenged DCM. Prior to initiating a pre-migration mobilisation phase, absolute clarity on any time-is-of-the-essence milestones, is a must. An immoveable deadline for completion helps gauge the time available for optimisation activity on the Source Operating Environment. If the deadline is the highest priority and limited time is available for optimisation, then the scope of the project is in a 'migrated on an as-is basis' territory, which further informs how the differentiated delivery organisation should be structured.

The commercials are closed off. The mandate has been secured. Money is made available. Scope is defined as much as it can be prior to kick off. Now you need a Data Centre Migration Delivery Management Team to make it happen. A world class DCM has 7 distinct functional teams. If you have a weakness in any one of these teams, then you've reduced your chances of success. I liken a high performance DCM core delivery team to the characters from the TV series 'The A Team' (1983-1987).

CLASSIFIED DCM INTEL	
Codename	Colonel John "Hannibal" Smith
DCM Function	Project Management, Project Management Office & Resource Management
Wise Words	I love it when a plan comes together
	Next time you think you want to take someone out, don't get yourself a good squad. Get yourself a team.
	Give me a minute, I'm good! If I got an hour, I'm great! You give me six months, I'm unbeatable!

Hannibal's strapline are the wonderful words you want to hear after a DCM has been delivered. DCMs are iterations of analysis, design, build, test and transition riddled with interdependency on organisational circumstances outside the team's control. The planning is complex and the plans complicated. Without best practise, pragmatic and agile project management, a DCM will fail. Always employ a project management team with a track record of delivery, using technologies in the Target Operating Environment, and technologies in the Source Operating Environment. Most importantly, the Project Manager must have an in-depth understanding of: 1) the organisation that the DCM will impact on; and 2) the supplier organisations delivering the DCM. They particularly need to know the barriers these organisations will put in the team's way. By barriers I mean: financial approval practises; change control processes; governance; HR; the way technology is deployed; resource management; prioritisation; the way power listens when the lesser mortals speak truth to Olympus; and the speed of decision making.

It's these barriers that will cause the exceptions. Knocking them down or knowing the workarounds before the project delivery hits them, clears a path for the team to deliver. A DCM can make liquid budget holders very poor very quickly. So robust financial tracking is the order of the day. A DCM requires many different types of resources, working in parallel and outside normal working hours. Resource management has to think many weeks in advance and continually check the resources will be there when needed. Given the business risk, level of investment and political visibility of the DCM, the PMO has to be able to present a true picture of project status against time, budget, quality, scope and risk at the push of a button. Configuration management is not a nice-to-have; it is an absolute must. An engineering team working from an out-of-date version of low level designs, will cost the project in terms of time and money.

CLASSIFIED DCM INTEL	
Codename	Sergeant Bosco "B.A." Baracus
DCM Function	Compliance & Risk
Wise Words	I ain't gettin' on no plane, Hannibal
	You're just a crazy fool, who's seein' things that ain't there!
	Quit your jibba jabba.

DCMs involve moving lots of valuable and sensitive data around. There are important policies around payment card industry standards and information security in the shape of ISO

270001. Public sector bodies are obliged to adhere to stringent Cabinet Office Standards whilst commercial organisations risk reputation, customer loyalty and profitability in the event of a breach against their security standards. Most mere techie and designer mortals are not versed in the Smiley's People world of information security. From a designer and build perspective, information security is boring. Compliance is something for risk-averse geeky people to worry about. Fortifying valuable information takes time and money. As a Project Manager, I want things to move fast. I'm not interested in lots of effort on the critical path, to mitigate a risk with less than 5% chance of happening when I'm long gone after the delivery. The problem is when the 5% probability becomes a reality -the stuff that makes the news. That's why you need a B.A. Baracus-type leading on compliance. Don't have the timid police-officer-type from Police Academy on the time. No-one will listen to them. They tend to reach a point where they explode with anger after months of not being listened to. B.A. Baracus had presence, charisma and authority to make it known the delivery team when they are delivering something, in a manner that is not wise from a compliance perspective.

As a PM, the temptation to drug compliance folk into a sleep, then put them in the cupboard, can be overwhelming. Don't succumb to it. A DCM is fraught with all the kinds of risk you can think of. It's easy to say we are managing risk but that normally means that on a failed DCM we just wrote them down. The project needs a B.A. to make sure the team and the outside world follow through on actions to close the risk. If your team is made up of people who have previously worked on a DCM gone bad, they are going to be wiser. That can mean more risk averse. It can mean greater propensity to suffer from confirmation bias. You will find the definition on Wikipedia. The risk register starts to fill with stuff, which is motivated by achieving closure on a negative experience. What's needed is Terry Tate's and B.A. Baracus' tough tender loving care to snap them out of it. It is a shock-and-awe communication to jolt them into proving why the DCM they are working on, is different from the last one. However, if it is not going to be different, then the team have every right to be miserable fookers. In those circumstances, an irrational leadership team is one that believes in doing something in the same sub-optimal way, over and over again, and then expecting improved results.

CLASSIFIED DCM INTEL	
Codename	Lieutenant Templeton "Faceman" Peck
DCM Function	Business Liaison
Wise Words	The key to any con is to place the mark in a position where he or she thinks reward will come or harm will be avoided if he or she does exactly as told by the conman.

The fourth necessary utility to keep a business going is its ICT. After all, it is what makes up the 21st century internet-of-everything. Screw up a DCM and you screw up business operations. When a business knows a bunch of ICT bods are going to be prodding and poking around the pipes and connectors, underpinning their business processes, business folk get nervous. The nervousness comes from being on the receiving end of 40 years of ICT function 'loonfestery'.

A DCM needs people to own and run with public relations (PR). There are politics to play out, to convince a business to take some pain while servers and networks are moved around. You cannot just send an email and tell them it is going to happen. Faceman needs to scout ahead and get to know the business. Communication needs to be constant and frequent. It would be easy to ramble on about what a Faceman should do and what he should say, but describing what he shouldn't do gets the point across just as well. The last kind of Communications Manager you need on a DCM team, is a Comical Ali. Comical Ali was the Iraqi Information Minister, Muhammed Saeed al-Sahaf, during the beginning of the Iraq war. Nicknamed 'Baghdad Bob' by the American press, Comical Ali appeared on television spinning fantastic spin about the war in Iraq. Comical Ali stated to the world that there were no American forces in Baghdad. Yet right behind him, American tanks were visible patrolling the streets. Telling the world it is raining while your audience can see someone urinating on your story, is a PR disaster.

There will be hiccups during a DCM. To maintain trust, it's best to be more honest than wise. The role of Faceman is not just to be a mouth piece. Most of the time should be spent getting the powerful in the business world, on board to make difficult decisions which won't be popular with middle management.

CLASSIFIED DCM INTEL	
Codename	Captain H.M. "Howlin' Mad" Murdock
DCM Function	Technical Design Authority
Wise Words	Say, are we a groovy, happenin' bunch o' guys, or what?
	You know Sarge, I had a cat once, but every time I tried to give him a bath, the fur stuck to my tongue.
	Nice drop, Kimosabe. (To Hannibal after he dropped a watermelon from a helicopter, and shattered the bad guy's windshield.)
	She's a beauty, Colonel. I'm gonna treat her like the proud lady she is.
	White paper, white paper, white paper...
	Pardon me Roy, is that the catatonic choo-choo?

They control the horizontal, they control the vertical, don't try to adjust. Yo

I merely relocated the aircraft with extreme prejudice because of a TOTAL LOSS OF THRUST AND LIFT FUNCTIONS!!!!!

I gotta tell ya, from up here the local flora and fauna are quite remarkable.

My size? My size is the amount of space I fill up. Thanks for asking.

That concludes your flight with Miracle Airlines, the only airline where Lady Luck is your co-pilot.

I don't suppose you've noticed that I'm wearing gold. You know why? I will tell you why. I got behind the wheel of this van here, and I noticed that she was shimmying a little, pulling to the left. Well it finally hit me; that ugly mudsucker tuned the suspension of this van to compensate for all that gold he was wearing. So I put on a few chains, a few rings, a bracelet and some bricks under the seat, and it worked.

Some of us won't be coming back, but those of us that do, will be back and those of us that don't come back, won't be coming back. Now, I point this out, because if you don't come back, you won't be back and if you do come back, you will be back. Any questions?

Apart from being completely bonkers, Murdoch was extrovert, inquisitive, communicative, fun to be around and loved being in the thick of it avoiding a crash. These are all qualities a DCM design team need to have. A DCM is won or lost in the way it conducts its design activities. Note I use the words DCM design team; a solution architect to lead on design, supported by experts in each architectural domain, found across the whole spectrum of IT at a high level, low level and implementation level. The spectrum includes: data; service management; security; network; applications; infrastructure; virtualisation; testing; and cloud. They have to be absolutely brilliant, and comfortable with white boarding their designs in front of those who are going to build it. If your designers are disappearing for weeks to draft a design document, only to throw it over the fence to the builders without any validation of 'can it be built' type questioning, your DCM will fail. A designer needs to ask some critical questions of their approach. Have I factored in the organisation's capability to build the Target Operating Environment and migration tools? Am I putting in the effort to pitch the design to the build-team, so I can factor in any low-level technical constraints only they could know about? The number one indicator that shows this self-reflection is not happening, is a design document appearing in your inbox accompanied with the following email message;

Dear Project Manager

I've documented the design but you will need to ask the other Murdochs about network and applications. I only do servers. Please can you pass it on to the engineers for review then send me the comments.

Yours sincerely

Murdoch

PS : The risk management dude I was working with didn't want to get on the plane. He told me to quit my jibba jabba, then slapped me. I am going to report him to HR.

Reading between the lines the design validation process has lacked any collaboration to ensure clarity, unity and agility. In the event this behaviour is left unchecked, you will get the following email from the builders;

Dear Project Manager

We rehearsed the SAN replication from the SOE to the TOE. It did not work and we don't know why. Spud has tried contacting the designer several times to discuss but we've not had a response.

Yours sincerely

Bob the Builder

P.S. Hope that black and white cat of yours is OK

We've assembled the DCM A-Team to move the project through the pre-migration phase.

DO YOU HAVE A DCM PROBLEM THEN HIRE THE DCM A-TEAM			
Project management PMO & resource management Hannibal	Risk and Compliance B.A.	Communications face	Technical Design Authority Murdoch

The first stage is called Source Base-Line Discovery. This where the team acquire a deep understanding of the Source Operating Environment (SOE) and I'm not just talking about servers. A DCM will go off piste during implementation if the team lacks an accurate picture of the environment being migrated. SOE Discovery is not a one-off task. While the design and build of the Target Operating Environment (TOE) is being done, the SOE will change. After all, it is a production environment for the business. The project requires a function and people who will keep a single accurate picture of the SOE. An SOE consists of data, network layers 1-8, applications, servers, system management tools, monitoring tools, people who use, people who look after it and maintenance processes in the form of service management architecture. A failure to understand it and maintain an accurate understanding, risks encountering a major curveball during migration.

Understanding the source baseline is detective work. The project needs detectives whose sole motivation in life is to communicate how the SOE is built. There are some people who should not conduct source baseline discovery, namely anyone with manager, accountant, finance, bid or sales in their job title. Firstly, they lack the technical onions to get hands-on. Secondly, they suffer from confirmation bias. The result is either optimistic assumptions or incorrect volumes to get the sale, meet a constrained timescale or come up with costs that magically fall within available budget.

What you need is a Columbo-type detective. Columbo was tenacious, and constantly asked the questions to identify the inconvenient truth. More importantly, he had an eye for joining the innocuous dots to identify the unseen important clues. The product from Source Base-Line Discovery is a detailed specification of the SOE, which can be maintained by the PMO as part of the configuration management strategy. It means the PMO needs technical resources to maintain the picture in the form of a Configuration Management Database (CMDB). This function is not an overhead or a nice-to-have; it is a necessity. Without this function embedded in the PMO, the project will have technical teams working from different versions of the technical truth. Without this function, the project becomes dependent on individuals who have the information in their heads. People become miffed off when all they do is spend time answering the same questions over and over again. They tend to leave the organisation for another role, which does not involve 40 hours a week being the Ministry of Information for an ever changing Source Operating Environment.

Pre-migration consists of 4 technical phases: Source Operating Environment discovery; design; build; and test. The greater the complexity and ambiguity, the greater the need to run the activities slightly overlapping and iteratively. Discover a bit, design a bit, build a bit, test a bit and then use the insight to improve the next iteration. The aim is to get all the advantages offered by an agile approach. Design is where the action really starts. First up is the design of the Target Operating Environment (TOE). The TOE design scope consists of all architectural domains for an IT solution. These domains are: data; network; service design; endpoint management service; servers; security; IT service continuity management; and applications. The design needs to contain the design of everything in the TOE. As soon as you make the DCM dependent on: a TOE solution that has not been built; a TOE solution that is not product proven; an inflexible TOE solution; or a TOE solution that does not fit the definition of the term 'turnkey', then the designers have just increased the risk tenfold.

An optimum contemporary TOE, will be a production-capable turnkey infrastructure, as a service cloud solution which has been tested a zillion times. Look for the following features;

Orchestration Features

Deployment

Provisioning

Authentication

Fabric Management

Process automation

Infrastructure Monitoring & Management Features

Back up

Firmware management

Patching & software updates

Anti-virus

Intrusion detection & prevention

Logging

Asset management

Configuration management

Capacity monitoring

Self Service Portal for:

Capacity management

Service level management

Access management

Provisioning

Decommissioning

CMDB

Request fulfilment

Change control

Incident and fault reporting

Service reporting

Utility based billing

The overall impact for the DCM project will be the acquisition of capability to build the TOE quickly, increment its capacity quickly and amend it quickly. Capacity-wise, you will only pay for what you use which is great for the project's financial health. The next important design product is the migration strategy and run books. The migration strategy is the product that answers the question how and what are we going to migrate. Essentially there are 2 approaches: a logistical move; and replication. Logistical approaches lift the servers from the source, shift them down the motorway and plug them in the target data centre. Replication approaches involve copying the source environment across a network to the Target Operating Environment. The norm is to use replication techniques that virtualise the Source Operating Environment and then install on the Target Operating Environment.

Extract, transform and load (ETL)

Manually take a copy of the SOE. Do some work on it to make it work on the TOE. Copy it to the TOE.

Physical to virtual (P2V)

Use a tool e.g. VMware to take a copy of the SOE from a physical server. Do some clever work with the image so it works on the target operating virtual environment. Install and check it works on the TOE.

Virtual to virtual (V2V)

Use a tool e.g. VMware to take a copy of a virtualised SOE. Do some clever work with the image so it works on the target operating virtual environment. Install and check it works on the TOE.

Virtual to physical (V2P)

Use a tool e.g. VMware to take a copy of a virtualised SOE. Do some clever work with the image so it works

> on a physical server. Install and check it works on the
> physical server on the TOE.

The run books describe a granular step-by-step painting-by-numbers method statement to migrate a workload. A workload is a logical chunk of data and application being migrated from the SOE to the TOE. The aim of the game is to script the migration method statement so that it can be automated and industrialised into a workflow i.e. push of a button, Service Orientated Architecture (SOA) that follows the principles of continuous integration (CI). Aligning to this approach reduces the number of manual processes required to complete a migration. It will be these manual processes that are a source latency, which in turn can create schedule risk.

Taking these run books and building the migration tooling in the manner prescribed, creates a reusable and repeatable lean migration assembly line. Migrations from an SOE to TOE never work first time. To assume otherwise and resource the project on this basis, is a recipe for disappointment. When first run, the process gets so far then hits snags. What follows is some snagging before the process is run again. Next time around, the process goes a bit further then hits some new snags. At some point it works. Going through this drama, using lots of manual intervention to complete the migration of the workload, is costly. Every new piece of complex software behaves like this when it is first executed. Tooling to automate this process for DCM is no different.

Testing a run book a couple of times pre-migration, results in early migration-proving. Early migration-proving generates data that enables the project to better estimate how long the migration will take and the likely technical issues. Successful DCMs are made up of people who believe in 'the more I practise the luckier I will get'. They are lucky because subsequent decisions are data driven, using information gleaned from an empirical process.

Think about the words 'data centre migration' and it will conjure up pictures of physical and virtual servers that need to be moved from one place to another. Perceiving a DCM in this manner will make the team underestimate the complexity. It's what's on the servers; how they talk to the internet-of-everything; and what those applications are used for, that should concern the team. Planning a DCM, based on server volumes, server types and the OS that's on them, makes the project look easy because it's everything else in the SOE that results in the complexity. Special attention needs to be paid to network layers 1 – 7, and the applications that use the network to move data around. If you've got 100 man-days for design focus 80 on these 2 areas, the likelihood is the software that sits on servers does not just talk to other software that sits on the same server. The project plan needs to contain the tasks to address this point or there is a significant risk of encountering a major technical 'gotcha' during implementation. Building a network for a DCM is a distinct project in its own right, and in terms of critical path it's the solution that needs to be delivered first: a) it's the most complex area of DCM; and b) every other technical component won't work without it.

Best practise would be to implement a gateway review between pre-migration and migration to determine readiness migration. Measureable conditions describing readiness for migration, need to be documented in the test strategy. The project will come under pressure to get the migration out of the way. The last thing an organisation needs is a production environment spread across the SOE, and a poor performing TOE. Share prices and profits get hit when that happens. If the project is not migration-ready, either request more time to get ready or de-scope the migration. If these opportunities are not offered, walk away and find another job. There is no glory in failure. If the migration presents a major business risk to the organisation, then best practice would be to bring in independent project assurance to assess readiness. An investment of 50k in independent advice to prevent a financial risk of millions and irreparable reputational damage, is money well spent.

The migration phase consists of 3 distinct blocks of: work migration control; rehearsal; and actual migration. Migration control is a hub delivering activities to script, track, communicate and control migration waves. A migration wave consists of a period of rehearsal followed by the actual migration. The rehearsal is a dry run in the operational environment to understand how the actual migration will perform. A rehearsal needs to simulate the operational circumstances that the actual migration will take place under. It's the last chance to get it right whilst identifying, and fix-forwarding, activities that will need to happen post migration. Rehearsal and migration normally takes places out of hours so the resources need to be scheduled well in advance. There will always be someone who won't be available due to a pet dying, falling off a trampoline while playing with the kids and damaging one's gonads, relationship problems or inebriation. So it's best to carry some over-capacity in the forward resource schedule.

Migration is about predicting performance and then reacting positively to unforeseen snags. Metrics and measureable acceptance criteria need to be produced that define what a successful migration looks like. Take all the run books, and the following conclusions will scream at you. Success requires achieving data accuracy in the requirements feeding the migration process. Success requires data accuracy in the interdependency between the requirements. Success requires complete visibility of workload interdependency, with all technical domains found across the whole spectrum of ICT project delivery. The performance and synchronisation of all technical tasks during migration must be measureable in real-time as the migration moves through the steps in the run book. A migration performance measurement and management system, provide visibility of actual performance against the said factors. If a process is not defined, it cannot be measured. If a process cannot be measured, it cannot be improved or managed.

Regular and frequent communication is an absolute necessity. The best means to keep everyone informed of progress is not email, call conferences or 1-2-1. It's social media. Think about the number of people interested in progress. It's probably in the hundreds for a large organisation. A Facebook page or Twitter are probably the best means to keep everyone informed.

The migration stage must have a rehearsed back-out plan. The best place to position the development of back-out plan, is to position it as a Major Incident Priority 1 Disaster Recovery Process. Developing a back-out plan in isolation to an organisation's DR and major incident management process, will result in it: having a lack of credibility; not getting the organisational attention it deserves; and a bypass of any corporate validation testing to prove both warranty and utility in the recovery process.

Post migration primarily consists of activities to achieve acceptance into service (AIS). Most DCM frameworks I have seen tend to have this box at the end, called 'handover'. These frameworks read like, "At the end of the migration, the Service Management Function will shake your hand and welcome the solution into service with a smile." They won't if the project has treated transition-into-service as some last minute after thought. Over the last 20 years I have worked with many an ICT Service Management Team, and the message is consistent. There is an undercurrent of ICT Service Management Teams being on the receiving end of incomplete ICT solutions that they have to fix, while the project team rides off into the sunset. Do not leave transition-into-service until the last minute. The likely outcome will be a high dependence on the project team for support, as the target operating model moves into early life-cycle support and then full acceptance into service. A service model that spans project and operational world tends to be inefficient and will increase project cost.

The halfway house introduces a rigidity, which prevents clean project closure and denies the operational world an opportunity to evolve its own performance. All of these problems can be avoided by making two key assumptions at the very start of the project. A DCM has the potential to be very disruptive to the Source Operating Environment's service design. A new service design is an integral part of the Target Operating Environment. Therefore, the project plan requires a tranche of activity across the time-line, that results in the organisation acquiring empirically proven capacity and capability to sustain the Target Operating Environment's utility and warranty.

The best way to do this is to run the ITILv3 life-cycle in parallel with pre- migration, migration and post migration. As a result of the approach, the project team is made to answer the key questions that are known to lead to best in-class transitions into service. Those questions cannot be answered without collaborative and constant dialogue with the world of operations. Absolutely paramount throughout this process is the transfer of knowledge about the Target Operating Environment, from the project team to the ICT service management world. For acceptance into service purposes, knowledge to support the Target Operating Environment needs to be put through its paces prior to completion of post migration activities. The best way to achieve this aim (whilst at the same time get the Target Operating Environment's service design match fit i.e. the required ITILv3 process scope), is to have all the ITILv3 people and process habbardashery in place at the point of migration rehearsal. In fact, I would advise assessing the state of operational readiness within the scope of the gateway review, between pre-migration and migration. As a result, the project increases its propensity to achieve a clean closure, it creates an opportunity for service validation testing and it proactively encourages collaboration with operations.

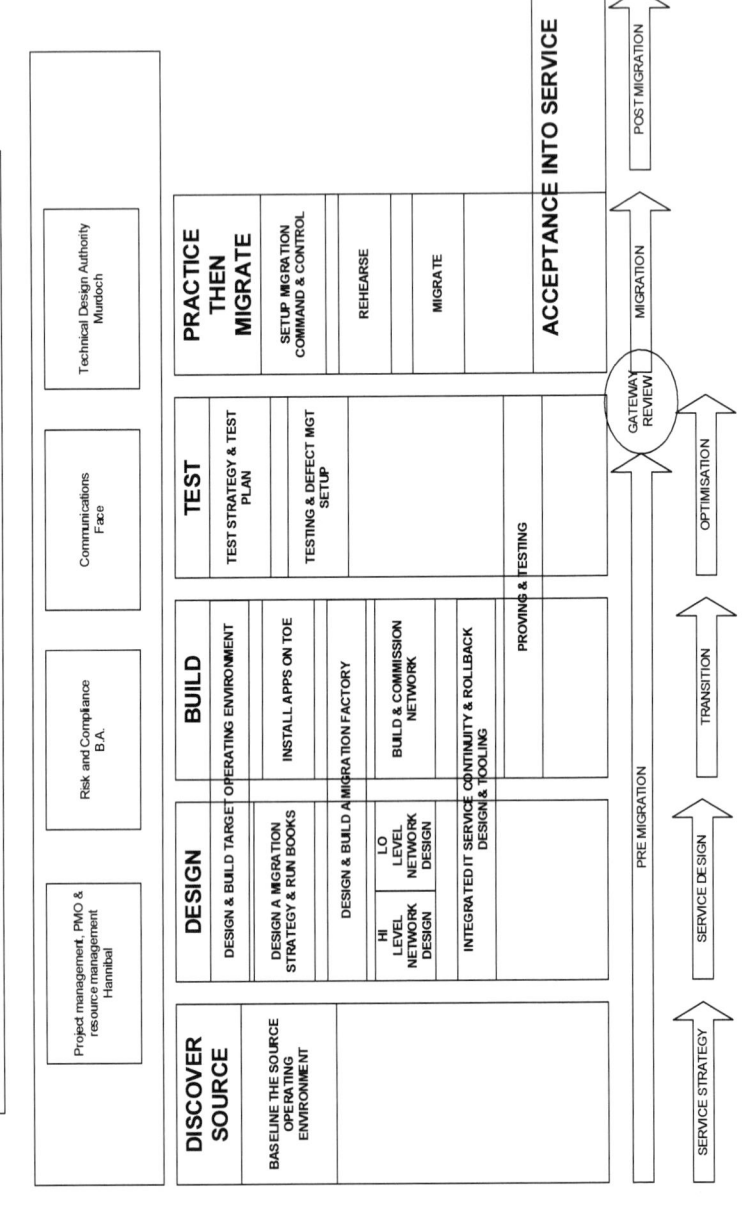

DO YOU HAVE A DCM PROBLEM THEN HIRE THE DCM A-TEAM

So there you have it - data centre project delivery framework. Its goal is to help you avoid the common pitfalls associated with failed data centre migrations. These pitfalls are namely: poor planning; a failure to establish pre-move baselines; not thinking through the totality of the solution; inflexible organisation; expecting complex stuff to work first; skimping on testing; applying complex upgrades throughout the migration; using unproven technology; and (probably the number 1 cause of failure) mobilising an inexperienced team. There is no substitute for experience.

Monkey Episode 26 : The End of the Way

GAMIFICATION FUTURE SAVY
PART 1: M.O.O.P.P

'Say, we can go where we want to. A place
where they will never find. And we can act like
we come from out of this world.'

The Safety Dance

Men Without Hats

COMMUNICATION ENABLEMENT IS MORE IMPORTANT than ever in the world of IT project delivery. So why is Microsoft Lync totally awesome, why should you use it and are you ready for life in a MOOPP?

It's 1979 and I'm staying over at my cousin's place for a couple of weeks down in Wiltshire. Off we go to Swindon for the day to see where my Uncle Andrew works. I think he worked for ICL. It is the first time I have ever seen a computer. I'm 9 years old and it is my first time on a mainframe. I feel like I have walked into a NASA control room. I will never forget that day. My Uncle Andrew was an avid Morris dancer. He appeared on MTV in the video for Safety Dance by Men Without Hats. I would not be writing this chapter if it were not for my Uncle

Andrew. He is a man of many talents. So my uncle parks me on this big office swivel chair in front of a monster keyboard and monitor with a flashing TCL>. Windows was still a pipe dream. I am Captain Kirk. Uncle Andrew loads up a game. It is called Adventure. No graphics just text. Adventure is part of the genre known as multi-user dungeon (MUD). In the game I am instant messaging (IM) other people playing the game. Four hours flash by in minutes and it will be another two years before I ever see another computer. A couple of weeks later when I'm back at school, all my mates think I am completely mad when I tell them what I saw at ICL down near Swindon. But 35 years later, instant messaging is all the rage and my son is playing Minecraft. I ask him what do you have to do to win the game? It is not a game. It is a virtual Lego set. You build stuff. The developers are millionaires.

5 years ago I am watching Peter Molyneux, a world renowned games designer. He started making computer games when I started playing them. Microsoft has given him a development kit for Microsoft Kinect. Peter Molyneux shows off Milo, a virtual character you can talk to using Kinect. The player draws a picture and shows it to Milo. The Kinect system virtualises it and Mike Teavee's dream from Willy Wonka and the Chocolate Factory (a book I read 20 years earlier) is on the verge of becoming a reality! I'm left wondering how great it would be if IT project planning was as interesting and exciting as life in a virtual world. In 2012, I start to hear about a product called Microsoft Lync on a daily basis so I check it out. I'm left with the feeling that email will be a thing of the past and good riddance to it. Nowadays, IM is just accepted as an everyday part of life. It is a core feature of a unified communications solution (UC). Used in the correct manner, UC has the ability to remove latency from a communications process. The features encourage far more interpersonal communication unlike email, which encourages latency and is less interpersonal.

A major theme throughout the book is the woes as a result

of poor communication because of tools like email. Nothing beats co-location of team but in an IT project delivery context, co-location of the whole team may not be practical. Virtual team working is the norm to overcome the impractical issues that accompany co-location. Latency, caused by the misuse of email and impersonal call conferences, can destroy clarity. UC, coupled with social media and cloud based collaboration tools, are a great enabler of virtual team working, a concept known as Massively Open Online Project Planning (MOOPP). It is not a new concept; the Rolling Stones sang about it in the 1960s. 'MOOPP MOOPP MOOPP MOOPP, please allow me to introduce myself, I am a man of wealth and taste.'

To understand the power of a MOOPP capability; you have to understand why Massively Multiplayer Online Role Playing Games (MMORPG), such as World of Warcraft (WOW) by Blizzard Entertainment and Minecraft, are so popular. If Adventure on an ICL mainframe was a troglodyte, World of Warcraft and Minecraft would be modern day man. 8 million people play WOW without being coerced. To become all powerful, players self-organise into clans to help eachother increase experience points. Now think about the nagging that has to go on to get a few people on an IT project team to collaborate on something like MS Project or even to attend a workshop to do a project plan. Here is the lowdown on how those sessions play out:

You invite loads of people. Only half turn up because planning is boring.

You sit there with your laptop connected to a projector with MS Project on the wall. As people talk you programme in the task to MS Project. The audience is falling asleep. Watching Dr Zhivago 50 times in a row is more interesting.

So you make it interesting using post-it notes and ask everyone to write down the tasks. The problem is that IT projects are complex and involve lots of people. You suddenly discover gaps; participants have to go back to their team to get the information.

Then you get the philosopher who asks the question, 'Why I am here?' As a Project Manager, you should know how long everything takes to do and what is needed to be done. The sentiment goes viral around the room. Manager-knows-all-and-knows-best on an IT project is a recipe for failure but that is what people sometimes expect of you. It is because you've got IT in your job title.

It never fails to amaze me how many people in those planning sessions play Warcraft or something similar, like The Sims. For the avoidance of doubt, the big guy who beat me at a rap contest one Christmas (rapping Rappers Delight by Sugarhill Gang) is not a WOW player. Those games are virtual worlds full of unified communication type features. Below are the features you would find in Microsoft Lync and Cisco Unified Communications. You will find exactly the same logical features in games like The Sims or World of Warcraft.

Instant messaging

Presence

Teleconferencing

Me area

Voice

Contact cards

Privacy and sharing controls

Meeting and conferencing

Integration with social media to share with the world
what you are doing and why you are doing it

What if it were possible to plan an IT project in a manner where the process felt like collaboration in an exciting virtual world? To beat the plan, you need to achieve clarity, unity and agility. If clarity, unity and agility represents the best three course meal in the world, then the question is what are the ingredients? They are all the ingredients behind the creation of the world's best players and teams in all those massively multiplayer on-line games. The virtual world and what you can do in it acts as a catalyst for all these ingredients.

Accuracy	Flexibility	Reliability
Assertiveness	Focus	Resilience
Aesthetics	Helpfulness	Respect
Balance	Honesty	Responsibility
Caution	Humour	Self-discipline
Cleanliness	Industriousness	Service
Commitment	Initiative	Simplicity
Confidence	Integrity	Skill
Cooperation	Joyfulness	Stewardship
Courage	Knowledge	Tactfulness
Creativity	Mindfulness	Thoroughness
Curiosity	Openness	Tolerance
Decisiveness	Orderliness	Trust
Determination	Persistence	Trustworthiness
Endurance	Pragmatism	Togetherness
Enthusiasm	Purposefulness	Vision
Excellence	Rationality	

A cursory glance over the list leads me to conclude that a challenged or impaired IT project suffers from a cumulative deficit in those behaviours. Let's go back to my planning session from hell. I have sought answers from the psychologists as to why people want to tap away at their smart-phones instead of participating. You need clever and talented people to attend those sessions. You'd think with all those clever and interesting people in the same room, the vibe would be good. The answer I like to take comfort from comes from Deci, Ryan 2004 Self Determination Theory. The theory goes that human beings are at their best when intrinsically motivated. Self Determination describes three main intrinsic needs. I have come to the view that when participants don't feel intrinsically motivated, the planning session won't go well.

Competence

The need for a person to experience oneself as capable in coping with the environment.

Autonomy

The need for someone to actively participate in determining one's own behaviour, with autonomous choice of actions.

Relatedness

The need to care for and be related to others, and to be involved in the social world.

Professor Steven Reiss 2002 came up with several innate desires guiding human behaviour.

Acceptance
The need for approval

Curiosity
The need to learn

Eating
The need for food

Family
The need to raise children

Honour
The need to be loyal to the traditional values of one's
clan/ethnic group

Idealism
The need for social justice

Independence
The need for individuality

Order
The need for organized, stable, predictable
environments

Physical Activity
The need for exercise

Power
The need for influence of will

Romance
The need for sex and for beauty

Saving
The need to collect

Social Contact
The need for friends (peer relationships)

Social Status
The need for social standing/importance

Tranquillity
The need to be safe

Vengeance
The need to strike back and to compete

So if the act of collaborating on a plan can meet basic human desires and intrinsic motivations, the planning exercise should result in 'beat the plan' type behaviours. Is it possible to socially engineer such a temporary management environment? Probably not. At one end of the scale there is anarchy and at the other there is total order. Both extremes are flawed. But according to the management 3.0 gurus, maybe with greater distribution/delegation of control and a greater allowance for self organisation, self direction and self selection, the management environment becomes more conducive to dealing with uncertainty and complexity. It sort of makes sense when you consider a law developed by Kevin Kelly (Out of Control 1994:469), an authority on digital culture. And note today's challenged IT projects are delivered in a culture of digitalisation.

Control from the bottom up

In a complex system, everything happens at once, and problems ignore any central authority. Therefore overall governance must be spread throughout its parts.

All this self organisation stuff sounds great in theory but would it work in practise? If you put the whole IT project team in a room and told them to get on with it, there would be anarchy. The first problem is the logistics; the second problem is regulation. There is not any of either of these things. The third problem is lack of opportunity to put self determination theory into practice. (However, you might get a few babies nine months later and a couple of fights.) What if I put the whole team in a MOOPP - an arms-length, managed, exciting virtual world where building the plan is akin to playing WOW and Minecraft? In a MOOPP, there are missions. Missions describe what you have to achieve. Missions describe products and deliverables. You can only attempt a mission if you have prerequisite experience points and an appropriate character class. These points are assigned to you by your employer. If you complete a mission, your experience points go up. The MOOPP has facilities to share your experience and achievement on social media. In the MOOPP you can look like whatever you want to. This makes planning fun and memorable. There are no GANTT charts in the MOOPP. In the world you pick a product from a mission. Your goal is to virtually arrange all the tasks to complete the product. There will be some tasks you can do and tasks you need others to do. When the player selects a product it comes with a default set of tasks with costs, duration, effort, resource requirements and constraints based on successful historical deliveries. For the tasks you can do, you describe what the task is and how long it will take. Tasks you cannot do are added to missions. In the world you will have to talk to other character classes to get information. There are shops run by suppliers who can sell you services to build better products, or build your products quicker than you can. They can generate quotes and proposals for approval. The system is constantly generating the information required to formulate a realistic plan. It creates an environment to encourage a self-organising, self-directing and self-selecting system; the ingredients required to solve complex problems. It starts to solve the problems caused by the Darkness Principle (Cilliers : 1998:4-5); Each project team member has an incomplete picture of what is required to achieve the project. Hence why planning together and deciding together is a critical success factor.

As I write this I can hear the howls of laughter. Will we ever see a MOOPP? Well, it may not be that far off if you look at the possibility of converging technologies.

Microsoft Kinect

Volumetric computing and motion sensing

Google Glass

Augmented reality

Wearable Computing

Context awareness, smart-phones just as powerful as
PCs, Pebble and Iwatch

Occulus Rift

Virtual reality

Unified Communications

Microsoft Lync, Cisco UC, Avaya & Social Media

Cloud based Collaboration Tools

Early generation self-service collaborative project
planning tools.

Agile Project Management

The transfer of agile practices and philosophy from
software development into all forms of IT project
delivery.

As we speak, I would bet a £1000 that Twitter is being used
to provide updates to anyone who is interested in an IT project's
status. Maybe a MOOPP is a blue sky pipe dream but there are
tools around today, like unified communications and intuitive
collaborative cloud based project planning tools, that could give
you some of the features and performance from a MOOPP; a
far more productive means of project planning than getting
everyone in a room to enter information into a tool like MS
Project.

DON'T PLAY THE GAME OF PHONES

'With nothin' to gain except killin' your brain'
White Lines
Grandmaster Flash

THERE WAS A TIME BACK in 1989, during the second summer of love, where techno addiction brought thousands of people together in a sea of happiness and oneness. 22 years later, I'm walking into offices housing IT project delivery teams rubbing shoulders with one another. Not enough desks and too many people; their heads down on a desktop or laptop. Some are talking to themselves into the ether on call conferences. When the aircon breaks you know about it. Most of the email activity in the office has one thing in common; differences of opinion. Differences of opinion over how to get things done, what needs doing, what was done, and when things need doing by. Unlike the techno induced oneness of the late 80s, there is an atmosphere of division in the air. This is what it feels like in one of those environments with a propensity to produce challenged or impaired IT projects. I'm constantly left wondering how different it would feel if email and ICT, to help us work smarter, did not exist. Then there are those who are worshiped by the consumer electronics companies and energy providers. They have a laptop, a tablet, a work smart-phone, a personal smart-phone, and a couple of monitors. Now I'm no time-and-motion-studyand-motion-study expert but I reckon they will spend 30 minutes a day recharging and synching their devices. That is 2.5 hours a week making money for the energy companies. You can spot the addicts. They phone you, leave a voicemail, then send you an email detailing exactly what was said on the voicemail. If you are unfortunate, they CC in every man and his dog. The CCs generate more emails and voicemails to deal with. On the upside, at least they phoned you. I get these emails from people I have never met before or spoken to, demanding immediate action without a please or a thank you. They end up in the junk folder. During meetings these days it is not unusual to see people texting away. Nothing wrong with any of this for social purposes but on an IT project, these behaviours create latency and reduce clarity.

There are forces at work that are seducing us into using technology when in the cold light of day it is not conducive to do so. An American TV company parked themselves outside the Apple Store in New York looking to interview the first customer of the Apple iPad. They caught their prey clinging to his purchase as he made his way home. They asked him, 'What are you going to do with it?' He said, 'I don't know'. He had purchased a solution looking for a problem. It's not uncommon for anyone working as an IT Project Manager or in a role on an IT project, to have a passion for technology. Had my parents not bought me a ZX81 back in 1980, I probably would not be writing this book. Just look at the tech I have desired and owned since 1980.

ZX81, Sinclair Spectrum, Commodore 64, Acorn Electron, Commodore Amiga, Atari 800XL, Sega Master System,

Nintendo Entertainment System, Super Nintendo Entertainment System, Sega Megadrive, numerous PCs, numerous laptops, betamax, VHS, ghetto blaster, Walkman, mini hifi vinyly, CD mini hifi, numerous TVs of all shapes, several mobile phones, PDAs, analogue modem, satellite TV, freeview, Playstation 1, Playstation 2, Nintendo Gamecube, 3DO, Nintendo 64, Xbox, Xbox 360, Nintendo Wii, Sony PSP, Nintendo DS, Nintendo 3DS, Xbox One and numerous broadband connections.

Whatever compelled me to own it and spend my time with it more than humans, may still be embedded in my psyche. In terms of owning all those gizmos, I am not unique. Anyone below the age of 45, has experienced an era of unprecedented technical innovations. Since 1980, the average UK household has gone from having only four TV channels to 100s. Throw the internet into the mix and we are bombarded 24/7 365 with marketing and peer pressure to own the next wonder gizmo. I'm left wondering how this desire to interact more with technology than with human beings, influences my decision-making as an IT Project Manager. Are these influences, coupled with human insecurity and lack of time, feeding a compulsion to use email instead of picking up the phone to talk it through? Are these influences, the human condition, and a passion for technology, compelling us to delivery IT solutions looking for a problem? If a source of IT project failure is over-engineering, could these influences be feeding a motivation to over-engineer?

Poor communication is pervasive on challenged or impaired IT project delivery. Yet you will find things like email and sharepoint used in abundance. On some of the worst performing projects I have seen, they have excellent documentation and thoroughly detailed risk registers. The bad news is there in digital black ink. Retrospective reflection on challenged or impaired IT deliveries always has a 'rabbit from the hat rabbit in the headlights' moment. Someone will produce a 'I told you so' email. The recipient will react like it was the first time they ever saw the email. Use of technology in this manner is an indicator that participants in the project delivery are not confident about the project performing. The result is avoidance of accountability, latency on the critical path, avoidance of conflict, and lack of trust. These are all traits prevalent on challenged or impaired project delivery and rigidities that reduce clarity, unity and agility. I will give you several real life scenarios where overuse of technology reduces clarity, unity and agility. This happens every day on an IT project.

The Meeting

When was the last time you saw a laptop, tablet or mobile phone on the table at one of those government meetings filmed on TV? The TV stations only film the really important meetings. It's all about human interaction to sort really important stuff out. The meeting room layout and all the equipment, if any, is designed to encourage collaboration. Technology is present but it is not obvious or placed between anyone in those meetings. Now think about the meetings you attend to discuss the delivery of an IT project. Recognise this meeting? Laptops out and tablets stood up like a range of mini pyramids. The owners clinging to them like the character with the comfort blanket from Charlie Brown. The factions that make up the project team, sit together facing off to other factions, and in between, there's a display of technology you would find at a consumer electronics store. People drop in and out of the meeting to take calls. Even with all the technology, someone is asked to write up the minutes. In this scenario, banning phones, laptops and tablets from the meeting would encourage behaviours known to lead to greater clarity and unity. However, you've still got the day dreamers and doodlers to deal with.

The Don't Have to Deal With People Task Allocation Solution

In the late 1990's, Microsoft released a version of MS Project that emailed details of tasks to the resources against the activities. I remember seeing how overjoyed a couple of PMs were when they discovered the feature. I actually heard one of them say, 'This means I don't have to talk to anyone.' He was so happy with the new feature in MS Project. I think it was because, in that particular environment, it was effort intensive to get various departments to do anything. Needless to say, the first project where this feature was tried resulted in nothing getting done. These systems come with the promise of greater efficiency, which is normally the case when used sensibly. However, these systems perpetuate problems when they are intentionally used to avoid conflict or keep an audit trail because you are dealing with people who tend to say 'yes' that becomes a 'maybe'. In environments where resources are constrained, requirements are complex and time is short, the allocation of work should be preceded by dialogue with all those involved. Allocating complex work without a dialogue with the team that's got to do the work, raises the risk of rework.

The 2me 2u 2me 2u Letters Delivered by Postman Pat

My children love the Chuckle Brothers. There is many a funny scene when they repeat the same action. Their catchphrase is 2me 2u 2me 2u. Then there was Postman Pat, the most helpful postman in the history of postmen. So I'm sitting at a hot desk and I'm surrounded by three teams; network, servers and applications. An email comes in from the applications team raising an issue that something, at OS level on the server, is preventing them from completing the install. The email details what and how the snag needs to be fixed. So being the helpful chap that I am, I saunter off to talk to the server team. I talk it through with them, go back to my desk and send on the email. The server time have some clarifications around firewalls. So being the helpful chap that I am, I saunter off to talk to the network team. I talk it through with them, go back to me desk and send on the email. I think to myself, I will just route the emails to each team as they come in. The emails are getting more complicated, as a result of the chinese whispers at the beginning of the first set. Email tennis ensues. The average time between the email timestamps starts to increase exponentially. To be frank, the whole scenario belongs in a Monty Python film. The irrationality moves to another level when I'm asked to log the detail in an email from the applications team as a service request that will go to the applications team. It is a scenario full of time-stealing, non value add activity. Firstly, why did the team email me when I was literally sitting next to them? Secondly, why did I instantly go into Postman Pat mode? Lastly, (the icing on the cake) these guys had known each other for the last five years. Why could they not phone or walk across the room to get the matter sorted? With the benefit of hindsight, 75% of their job was high volume and low complexity repetitive IT work. Their systems were designed for this type of work. The work I wanted doing was far more complex and required a collaborative effort. However, the reasoning does not explain why they preferred emailing me to pass the email on, when they sat practically next to one another. What would they have done if there was no such thing as email? Nowadays, I don't succumb to the urge to play Postman Pat. The scenario shows how propensity to use email can cause latency. The process to complete the work was not communication enabled. Readily available technology,with the desire to use it to avoid dealing with people, actually disabled the communication. The end result is a reduction in clarity, unity and agility.

How to Increase Mistrust Using the Sharepoint Action Log

PMO - three letters that strike fear into the hearts of an IT Project Manager. The project management office is the seeker of truth and proponent of data driven decision making. Every portfolio of IT projects needs a PMO. They are an IT Project Manager's conscience. PMO people love Sharepoint and so does everyone else when it used appropriately. During my career, I had the honour of working on a project team with a track record of delivery, namely, because they had worked together for years. On this particular programme, the team met weekly for risk management purposes. Only this time around it was the first time the team was working with a much more formal PMO. The PMO insisted on recording all risk management actions on the Sharepoint action log. For those unfamiliar with the Sharepoint action log, you log an action, assign an owner and Sharepoint sends the owner an email with a hyperlink to the record. The owner then maintains the record. The team could not understand why their actions were being tracked when the Project Manager knew full well they had an excellent track record of doing what they say and saying what they mean. For compliance purposes, the Project Manager insisted on using Sharepoint in the manner prescribed by the PMO. The impact was the creation of a perception; that the PMO and Project Manager did not trust the team to do what they said they would do. A lack of trust is known to reduce the performance of the team on an IT Project.

Crackberry

At the end of the working day, I used to send a few non-urgent emails out keeping everyone informed. Normally I do this between 5-7pm. I can guarantee I will get a phone call, usually from someone with 'manager' in their title, to discuss something. Why? In the background, I can hear the sound of family dinners, sports halls or bars, all the good stuff associated with work-life balance.

Omnipresence

Why do people send you emails while you are on holiday? By the time you get back the information is out of date. If it is urgent, it won't get done because you are on holiday. Your 'out of office' message says you are on holiday. The most organised people list points of contact to substitute. Yet, even though they have seen the 'out of office', they continue to send you emails. Maybe they wanted to make sure you knew they were working while you were on holiday. Sending urgent emails to people who are not going to read it for a week or more, is pointless. It indicates that people working on the project have no problem doing something pointless, which means they are not doing something with a point i.e. doing stuff to make the project happen. Have a rule on the project. Do not send emails to people who are away for a week or more. The result will be to make the mythical man-day a little less mythical.

The Men in Black

What is the most professional voicemail greeting you could hear from an information security consultant? 'Please leave an encrypted message after the tone.'

Techno addiction is a productivity killer; just say no. Get disconnected! Have a 'no email day' on your IT project. Use above examples to spot the same behaviours on your IT project. Challenge the root cause behaviours. The technology is the catalyst. The result will be behaviours more conducive to beat the plan.

A VISIT TO THE WILLY WONKA SCHOOL OF CONTRACT & SUPPLIER MANAGEMENT

'Luck has left me standing so tall.'

Gold

Spandau Ballet

N THE HARSH ECONOMIC CLIMATE, unique, rare and specialist suppliers will attempt to do as little as possible for the most possible. They want zero risk and high return. Knowing about contract management and supplier stratification is your defence. Every character from Roald Dahl's Charlie and the Chocolate Factory, is a metaphor for poor supplier performance in the world of IT project delivery. Make sure you get Charlie Buckett. There is a scene in the film where Willy Wonka takes his visitors on a psychedelic tour from hell. That scene scared the wits out of me. I know some people who have watched the 1971 version of the film after taking something they should not have. They only did it once. When your IT project is going pear shaped because of poor supplier performance, the experience is akin to a bad trip on the Willy Wonka psychedelictram. If there was ever a scene in a film or book portraying the sheer joy of being the luckiest person in the world, it has to be when Charlie finds a golden ticket. Right now in the current economic climate, finding the right supplier in the world of IT is like finding a golden ticket. Getting the most from a supplier is really monotonous hard work when you pick the wrong one. It takes an army of Oompa Loompas to clean up the havoc they can cause. A couple of things have happened in recent years that has resulted in this situation. One of these things is the financial crash. There are too many suppliers and not enough money for everyone. The watering hole used to have enough water for the herd. In current economic times, organisations will do anything to avoid spending money and will encourage suppliers to go that extra mile before payment is made. So the suppliers out there are feeling ripped off. We have buyers on one hand who want more for less, and suppliers on the other hand trying to do less to get more. It is a pretty naff situation. I'd like to live in the world of the management consultant's 'symbiotic catalytic mutuality partnership' but poor supplier performance is a major theme running through impaired and challenged IT project performance. These projects suffered from adversarial supplier customer type relationships or lack of incentives for the supplier. Given the vast amounts of money involved as a buyer you need to protect the project budget from the unscrupulous supplier. Maybe the word 'unscrupulous' is too harsh but there is no doubt in my mind that I have seen many inadvertent poor behaviour from IT suppliers.

Charlie and his Grandad walk into a room full of bubbles. The sign clearly states 'do not drink from the bottles'. Charlie and his grandad think they have gotten away with it until Willy Wonka whips out the contract and points to the small print. Willy Wonka had it covered then Charlie, bless him, owns up to taking something he should have not taken. Willy Wonka proceeds to offer him the world. The best suppliers are like Charlie Buckett: humble, unassuming, hard working, they listen, only ever so slightly dishonest, more honest than wise, and always ulterior. To beat the plan, you need a supplier who will behave in this manner.

So what was in those reams and reams of contract speak that Willy Wonka so painstakingly put together? Contract and supplier management is a world in its own right. So I have attempted to surmise some basics. My first starting point is to understand the term 'supplier relationship management' (SRM). SRM acquires, then retains, partnerships that add value and to cut lose the suppliers that don't. The same principle applies on an IT project. IT projects fail in environments not structurally conducive for their delivery. If an organisation lacks maturity in terms of SRM, then an IT programme with a high dependence on multiple suppliers will have a high propensity for failure. It is an Augustus Gloop situation. Some suppliers get into a position where they manage the organisation to drain money. The chocolate lake is the accumulation of all those IT project budgets. You gave them a taste but you let them take more than they were entitled to. It can get to the point where they don't even ask before taking a drink!

The next big word is 'stratification'. Stratification is a process that seeks to categorise the criticality of the supplier to the project. Essentially, there are two key questions you need to ask: How easy would it be to substitute the supplier? nd what would be the switching cost? This process will help you identify the rude, pushy ones who constantly make demands because they reckon they are unique and irreplaceable. As far as they are concerned, you need them more than they need you. You know the one, the Veruca Salt type character? In a multi-source environment it is easy to become the accidental vendor manager. When you've got to evaluate or manage lots of critical suppliers, you should really consider getting an experienced commercial and vendor manager on your side. A good vendor manager is like one of those squirrels that Veruca encountered. As far as they are concerned, there are quality nuts, poor nuts and no nut is irreplaceable. Man, those squirrels gave me nightmares for years. The point was those squirrels were experts in nuts. Willy Wonka was not an expert in nuts. He did not check all the nuts. He employed experts in nuts to check the nuts. Those squirrels were devoid of idiot compassion.

In a contract, there are a couple of innocuous clauses known as condition precedent and condition subsequent. These are the conditions that you, as the customer, have to put in place before (precedent) the supplier can deliver and sustain (subsequent) service you have asked for. Extensive use of these terms is a really good way of reducing contract frustration i.e. conditions that prevent one party from fulfilling their obligations. Mike Teavee is the character that constantly criticises Willy Wonka's business as they tour around the factory. Mike Teavee moans about everything. Whatever Mike Teavee wanted in place, Willy did not put in place. Throughout the whole tour, Mike Teavee is a constant sourpuss about everything. His whinging starts to put a damper on everyone else's day. Willy Wonka might have experienced less whining had he explained to Mike Teavee up front, what to expect from the tour, whilst taking some time to understand Mike Teavee's expectations of the tour. Had such dialogue taken place, maybe Willy Wonka would not have let him in the factory. Finally, Mike Teavee gets to try out one of Willy's invention he truly appreciates. Unfortunately, Mike Teavee gets miniaturised. His mum blames Willy Wonka for her son's predicament. Condition subsequent and precedent clauses are an opportunity for the supplier to offer clarity on what they need from you to do the job you want them to do. If a supplier does not proactively communicate what they need from you in a contract, then you will have a whole series of episodes from Mike Teavee to deal with.

Effective supplier relationship management requires you to articulate what you don't want from a supplier, for example, trialling with new alpha state technology using a business critical IT project as a laboratory. Say hello to Violet Beauregarde. For those unfamiliar with the story, Willy Wonka invents a stick of gum that tastes like a three course meal. The gum is still in a state of invention but despite professional advice not to try it, Violet is determined to give it a go. Violet turns into giant blueberry. It is Willy Wonka's organisation that has to invest its own resources getting the de-juicing Violet. I can recall many an Oompa Lumpa moment over the last 10 years when a supplier has gotten themselves into a technical pickle. The root cause is a lack of clarity around the technical and organisational constraints that the supplier will need to work with. It is easy to fix; just get your lead designer to play back the design and technical constraints. I have outlined below the top four I tend to encounter during implementation because the supplier lacked understanding of the technical constraints.

Breaches information security management system guidelines

Incompatibility with virtualised servers

Incompatibility with the desktop image

Network capacity and capability

Contravenes service orientated architecture principles or data management guidelines

In the 1971 version of the film, some of the parents threatened to sue Willy Wonka for the predicaments their offspring got themselves into. But Willy Wonka was a wily old fox. He had them all signed up to a 'cover every angle' contract before they entered his factory. He made it absolutely clear to everyone. Suppliers nowadays don't carry over-capacity. Everyone has gone lean. They use over-burdening to keep utilisation on chargeable work high; great for the supplier but not so great for their customers. Over-burdening results in fractional assignment i.e. when a key third party resource for your project is spread across too many projects. The impact is a deterioration in productivity and output. To avoid this problem, insist on conditions in the contract so that there is disincentive for a supplier to spread their resources too thinly. Ask for named individuals in the contract with a track record in whatever they are delivering. Remember when you were a kid playing a game on the park. Two captains would pick teams; the not so talented ones are the last ones to be picked. This is just like your suppliers applying stratification. Suppliers group customers into gold, silver and bronze, based on profitability and up-sell potential. Then they allocate their best staff accordingly. So when you offer a supplier a wafer thin margin, unless the customer is strategically important, a supplier is more inclined to allocate less able staff. I have never met a supplier that told its customer they are not strategic. Use of materially high delay payments are a good way of incentivising suppliers to provide competent staff. The salesperson, whose bonus depends on delivering against plan, will make it their life's work to get quality people on the delivery.

There is one contract Willy Wonka got right - the one he had with his team of Oompa Loompas. The Oompa Loompas knew exactly what was expected of them. They were satisfied with the incentives. Willy Wonka played them to their strengths. He must have evaluated the Ooopma Loompas against a model called the 10c's (Carter, R. (1995) 'The Seven Cs of Effective Supplier Evaluation,' Purchasing and Supply Management, April 1995, 44-45, note 3; more were added later on). The 10c model is an excellent and easy-to-use tool to evaluate IT suppliers.

Competency

Capacity

Commitment

Control

Cash

Cost

Consistency

Culture

Clean

Communication

Exemplar supplier performance helps you become an emphatic exemplar performer.

Gene Wilder

"When I make my first entrance, I'd like to come out of the door carrying a cane and then walk toward the crowd with a limp. After the crowd sees Willy Wonka is a cripple, they all whisper to themselves and then become deathly quiet. As I walk toward them, my cane sinks into one of the cobblestones I'm walking on and stands straight up, by itself... but I keep on walking, until I realize that I no longer have my cane. I start to fall forward, and just before I hit the ground, I do a beautiful forward somersault and bounce back up, to great applause."

DON'T DO SHADES OF FADE TO GREY CRM IMPLEMENTATION CLICHÉ

'This Means Mothing To Me'

Vienna

Ultravox

THE STORY STARTS WITH A trip to local garden centre. The wife has made me go. It's a kind of practical date. Have a romantic coffee moment together, then buy some compost. Mr Grey would not be that practical. As I'm waiting for my darling wife, I have a look through the books on sale: 500 Interesting Facts About Trains; How to be Great at Being Grumpy; and Learn to Play a Guitar in 5 Minutes pulp etc. I happen to pick up a book 'Clichés: Avoid Them Like The Plague' by Nigel Fountain. It is a great book by the way. Having read the book I have concluded I hear what's in it on a daily basis, particularly on customer service transformation programmes, which involve implementing CRM applications with lots of integration. Every cliché in that book reminds me of life, delivering ICT on those customer service improvement programmes.

The author, Nigel Fountain, has kindly given me permission to use his book as a reference point for this chapter. Nigel Fountain is a writer, broadcaster and journalist who has written for many publications, including The Guardian, The Observer, The Sunday Times, The New Statesman, The Oldie, the London Evening Standard, the New York Soho Weekly News, History Today, New Society, Oz magazine and Time Out. In this chapter I will take every single cliché known to man. I will then proceed to explain its true meaning in the context of a CRM application project delivery. Nigel Fountain's book has a powerful message. Avoid acting out the clichés. My message is: avoid using them to justify how and why the IT project is being delivered. Enacting them indicates the presence of irrationality.

The chapter is not about a prescriptive methodology showing how to implement a CRM application. If you visit the Microsoft Download Centre, they have lots of information and tools for implementing any CRM application. http://www.microsoft.com/en-us/download/details.aspx?id=8162. The chapter is about imparting some lessons learned from several CRM programmes I have worked on. Those programmes struggled because they enacted some of Mr Fountain's clichés. While I was writing this chapter, a 1980s icon, Steve Strange, sadly passed away. For those who don't know Steve Strange, he is credited with starting the post punk new romantic movement in the early 80s. His club, the Blitz Club, caught the mood of the moment. He knew what his customers wanted before they knew it. Now that is what I call CRM. Successful IT project management in some ways is the same. Understanding the true customer requirement and then delivering it. CRM projects can fail because the IT team failed to understand the customer requirements. The information driving those requirements comes from customer insight and customer experience management. If not, the requirements will come from those interpreting or assuming what the customer wants, desires or needs. So the customer is not the person buying the IT solution. The customers are the people using whatever goods or services are being offered by the organisation implementing CRM. It is a subtle difference that needs to be fully understood by the project.

It's six hours before a go-live of a CRM system on a hot August day. When anyone logs onto it, the screen goes pure white. The urge to quit and just get on a train is overwhelming. But I won't because even though last minute white screen moments are entirely preventable, they are an occupational hazard. I expect them, given the complexity and ropey old IT infrastructure that organisations use to run their applications on. I need to chill my beans in the hope that my sense of injustice for being dropped in it through no fault of my own, will dissipate. This will allow me to focus on doing whatever to stop the screen going white. Time for a coffee and a listen to whatever is on the ipod. As I walk towards Costa, the sky is all shades of grey - not the sexy kind either. The words from the first song play out - "One man on a lonely platform." My mind drifts back to 1982 when I first heard Visage's 'Fade to Grey'. It starts to chuck it down with rain as Steve Strange sings, 'Feel the rain like an English summer.' Then the sexy French lady on the track does her thing. There was nothing cliché about Visage. The same cannot be said for my CRM project. The techies fixed the white screen bug before the 11th hour. Was pursuing the requirements that led to the white screen moment worth it? Absolutely not. Lots of wasted effort and money for little benefit. Just collecting data without the business having the organisation and means in place to act on the insight from it. It was only 4 years later from that point when I started to view those seat-of-the-pants moments with hilarity; I had a serendipity kismet moment. IT projects are full of people using big complicated technical words - for a couple of reasons: to make the technology sound interesting, complicated, powerful and exotic; and to convince the outside world one is an expert and one knows what one is doing. It's not the technical verbiage on IT projects which is the problem; it is the prevalence of the cliché. The run up to those white screen moments start with a conversation about whether or not it is worth doing the doings that led to the 'snatching victory from the jaws of defeat' moment. If a bad idea gets the nod, then the prevalent use of the cliché will ensue to justify making the bad idea happen. A cliché is a phrase or opinion that is overused and betrays a lack of original thought. The use of a cliché on an IT project is an early warning indicator that the project is trying to convince itself a bad idea is a good idea.

All the bells and whistles

Nobody writes their own CRM application anymore. There is no need to. Most organisations will purchase off-the-shelf software or use a CRM Software as a Service (SaaS) solution. Bells and whistles are features to meet nice-to-have requirements. That's OK as long as there is clarity on the must-haves and should-haves. Secondly, deliver the must-haves first, before spending time on the other types of haves. Avoid any bespoke development of the packaged software. It's a risky and a costly business. CRM projects contain an iterative configuration process involving the activities below. Invasive development often risks storing up technical debt that gets discovered in the configuration process.

Application User Interface Creation, Application Data Administration, Source Data Conversion, Recurring Interfaces, Workflow Rules Creation, Integration, Integration Customization

Bells and whistles is a term you don't need to hear on a CRM project. It indicates the requirements have not been properly thought through. Extensive bespoke development of the vendor solution indicates the wrong product has been selected. Changing business processes to avoid bespoke and invasive software development, is by far a more pragmatic choice. Don't bespoke unless the enhancement can be directly linked to achieving one particular measureable business benefit - namely, acquiring or retaining profitable customers.

All Things Being Equal

'All things being equal' is a phrase whereby its true meaning contains 'if nothing happens to complicate things'. When someone says 'all things being equal', you need to ask yourself: what are those things? 'Things' are assumptions. The one thing that cannot be equal on a CRM implementation without testing the waters, is assuming the project is customer-management driven. A frequent cause of CRM project failure is when the organisation approaches the CRM project as a software project. This is what happens. The IT team installs the hardware and application software and then wonder why the benefits fail to materialise. The ICT tranche of a customer service transformation or improvement programme needs to start with an envisioning phase. But it should not start until the organisation's capability and capacity to deliver the business-change management scope, is in place. Without it, the IT team will be conducting the following in the dark and will have to make too many validated assumptions. The result is a technology-driven project, without the means to transform customer-management processes disconnected from the business and its strategy. Don't let this happen.

Initial Project Discovery; Identify Technical requirements and Architecture; Identify Functional Requirements; Identify Acceptance Criteria; Integrate and Approve Requirements

Baby Boomer Generation

This cliché gained popularity in the 1970s. It is a term that describes a specific demographic of customers. When the term 'baby boomer generation' caught on, customer segmentation emerged as a critical strategic marketing tool. My 14 year old son thinks I'm from the baby boomer generation. He blames my generation for the woes his generation now face. When I was the same age, I said the same thing of my parents. I think they call this inter-generational blame game equity. What this little ditty shows is our inherent human ability to stereotype groups of people. Since the dawn of digitisation, there have been many more clichés to describe customer segments. Generation x, generation y, achievers, socialisers, digital divide, no shows, newcomers, onlookers, grey surfers, cliquers, sparks, mix n minglers etc. No day goes by without some think-tank putting us in a segment. I am wary of the over use of terminology to describe customer segments on a CRM project. Customer segmentation provides the insight, known as customer insight, that drives requirements for integration customisation. In today's world, this means integration into digital channels; web, mobile, email etc. If there is one thing that excites purveyors of CRM technology, it is creating digital channels. Now that's OK if that's what customers want and it can be proven that is what customers want. A combination of a lack of data-driven customer segmentation and a eam, passionate about CRM technology describing those segments, is a recipe for over-engineering. They could inadvertently tell some white lies to describe the segment in a manner to justify the investment in building something interesting, like digital channels. Nothing kills a company more than investing in anything to meet the needs of a market that does not exist. The diagram below shows the phases in a CRM project. Use of inaccurate data from the customer segmentation exercise, risks building a CRM solution that will fail.

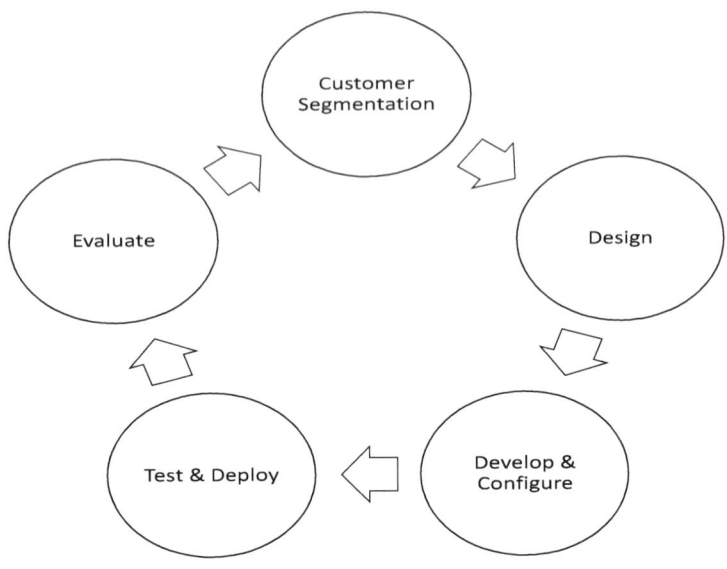

Back to the Drawing Board

The words 'back to the drawing board' are OK if a few people are 25% of the way through a design stage. It is healthy to fail fast before the project spends a fortune on hardware and software. Getting to the parsons nose-end of the project only to discover we have to go back to the drawing board, results in white screen moments. Discipline yourself to ask this question of everyone in the team a couple of times a week: Does anyone think we need to go back to the drawing board and why? Learn how to spot body language indicating they don't believe what they are saying.

Bad Hair Day

A 'bad hair day' is a day when everything seems to go wrong. If your CRM project team is a team of 20 and a couple of them moan about having a bad hair day once a week for 3 months, then the other 18 in your team are having good days. It's when most of the team talk about bad hair days every other day that the alarm bells should starting ringing. Bad hair days can be avoided by asking the following questions before the project starts. The team needs to imagine the project has been delivered. The answers the team come back with will indicate whether or not the project will be one bad hair day.

Was this project co-ordinated by the end-user organization? If so, was it their first time?

What were the root causes of significant failures outside of the CRM system i.e. applications, infrastructure or were they in external databases or data feeds?

Did we encounter any significant internal forces trying to put up barriers to the success of our project?

Was our CRM implementation political, and were there any users who don't want a project to succeed?

Better Late Than Never

'Better late than never' is a cliché one will hear on many an IT project. The phrase appeared in the English language around the 14th century - probably about the time Pillars-of-the Earth-type construction projects for the church became all the rage. If Ye Olde Standish Brotherhood were around, they'd be reporting about the performance of construction projects. 'Better late than never' actually comes from first century BC Greece. A Greek historian Dionysius of Halicarnassus wrote, 'It is better to start doing what one has to do late than not at all.' This is probably the first recorded excuse for a late project in the whole of human history. The one set of activities you don't need to be 'better late than never' is master data management(MDM). MDM is an ongoing initiative in its own right. It is not a one -off set of activities. Master data management (MDM) is an instrumental success factor in building successful customer relationship management (CRM) processes. Gartner have said, "CRM leaders who avoid MDM will derive erroneous results that annoy customers, resulting in a 25 percent reduction in potential revenue gains."

"Over the last several years, CRM software sales have outstripped overall IT spending," said Bill O'Kane, research director at Gartner. "CRM leaders must understand the benefits of the MDM discipline to CRM and make it part of their CRM strategy. MDM is critical to enabling CRM leaders to create the 360-degree view of the customer required for an optimized customer experience." Bounding the scope of an MDM exercise that can evolve from a project basis into a BAU activity, is difficult. There is so much to know about known customers and potential ones. Here would be my starters:

Accounts, Activities, Competitors, Contacts, Addresses, Cases, Discounts, Invoices, Leads, Opportunities, Price lists, Products, Quotes, Sales orders, Subjects, Substitute products, Units, Unit groups, customer sentiments, customer behaviours, places they visit, organisations they belong to.

The second most important thing about an MDM exercise that cannot be 'better late than never', is a transition state. MDM is not a one-off exercise. See the project scope as establishing the tools, capability and establishment of a business improvement function within Customer Services. In the plan, implement a gate to handover into BAU. If the project or programme does not do this, the project cannot be closed because MDM is an activity that has to happen iteratively all the time across the whole life-cycle of the CRM solution.

This is not core business for an IT project delivery team. This is the performance improvement with data management business programme, whose home should be in marketing and customer service. Outlined below is a framework describing MDM delivery. Delivering MDM lends itself to agile because of the uncertainty, complexity and the need to continually demonstrate value. One way of bounding the scope and then handing over to BAU would be to deliver a couple of iterations on a project basis. Then during one of the last iterations, transition into BAU, which is based on a clearly defined set of exit criteria, describes in measureable terms the establishment of the MDM capability. Exit following an evaluate and control stage, is considered pragmatic. MDM is one of those solutions that encourages 'happy ears'. There is so much an organisation can do with MDM, and trying to do everything possible MDM -wise on an IT project basis, is risky.

Iterative Stages and Things To Do in a Master Data Management Delivery

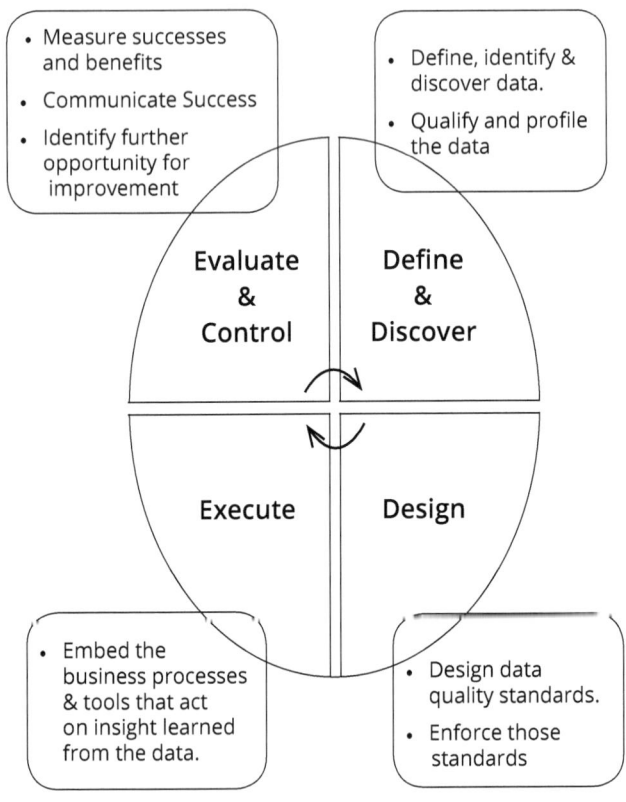

Blamestorming

The term 'blamestorming' first appeared in Wired Magazine in 1997. Basically, it means meetings where everyone talks about why dead-lines were missed, a project failed or who is responsible. Blamestorming during a CRM delivery is not pragmatic as it diverts attention away from fixing the problems. Ban blamestorming! Discussing CRM project failure is quite popular. Doing a google search on 'CRM Project Failure' yields about 669,000 results in 0.31 seconds. Blamestorming on a CRM project becomes the norm when a number of challenges are not overcome. Overcome these challenges below and the likelihood of blamestorming goes away:

Populating and correctly maintaining accurate data

Achieving end user acceptance

Putting in place adequate funding

Ensuring and keeping executive sponsorship

Looking after remote users and project workers

Matching the technology to the process problem

Getting the end users productive rapidly

Customising only when it makes sense to do so i.e. the business case stacks up

Failure is Not An Option

Back to the google search on 'CRM Project Failure'. Failure *is* an option, particularly, when implementing a brand new cutting edge CRM bag of technical tricks in today's organisation. Fail fast early and your project won't be in those google search results.

Catalyst for Positive Change

Many a challenged IT project starts off being referred to as a catalyst for positive change. The IT portfolio within the scope of a customer service transformation, is chemically inactive without the business change management to trigger the synergistic paradigm shift inculcation into the corporate DNA. I learnt these words listening to management consultants. Roughly translated it means:

'If you don't constantly transform your: business processes; organisation; and culture; the investment for implementing a new CRM system will be a complete waste of money.'

So what is it that will make our chemically inert portfolio of hardware and application delivery become part of the catalyst? Implementing a CRM application without Business Process Management (BPM) is like buying a Ferrari, driven by an ugly person who cannot drive, trying to impress the ladies at the Blitz Club back in 1982. According to Wikipedia, Business Process Management (BPM) is a field in operations management that focuses on improving corporate performance, by managing and optimising a company's business processes. It can, therefore, be described as a process-optimization process, which includes reorganisation. BPM sits in the same world as MDM, preferably in the same operational team. Wherever it sits, the success of your CRM application and infrastructure delivery is dependent on it. Here are 6 questions that need a 'yes' before implementing a CRM application.

Do your sales, fulfilment, and service managers have a complete understanding of what CRM can do, and what it can't do, out-of-the-box?

Have they visited an organization using the same CRM solution or used a proof-of-concept CRM system?

Do your business processes match the processes used in the CRM?

Do you have a process in place to resolve issues when deciding if your business practices have to change to conform to the CRM solution?

Do you already have a well-defined policy of who in your organization can view and modify master data management?

Do you have a team who can train your sales,
fulfilment, and support staff?

The questioning proves that the organisation has some BPM capability to sustain the rollout of a CRM application. Outlined below is a diagram that shows the stages within a business-driven and customer-insight-driven CRM project. It is a combination of the customer experience management (CEM) activities, providing insight into customer management business process management (BPM), which shapes the technology scope.

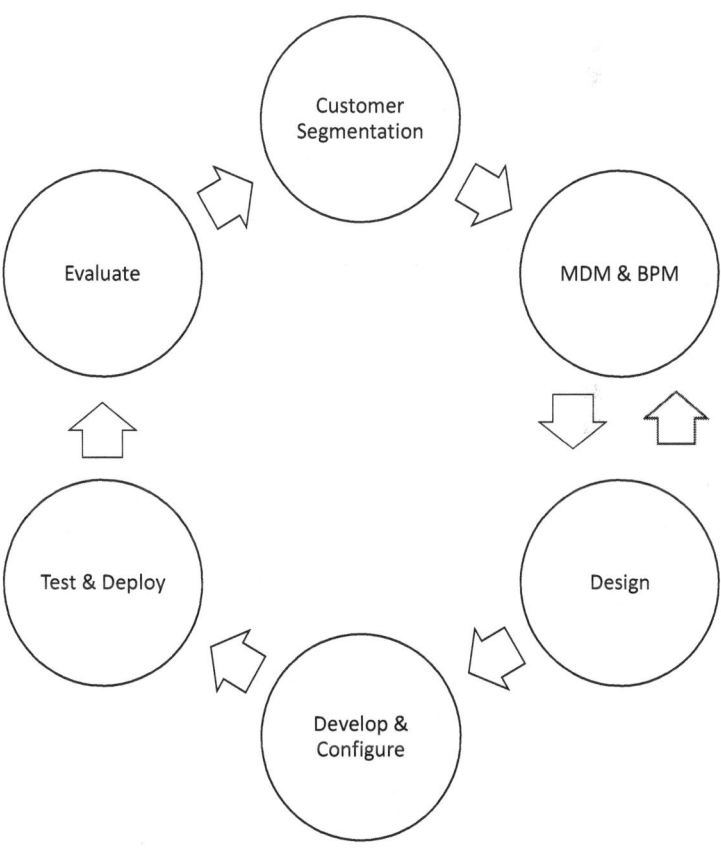

The Elephant in The Room

"A colourful expression used to mean any obvious problem or controversial issue that is ignored or avoided, usually because to discuss it would be uncomfortable." CRM is a sales and marketing capability. Historically, organisations invested on marketing and not on the customer. The goal was to market across all channels - the consumer had little choice but to notice the organisations direct marketing. The consumer became aware and the awareness created demand. Demand converted into sales. It was a pretty linear process and, from a Conway Law perspective, relatively straightforward to derive an implementation for CRM ICT. But something has happened to blow that paradigm out of the water. Consumers nowadays could not care less about all this advertising, so why continue to design and build technical solutions that achieve this aim? Generation Y live their lives ignoring the direct marketing and the phone calls. They've got a smart device with access to connections, conversations and information, to look for what they want, when they want it. Generation Y uses multiple touch points and want to be 'omni present' every time they visit them. Nowadays, CRM technology is about creating the technical means for listening to the customer's digital body language, so the organisation can find ways to become relevant in the customer's everyday life. Once the organisation has Hadooped the data several times over, with sentiment-analysis overload, they will come to a conclusion - all customers want is convenience, efficiency and quality services at a price they consider fair. Don't deliver any CRM technology project that will tell an organisation what it already knows and what its customers knew before the organisation knew. It is a wasted effort.

"It was about showing your creative side, and about showing that you'd taken time and effort in what you had created."

Steve Strange RIP

AN APPETITE FOR DISTRACTION, THE GUNS N ROSES MAN DAY

'Fritter and waste the hours in an off-hand way.'

Time

Pink Floyd

PARTY ON, EXCELLENT AND SCHWING. It's the late eighties with hair rock spandex overload dominating the charts whilst Kevin Bacon prances about with Sean Pen's brother. Ten years later I'm getting a reality check. My first role as an IT Project Manager is a disaster. Someone wiser than me, questions my first project. Work I thought had been done has not been done. Work that needs to be done is news to me. I've fallen foul of the mythical part of the mythical man-day. Rewind 10 years and I am in aural heaven as I listen to the Guns N Roses 1987 album, Appetite for Destruction. Those guys made six albums. They have sold over 100 million records. In September 1988, GnR play a gig at the Texas Jam in Irving Texas. The headline act is INXS. Before GnR play Welcome to the Jungle, the lead singer Axl Rose says, 'Apologises if I sound like shit but too many planes and too much cocaine, but you know where the f**k you are?' I am left thinking how the hell did that band come up with great rock 'n' roll music with all those career limiting temptations around them; drugs, beautiful women, alcohol, cars, food, band politics and all the fun things you can do because you can. Maybe the truth is that some of the work GnR had to do was boring and some of the work was interesting. The mythical parts of the mythical man-day are the non-productive things we gravitate to because we are not in the right frame of mind to tackle the mundane work we have to do, or they are forced on us by shouty folk whose motivation is not the success of the project..

It's March 2014 and I've been handed a 'I'm a professional get me outta here' agile development project. Now for some strange reason the project team reminds me of GnR. Once the interesting distractions are out of the way, the team is actually very productive and creative. So my game plan is to remove all those interesting distractions from the workplace. Unfortunately, I can't because it would mean a few sessions in HR related discussions and a breach of their human rights. I think back to that first project when I got a kicking for cocking up my first project. The behaviours on the team that led to that moment of kismet are prevalent on my latest engagement. I'm left with a feeling in my gut that organisations expect people to stop behaving like human beings after they swipe in. However, it is some of those behaviours that make up the mythical part of the mythical man-day, and your project's budget is funding people to do it. This chapter is not an opus on how to stop human beings from being human beings. The most positive person I know on this planet once told me you you'd be much happier focusing on changing your own behaviour than others. His message was that you can't control people and circumstances. You can imagine the discussion about theory Y vs theory X with that guy. Firstly, the chapter is about taking each track from the GnR seminal album, Appetite for Destruction, and using the track as a metaphor to demonstrate ways of conducting the delivery you need to temper in yourself and, if you can, in others around you. The time spent indulging in these behaviours could well be feeding the wasted time when you ask yourself the question, 'What has everyone been doing?' Secondly, the piece is about paying homage to the most productive time wasters in rock 'n' roll, Guns and Roses.

Welcome to the Jungle

We've got fun and games... In the south of England somewhere near London there is an IT transformation programme. The first I heard of it was back in 2004. It is still going on today. Back in 2004, I was asked if I wanted to go and work there. Being keen because I was new to the organisation, I was positive about the idea. When I mentioned this to a number of people who had been around the block I got the 'You don't want to go there wink wink nod nod'. It transpired that I never did get to work on that particular engagement. Over the years, I encountered people who did work there. All they did was moan about how bad it was. Ten years on and I'm working with a guy who worked on that engagement. He doesn't work there anymore but still moans about it. I'm left wondering how much time was wasted if I added up all the time over those 10 years, that those working on that engagement complained about how bad things were. Now don't get me wrong; everyone should be encouraged to raise concerns and everyone involved has a responsibility to redress. But what if things are the way they are and cannot be changed? There is no point continually moaning about it. Constant moaning about something that cannot be changed is a waste of time, particularly if the moan occurs between doing boring mundane but important project work. Going into that piece of work, off the back of a moaning session will more than likely result in a less than productive outcome. A climate of negativity has four guaranteed outcomes. The first outcome is that your project won't attract or retain talented people. Talented people have choice about where they work and they will do their homework before making decisions about where they ply their talent. If they hear a constant stream of negativity about the project, they will work elsewhere. The second outcome is that productivity will be low. The third outcome is that the only people you will have access to, to complete the work will be those who are available. These are the mediocre performers with nowhere to go but where they are is more than comfortable. The fourth outcome is that you will have to either de-scope or spend extra money to deliver the project. Welcome to the consequences of tolerating the 'negativity addict'. Negativity addicts are people who constantly communicate how bad things are, yet stay on the project and do nothing about it. They have this equation in their heads : Happiness = Reality – Expectation. Their score is always less than zero. From their point of view, management is responsible for both their happiness and everything that's wrong in their working day. How do you spot one? The first method is to take them out for a drink and introduce them to someone who may be joining the team. If their first words about the project are negative i.e. 'Welcome to the jungle we've got fun and games' type of conversation, then you've got yourself a negativity addict. Now you've got 4 choices for dealing with negativity addicts. Option: understand the history and fix their problems. Option 2: change the way they are rewarded and recognised. Option 3: get rid of them. Option 4: change the way they think. Whatever option you chose, do not chose to tolerate them and play to your strengths. Just bear the following in mind; all the great management trouble shooters, Gerry Robinson, Sir John Harvey Jones, Gordon Ramsey et al in their field go into troubled businesses, understand the history, and on nearly every occasion they change the team. You are unlikely to have significant influence over the way an organisation goes about reward and recognition. Changing the way people think takes up a lot of time. That's less time running the project. It is within your gift to tackle blockers that feed negativity. On an IT project, these blockers are poor tooling and weak clarity as a result of silo mentality. It is within your gift to ensure clarity over requirements so designers can solution effectively. It is within your gift to ensure clarity over the design and that the tools are in place so builders can build effectively. It is within your gift to put the team in situations where positive conflict can bear fruit. It is within your gift to get someone very important to come and talk to the team about why what they are delivering, is important.

It's So Easy

When everyone's trying to please me... Back to 1998, when I'm getting the hairdryer treatment for some schoolboy errors. The source of my woes was not actually listening and reading the situation correctly. The project needed a guru level SQL developer. I'd ask him how it is going he'd say that everything is going well. I'd walk away thinking this is so easy. The reality was I'd only known this guy for 5 minutes and knew nothing about Microsoft SQL server development. I heard what I wanted to hear. It turned out this guy's confidence was higher than his ability. Having people around you who tell you what you want to hear, is awesome. The working day is a joyous occasion. GnR were surrounded by people who gave them everything they asked for as they imploded. There is a difference between people who keep people happy, and critical friends who offer you tough love. Always fill those important technical positions on your IT project with people you know you can trust, and people who will tell you the truth. Fast forward seven years and I'm working on a migration of a revenues and benefits systems for a major local authority in the Midlands. I worked out that there were 15-20 complicated interfaces into the new system. On the supplier's plan was a duration of 5 working days to couple and test all these interfaces. I kind of felt the need to check this out. My questioning started along the lines of, 'This looks very easy; are you sure about this?' Of course the answer came back along the lines of, 'It's easy for this reason and that reason and we've done it a million times before.' I left the call unconvinced because on every IT project I had worked on, no interface had ever worked first time. Second phone call later, I changed the question. 'What do you need in place so that when you come to couple all the interfaces, it only takes you 5 working days?' That's when a whole raft of assumptions, in the shape of external dependencies about what would be put in place, came out. My third question was, 'What is the probability of all those prerequisites being in place?' The answer I got back was, 'I don't know'. There was an implicit assumption about all the precedents being put in place. I would say that the most gifted technical folk do have a bit of a prima donna about them. They know managers need them more than they need managers. They seem themselves as artists and rock stars and so they should given their unique gifts that everyone wants access to. They remind me of Shirley Bassey and Mariah Carey rushing onto stage when everyone else is moving the wires out the way so they don't trip over. It means they kind of expect everything to be in place so they can perform. What they do looks easy on paper because they assume perfect conditions before they do their work, while they are their doing the work, and after their work has been done. The starting position from a managerial point of view is it's not easy until there is clarity around the 'how' and clarity around the 'what'. This means no assumptions and deep diving prerequisite conditions for success i.e. condition precedents that have to be in place for any kind of technical person to thrive at what they do. The unsaid un-validated assumptions made by those on the critical path are the bottlenecks you cannot see, that will extend the project's critical path at the most inconvenient time.

Night Train

Loaded like a freight train. Feeling like a space brain... Yes it is a song about the misuse of alcohol. If there is one crutch I'd like to ban on any IT project, it would be alcohol. Tumbleweeds blowing across the office on a Thursday or Friday morning; a scene from the series Walking Dead. But instead of energetic creatures of driven fury, perfectly still zombies are staring into monitors. Phones are full of interesting texts and voicemails recorded or sent in the midnight hour. When I look back on those moments, it is not with nostalgia - it is with despair. Teams working constantly for weeks on end at an unsustainable pace, inter dispersed with nights out to let off a bit of steam, which normally involved drinking a vast amount of alcohol in a short space of time; intelligent and clever people binge drinking to relax. I was once told a story. It is a story that won't win me many friends with UKIP. Once upon a time there was a team full of guys in their mid to late 20s. Their code was poor. No one hardly ever hit their estimates. The incoming development manager swapped them all with developers from India. Productivity and quality went through the roof. It is a different mindset over there, when it comes to thinking about your well-being. So it should come as no surprise that countries in the far east have a lower rate of poor project performance. Maybe it is because those guys have not been brought up in a peer pressure drinking culture. High performance teams are made of people who understand the importance of both physical and mental well-being. They have hobbies and other things going on their lives to help them relax. They don't need to have a drink to chill out. Complex technical work requires people who can think clearly all of the time. It is a medical fact that a couple of units of alcohol changes your perception filter, not to mention your energy levels, the morning after. The Ultimate IT Project Team does not drink during a delivery and does yoga every morning.

Out Ta Get Me

They won't catch me. I'm f**king innocent, man. Sometimes it is easy to forget where you are going…Welcome to the Henry Ford school of resource allocation and time recording systems. If there is one culture I'd get rid of in any IT project, it would be the following: 'Thou shalt command and control culture around timesheet and resource management systems. Thou shalt not book unproductive time on your timesheet. Thou shalt not book travel time. Thou shalt not book time not budgeted for. Thou shalt not book the time spent at meetings. Thou shalt equate utilisation with the delivery of value. Thou shalt be bombarded with pointless reminders to input your timesheet daily should thee contravene the commandants'. I would say 15% of my managerial life has been spent dealing with the negative politics and consequences of equating utilisation with value, where the primary measurement tool is the timesheet/resource management system. The source of my contempt is the way these systems are used in matrix managed organisations. Matrix managed organisations in the IT project delivery game are essentially resource pools of distinct functional teams: testers, developers, network engineers, architects of all variations, project management, and data centre folk. These teams tend to be measured against two things: performance against the housekeeping rules; and utilisation. So as long as everyone in the silo is booking chargeable time, the 'chain gang chiefs' are happy. In my experience, these functional silos all have a bespoke resource management system. What ensues is an unproductive focus on making an inefficient system work, and their people becoming paranoid about being caught out not following the system. Secondary consideration is given to matching the right person to the job that is going to float their boat. High volume and low technical complexity IT project work tends to involve: build a bit; test to ensure the build of whatever, fits in with everything else; and then optimise it.

Successful IT projects maintain continuity of resource across multiple iterations of build a bit, test a bit and then optimise. They have a core team of network, testing, design, development and infrastructure personnel across the iterations of high volume and low/high complexity work. The problems occur when the project cannot secure the technician that did the work on the last iteration of work. It reduces the effectiveness of the critical chain. There is no incentive for the 'chiefs' to maintain continuity of resource. That's not how their success is measured. Their focus is chargeable time. Matrix managed organisations have responded to the economic freakonomics by turning their professional services functions into employed consultant model recruitment agencies. In the mind of the utilisation mad resource manager, IT projects are assembly lines made up of simple tasks done by resources in a predictable time box. In my world, IT project work is knowledge work conducted in a climate of technical uncertainty where the goal is to get people who enjoy what they do, to move at a sustainable pace. It's a clash of cultures. The time stealing negotiations and escalations ensue. Endless meetings of explaining to resource managers why the way the work, that needs to be done, is not akin to the way they work, is done in a Mcdonald's. There is only one sure fire away to avoid this distraction - The Genba Principle. Genba is a Japanese word which means to go and work where the value is. A technical person delivering remotely on the critical path, locked away in a functional silo with their resource manager acting as a gate keep, is not 'genba'. Business analysts need to work with end users on the coal face. Designers need to work with builders, together imparting knowledge and insight about the design. Testers need to work with developers. It's all about close proximity to where the value adding work has to be done. Challenged IT projects delivered by matrix managed organisations have a common theme; getting hold of the specialists at the point you need them, and a lack of collaboration between the specialists when you've got them. They have to be freed from their lair of despair. Identify the person you need, make sure the work fits with their aspirations, offer opportunities to learn new stuff, bring them into project team to work hand-in-glove with those who provide the information for them to do a great job, make them directly accountable to a lead who is both technical and a great coach for the duration of the delivery, talk to them daily and measure their performance based on output. Lastly, give them a timesheet code to keep the 'chiefs' out of the productivity equation and never ever check the hours booked. It never fails to amaze me when I'm asked to sign a timesheet for the first time. I just sign it. The recipient asks, 'Are you not going to check it?' I reply, 'No, I checked it before you gave me it to approve.'

Mr Brownstone

I used to do a little but a little got more and more....Mr Brownstone is about substance abuse class a-z drugs. Now clearly, the last person you want on your team is anyone indulging in illegal substance abuse. However, there are plenty of other legal stimulants in the workplace. I'm talking about sugar, nicotine and caffeine. IT project delivery teams get through a tonne of that stuff. The sugar, tobacco and coffee industry love the IT industry. Now I've worked on some crazy train deliveries and the working environment looks like this: an average of 4 people every 20 minutes outside puffing on cigarettes; pockets of cakes, biscuits and chocolates all over the office constantly being grazed upon; fridges full of cans of energy, diet and sugary drinks; desks strewn with the empty cans. These are all stimulants to keep us going. Now I'm no doctor but a constant exposure to this stuff cannot be performance enhancing. Our sleep patterns must be suffering, impairing our performance the following day. It must make our internal workings feel like a pinball machine on acid which, in turn, influences the way people behave. If you look at a high performance sports team, there is a nutritionist looking at what the team consumes and when they consume it. High performance individuals take regular exercise and do not overload their systems with caffeine, sugar and nicotine. At some point in the last 30 years, it became the norm to binge on stuff that is clearly bad for us to help us perform better in our jobs. As a result, I wonder how many mistakes people make because they are hyper or because they are on a downer? The truth is this stuff is toxic to our bodies. An IT Project Team that views this stuff as toxic whilst significantly reducing its intake in favour of super foods, herbal teas, fresh water, fish, vegetables and salad greens, will boost their natural energy levels, which in turn makes the team more resilient to the stresses of today's delivery climate.

Paradise City

Where the grass is green and the girls are pretty...A song about paradise view and a vision of perfection. The mid 80s onwards saw the rise of total quality management (TQM). It's drilled into us. Strive for high quality at all times. Quality is the last tolerance a Project Manager should compromise. But when is 'just good enough' enough? And when is perfection a must-have? Challenged IT projects consist of design and build decisions where 'just good enough' was not enough and perfection was an unnecessary luxury. We want our developers to be craftsmen. We need our designers to be visionary. We want to see our engineers take a design and make it better when they build it. We need our testers to set up and run the perfect automated test. The temptation to customise an off-the-shelf package to please the end users can be compelling. After all, we all want to see customer satisfaction. However, striving for perfection when 'just good enough' will do is a waste of time. Only strive for perfection when you need to. Technical people who are passionate about a product or who are learning to use the next big thing have a propensity to over-engineer. Watch for changing the problem definition or the requirements to expand the use of the product's capabilities. Always ask the question: What is the value (time saved, revenue generated, competitive advantage, reduced business risk, money saved, increased capability etc) if we build or configure the feature in the manner proposed? If the question cannot be answered quickly, don't do it.

My Michelle

Your daddy works in porn! Oerrr that's controversial. Don't employ people on the project team who have liberal erotic pastimes. Topics about sex are far more interesting than anything IT project related, like how we are going to configure VMware vs the topic of crotchless underwear. Secondly, it is a UXB in a HR minefield. Pastimes you need your project people not talking about include dogging, swinging, escort work, stripping, open relationships, lap dancing, anything tantric, nudism and sex therapy. If there is a choice between talking about IT project work, or talking with the person on the team with those hobbies, the latter will win every time. The evidence is only anecdotal and I cannot prove it but teams on challenged IT projects talk about sex more than teams on successful IT projects. All I know is that a team full of Mr Lover Lover Bombastics have their brains in their pants. Read into that what you will. I'm happy for Channel 4 to give me loads of money to make a documentary.

Think About You

People who have just fallen in love or are on the verge of falling out of love whilst on the critical path, is a recipe for disaster. Their minds are totally focused on spending time with their new found soul mate or, in a break-up situation, dumping them. And boy do they like to tell everyone about it. Cupid's arrow is one big time stealer. When you write a project initiation document, one of the constraints that everyone has to sign up to is that no one falls in love or out of love during the delivery! Joking aside, my advice is that it is difficult to be an effective 'beat the plan' IT Project Manager if you have just fallen in love or you are about to go through a break up in a relationship. Your hormones are all over the place.

Sweet Child of Mine

Where everything is as fresh as a bright blue sky... Challenged IT projects suffer from creating a form of future failure demand, a constraint which introduces unforeseen effort. The last thing an IT project needs is its star players leaving the team at a critical time. It happens because, as managers, we have a natural tendency to give important work to the people on the team who will never moan, do a great job and always deliver. They are the favourites. In simplistic terms, IT project teams can be split into radiators and drains. The radiators are the star players. The drains are a drag to manage to get things do. The reason we want to give all the work to the radiators is because of expediency and reduced uncertainty, whilst avoiding the hassle incurred by dealing with the drains. However, even though the approach pays off in the short term, in the long term the approach is creating a weak link on the critical path. At some point it becomes unfair to burden the radiators with all the tough difficult technical jobs. Under these circumstances the radiators tend to leave. Drains are akin to a lion in a cage being fed steak from seven months old. On the first day of the eighth month, the keeper says to the lion, 'You can have your steak but we want you to perform.' The lion opens one eye and goes back to sleep. Don't over-burden your radiators with boring technical important work. The load has to be spread across the team. Spot the drains early, let them go and get yourself a radiator.

You're Crazy

A song about people who do the exact opposite of what everyone expects they should do. My opening gambit for this piece: if there is no incentive for finishing early then why finish early? When was the last time you worked on an IT project where its people were rewarded for finishing early? Could it be the norm whereby people think if I finish early and tell someone then I'm going get a load of uninteresting mundane firefighting work to do? Organisations reward project teams for following the rules, filling out timesheets on time, completing the company mandated training, and getting great feedback from end users. But I have never worked for, nor seen, an organisation go out of its way to reward an IT project team for delivering early. Maybe I'm just unlucky. It is no wonder then that no one shouts from the highest rooftop, 'I've finished early.' Crazy is it not? Well, according to a bunch of academics and scientific types who specialise in statistical process control managementology, there are equations that prove what I've just said is true. Now take an organisational climate with a primary focus on cost management and ask someone in a technical role to estimate the effort it will take them to do a complex technical task in an uncertain environment i.e. software development. Now ask them what is the probability of achieving the estimate. Let's for argument sake say they reply that it's 80-90%. Now if you could go an ask another 99 people with similar experience the same question, then calculate the average of the answers, what are the chances the average would be between 80-90%? Would you bet £100 on the answer being 80-90%? Probably, not. Let's go back to the first estimate to understand what the thought process is behind the estimate.

Is it a task I'm familiar with? No. Best add a bit of safety also known as 'fat' to salespeople who have no idea how the work is done.

What happened the last time I did something similar? Well

it's the same location and the traffic is pretty bad on the way to client site. The last Project Manager was pretty naff at arranging physical access so I was hanging around for a while. Now I remember a couple of things were not configured on the active directory and reverse proxy. Best to add a bit just in case.

Is it a task I'm going to enjoy doing? No. Not really going to enjoy doing that. I will overestimate so they find someone else, knowing full well there is no one else readily available.

Do I work for a management team who always reduces the estimates to keep the costs down? Yes. Best to add a bit of a buffer so that when they hack and slash, my contingency does not get touched.

Hey presto, I've got lots of buffer in my estimate. Think I will leave it to the last minute to start the work. Must be suffering from student syndrome.

The estimate is padded with time that be might be needed. However, with no incentive to finish early it gets magically used but not on activities to recover from over-runs. When someone finishes early, when there is no incentive to finish early, the hidden time just gets used up doing things other than recovering from delays. I never understood Parkinson's Law until I heard about the whole 'no incentive for finishing early' theory. My first instinct was to declare war on padding. My second instinct was to be pragmatic. Let's just accept the fact that all estimates contain an element of natural padding. After all, estimating is not an exact science. So how do you use all time we might need in an estimate, wisely? Firstly, there has to be an incentive for using the buffer for value adding work, which means the project must incentivise participants for finishing early. Secondly, take the budget that is not being used as a result of finishing early, and invest it in strengthening the weakest links in the project's critical chain. Pursue Kaizen, which is Japanese for 'change for the best'. This will mean applying improvement to IT project work centres whose performance, with high volume and low complexity work, is causing quality or schedule risk: too many network devices to stage and not enough network engineers; too many test scripts to be run and not enough testers or lack of automation; lots of design to be done but not enough designers. Every IT project has inefficient work centres. Thinking in this manner requires the IT Project Manager to focus on throughput and not cost management. In practise, the organisation must delegate approval to spend, to the IT Project Manager, thus empowering them. Challenged IT projects tend to suffer from significant lag and latency between the request to spend, and approval being given to spend.

My Way

Your way anything goes…It's the song I hear when I'm stuck in, what seems like, a never ending debate about what tools the project should use between the fanboys of one tool and the fanboys of another. Nothing eats up more time than trying to get technical folk to decide on what tools to use, particularly in the world of software development. I recall a project where the choice was between Red Hat Linux and other versions of Linux. It was called Gooneegugoo or Ubuntu or something like that. The process was like one of those forensic fraud investigations chaired by a government select committee. In the end, the project reached a point where a decision had to be made. It was a 'thou shalt not useth Red Hat'. Now from a layman's point of view, the evidence suggested there was not much to choose from in terms of performance or functionality. Every time there was a bug or something did not work quite right, the Red Hat Harry Enfield brigade would pop up and say, 'should have used Red Hat'. Then a repeat of the Red Hat vs Cat in the Hat Linux debate in the technical team, would ensue. I could never quite frame where this time stealing behaviour came from until I watched the film, Ted. No, not the film about the sex-crazed potty-mouthed, heavy drinking teddy bear. It was an episode from TedTalks called The Paradox of Choice.

The theory is that because there is so much choice, we can't help but think the alternatives to our final choice could be better. It's a nagging doubt that lingers throughout the duration of project. In the good old days, there were not that many software development stack tools to choose. Now, however, the choice is vast and everything in the apps stack can talk to everything else. Today's software developers are literally spoilt for choice and, boy, they are passionate about choosing the right tool. Generation Y software developers are being taught to be craftsmen and like all good craftsmen the choice of tool is an important decision. However, the organisation's corporate IT strategy makes that choice for them. Otherwise, there would be chaos. But the paradox of choice remains at large, torturing the software developer forced to use tools they had no say in. John Seddon is a leading systems thinker and keen critic of command and control. The message from his books is that poor quality is the result of not empowering those who do the work, to decide how the work is done. Poor quality in software development normally means a build-up of technical debt that will have to paid off later on. So here is the quandary. Giving software developers too much choice results in a free-for-all. Not giving them enough choice in the tools, disempowers and can instil a sense of powerlessness, which can be used to avoid accountability. 'Management choose the tools. I just work with what I'm given.' That's the language of poor commitment and avoiding accountability. I call this paradox of an imposed choice. It has the same effects as the TedTalks paradox of choice, with the added bonus of more disillusionment because the choice was made by someone without the responsibility for doing the actual work. So how can we reduce the time stealing impact associated with the paradox fo choice? Jet fighters cost a fortune to make. They contain critical parts. What if there was a choice between three critical parts for our jetfighter? How would we empower the engineers so that they are brought into the final decision? Or should the lead engineer or Project

Manager do a King Solomon and decide for the team? In high-end manufacturing, such situations are dealt with using concurrent set theory where experience is considered the purest and truest from of knowledge. The approach involves splitting the engineering team into three, and giving each of them a part to evaluate. Halfway through the evaluation, each team swaps parts and the evaluation is repeated. At the end of the evaluation, the team decides on which part to use. This approach reduces negative consequences associated with the paradox of choice, whilst putting the engineering team in an informed position to choose the correct tool. On any strategically important package implementation (ERP, CRM etc) or software development (.net, J2EE etc), the team will be faced with a 'what tool should we use' type of evaluation. With the advent of everything as a service (XaaS) cloud solutions (SaaS, PaaS, IaaS, DBaaS) and open source, it won't cost that much to deploy environments to allow the team to deep-dive, run model office type pilots with end users, and get hands-on with the tools. It will be your job to create the climate and to convince the project paymasters that working in this manner is a great thing to do. This whole approach significantly reduces the need for management intervention to dictate to technical teams how the work should be done. That's a command and control way of working known to result in poor quality, which in IT project management, normally means the acquisition of schedule risk that will ultimately convert into over-run on time.

Rocket Queen

Content removed due to risk of litigation ;-)

BE KEN KUTARAGI: THE ULTIMATE TECHNOLOGY PROJECT MANAGER

'Now it's history I see '

Big In Japan

Alphaville

FOLLOWING THE RELEASE OF THE potentially marriage-wrecking, transactional life-inducing Sony Playstation 4, what valuable lessons can we learn about Technology Project Management, from Playstation's inventor and the master of Moore's Law, Ken Kutaragi?

I have always loved video games. Since the late 70s, my hobby has been computer games. I have lived through, and experienced, all generations of technology. If it were not for video games, I'd probably not be writing this book. The innovators behind the hardware and the iconic games fascinate me. Most of them started from their bedroom or garage. What happened all those years ago still has repercussions today. As I write this chapter in June 2013, there is a story on Sky News. When the film ET hit the cinemas, Atari planned to release en masse, a cartridge-based game for its 2600 system. Unfortunately, that particular console was coming to the end of its life. The market for all those ET cartridge games was not there; Atari had missed the boat. IT project failure has two things in common with the mistake Atari made. IT projects fail when nobody wants what they have produced. The IT project delivery team fail to understand the needs of their market audience. Another reason for failure is releasing a solution that is not quite ready. Yet video games and the most successful games consoles are far more complicated than any IT project for either the public or the private sector.

So what can we learn from the innovators who ushered in the digital entertainment era? Well, there are hundreds of lessons to learn. Not far from where I live is a company who developed software for the Sinclair ZX Spectrum in the early 80s. Fast forward to the 21st century and Microsoft have purchased them to develop software for the Xbox 360. I'm going to put the spotlight on Ken Kutaragi, the grandfather of the Sony Playstation. He rose from an engineer in Sony's analogue hey days to Vice President of Sony Computer Entertainment (SCE). At one point, SCE's contribution to Sony's profits reached 23%. My starting point is one of Kutaragi's quotes. It oozes 'beat the plan'.

> "I wanted to prove that even regular employees – no, especially regular company employees – could build a venture of this scale with superb technology, superb concepts, and superb colleagues."

Ken Kutaragi

If you want to be emphatic and get noticed on a run-of-the-mill IT project, use a variation of Ken Kutaragi's words in front of your project team and key stakeholders. The catch is that you can only say this in the project closure meeting.

"I wanted to prove that even regular employees – no,
especially regular company employees – can deliver an
IT project of this scale with superb technology, superb
concepts, and superb colleagues."

Future you

That's the first thing we can learn when attempting a difficult
IT project with 'beat the plan' in mind - you've got to be a man
or woman with a mission. It is important to note that when
Ken Kutaragi decided he was a man with a mission, he was
just an engineer. At the time, Sony was a business designed to
build, mass-produce and market products for the analogue age.
Can you imagine the first reaction Kutaragi got when talking
about a video games console using digital signal processing and
CD ROM? Probably a similar reaction many of us see on IT
projects when there is the merest suggestion of using a different
technology; the NIMBY syndrome – not in my backyard. At the
heart of this response is the natural fear of radical technological
change. The motivation is entirely appropriate. It is born out of
not wasting organisational time and money. Given the reputation
of IT project delivery, it is no wonder business representatives
are fearful of the potential disruption to business operational
stability. When I've encountered this reaction, it feels like Alice
in Wonderland when Alice meets the Red Queen.

"A slow sort of country," said the Red Queen. "Now here,
you see, it takes all the running you can do to keep in the
same place. If you want to get somewhere else, you must
run at least twice as fast as that!"

Lewis Carroll, Alice through the Looking Glass

Ken Kutaragi was an Alice looking for a wonderland - and he
found it. So what did he do and what has making video games

consoles got in common with IT project failure? IT project failure has nothing in common with the birth of the Playstation. If there were commonalities, I suspect the launch of the Sony PS4 would be a chapter in a science fiction novel. The successful birth of the Playstation has a lot in common with the 33% IT project success rate. Ken Kutaragi managed his project with critical outcomes in mind. Ken Kutaragi maintained a link between his process of innovation and the needs of the business he served. A successful IT project is a business-driven product development process that goes from development to maturity. Successful IT projects can empirically predict, with certainty, the end point where the solution is mature enough for release. From the point Ken Kutaragi envisioned the original Playstation, he accurately predicted it would be 10 years before technology was mature enough to build a mass consumer product. Basically, he surrounded himself with expert designers and builders he needed to make it happen. IT projects fail because of the latency involved in getting hold of expert designers and builders to create momentum. Ken Kutaragi's innovation process was technology fusion friendly. Although the playstation has a distinct identity, his technical solution was the result of ease of convergence between different technical streams. IT projects can fail because the project team does not think through how their technical solution will converge within the overall technical environment in which is operates. For example, hosting is not designed with the networking in mind or when the application is not designed with the hosting arrangements in mind. Ken Kutaragi ensured the design process was robust. Robust designs can be extended without breaking everything else. Many failed IT projects are the progeny of poor design. When trying to execute a complex activity in an organisational environment that is not designed to be conducive, assiduously feeding knowledge into the process is paramount. Ken Kutaragi did the exact opposite. He did not have it all his own way though. Ken pursued a relationship with Nintendo but failed to appreciate

Nintendo's true intentions. Nintendo pulled out of a potential partnership with Sony and pursued a similar venture with Philips. IT projects can fail when the various partners perceive the benefits as unequal. Such perceptions create disunity and discord. Nintendo's u-turn came as a bit of a surprise to Ken. He found out about Nintendo's intention on the media grapevine. Infrequent communication between partners, in particular between each third party technical team, is pervasive on failed IT project delivery.

So what did Ken do so well that we can learn from? The one feature of his success that stands out the most is the people he surrounded himself with. He actively sought them out. How much thought did all those IT projects in the 66% failure category think through the governance or team make-up? Ken could not deliver his vision alone. He had a coach who guided him managerially. More importantly is that he recognised he needed one. He also brought along a trusted confidant. How many of us IT Project Managers have a coach or confidant to show us where we may be going wrong? Ken surrounded himself with experts in the fields of distribution, marketing, ergonomics, production and engineering. He made it his mission to get the attention of Sony top management. Failed IT project delivery experiences middle management inertia that just gets in the way and slows the project down. Ken Kutaragi learnt that lesson very early on in his Sony career that started in the mid 1970's. Successful IT Project Managers behave like Ken. They don't make the same mistake twice and they don't solve problems with the same thinking that created it. Ken was passionate about the actual solution he was delivering. Would it be surprising to assume that failed IT projects may be led by IT Project Managers who are dispassionate about what they are delivering? I have worked on several challenged deliveries and, on reflection, I was indifferent about the technology involved and the aims of the project. Anger at Nintendo's betrayal was a source of motivation for Sony to press ahead with their own venture. Successful IT projects deal with let downs effectively, efficiently and ruthlessly. Someone agrees to do something. Then they either don't it or they do the wrong thing. If you let it go, history repeats itself. Getting angry about what happened to spur the necessary corrective action, can only be healthy for the project. The venture to develop the Playstation was separated from Sony. It was a deliberate decision to protect the venture from the status quo. Is it a coincidence that matrix management is at play in the environment where failed IT projects are delivered? In my experience I tend to find that the resources and skills to effectively deliver an IT project are locked away in organisational silos. I say something along the lines, "Wouldn't it be great and optimal to pull everyone into a single team?" Then everyone nods in agreement but then says, "But that is not how we are organised." Ken did not blindly accept that the status quo organisational design was going to enable the delivery. He sought executive level support to change it. In the video game console industry, your console is a white elephant without games. Game developers are just as important as end users. To get them on board, Sony put on 'an astonishing demonstration'. It is the word 'astonishing' that interests me the most. The most publicised root cause of IT project failure is lack of end user involvement, which has connotation with poor communication selling the solution. Anecdotal feedback includes, 'Nobody spoke to us', ' We didn't see it before we got it', or 'That demo was so boring and flaky'. The 2 principles at play in the Playstation communications strategy were: make the demos astonishing; and advertise only if the product is interesting.

I hope that one day I will meet Ken Kutaragi. When I fall out of love with my job, I think about what Ken Kutaragi would say to me. That was after Marlon Brando, in his role of Godfather, had finished giving me some verbal slaps because I felt like Johnny Fontaine who'd just been dumped as an actor! I think Ken would say, 'You fell out of love with your job because.......

You convinced yourself perfection was not attainable.

You did not use all the resources at your disposal.

As a worker bee, you thought you felt you could not work independently of the hive.

Your project teams were not formed by like minded individuals.

You blindly accepted ways of working that stopped you striving for quality.

Those are not 'beat the plan' behaviours in the little-big-planet-world of contemporary business.

HOLLYWOOD MANAGEMENT SCIENCE PART 1: LEARN THE WAYS OF LEE JUN FAN

'I know not what trouble lies ahead. Before you fight, use your head.'

The Last Dragon

Dwight David

ORN LEE JUN FAN IN November 1940, he went on to become the most influential martial artist of all time. He changed the way the world thought about Chinese culture and martial arts. Tragically, he died at a very young age in August 1973. He'd just finishing filming the movie that made martial arts become mainstream Hollywood material - Enter the Dragon. Bruce Lee gave us the quote, 'Be like water'. If you pour water at the top of a hill, it will find the shortest route to get to the bottom. Yet the water has no knowledge of the obstacles it will face. What a great way to run an IT project.

It's 1980 and I'm hanging out in the park on a Raleigh Grifter with my mates. Here comes Franny. Franny thought he was born to be a ninja. Out of a plastic bag he pulls out a pair of homemade nunchucks - two bits of cylinder-shaped hardwood joined together with a piece of washing line. He starts swinging them around while making noises like an owl on acid at a rave. There is only going to be one outcome - the achievement of self actualisation and a higher state of consciousness? No.

10 – 15 seconds looking at gold stars and a moment of breathlessness curled up on the floor? Self contemplation as a result of nunchucking ones crown jewels? Yes.

26 years later, I've been asked to help on a project. It is all last minute rush rush. Today's issue is a missed requirement to setup some networking to get a load of data from A to B; from the Midlands to Kent then back to the Midlands. We come up with a cobbled together VPN solution. Pull this off and we will look very impressive. However, I start to feel like Franny before he started to show off with those homemade nunchucks. It is not going to work - and it didn't - but we tried anyway just to look proactive. We'd fallen into the must-be-seen-to-be-doing-something trap. Children of the 70s grew up watching Bruce Lee films and all of us at some point tried a dragon-whips-his-tail moment, only to fall flat on our faces. In real martial arts, every action has a purpose that leads towards a goal. The same cannot be said of challenged IT projects. They become challenged because every action did not have purpose that led towards the goal. Bruce Lee once said 'Where there is freedom from mechanical conditioning, there is simplicity.' Leonardo Da Vinci said something similar several hundred years earlier. Just goes to show Bruce Lee had studied topics beyond fighting. This is one of the many lessons IT Project Management can take from the Tao of Jeet Kune Do. Every scene from the greatest martial arts film ever made, Enter the Dragon, has a lesson waiting to be taught. Project boards that don't hit back and the art of managing without managing.....

The winner

In the first scene, Bruce Lee's schifu, coach and sensei watch their star pupil take part in a practise contest. During his career, Bruce Lee had many teachers; he did not achieve excellence on his own. You can't keep winning difficult contests without a strong mentor on your case who expects no less than the best of you. To become excellent, you need someone more excellent than you, more wise than you, not afraid to put out your weaknesses and knowledge enough to show you how to turn those weaknesses into strengths. Every successful person in business has a sensei. Get one.

A martial artist's responsibility

In this scene, Bruce Lee's schifu asks him, "What is the highest level of technique you hope to achieve?" Bruce Lee responds, "To have no technique." It's an ability for a person to instinctively know what they need to do. The ultimate form of Project Management is to achieve project success by eliminating the need for management. This can only be achieved through an understanding of what it takes to create a self-directing team. Surround yourself with highly trained people and motivated people you trust. Instil a sense of common purpose across the project team. Make them all accountable for a common goal. Make this your primary responsibility.

Emotional requirements management content

Requirements management is like a finger pointing to the moon. Don't concentrate on the requirements or you will miss all that heavenly glory. Requirements will change. It is a given. You cannot change the reasons why requirements change. Expecting otherwise is like going into a fight expecting not to be hit. There is an old saying in the trade that 'the project didn't become late in the last month; it became late in the first month'. This rings true. The seeds are sown for challenged projects during the formative moments of the requirements. Always invest time, technology and the creation of robust processes to facilitate accurate requirements right from the off.

A Lalo Schifrin mindfulness moment

The musical score for 'Enter the Dragon' was composed by Lalo Schifrin. He wrote the scores for many a great film like Bullit and Mission Impossible. Lalo Schifrin was one of cinema's greatest composers for movie themes. Producing and communicating a project plan is like composing. When producing a plan, think like Lalo Schifrin. Be conscious of the people who will read it and listen to it. Lalo Schifrin once said , "I don't write in an insular way or in an ivory tower, because that would be selfish; that would be an exercise in self-indulgence. The public is the ultimate goal of any communication. The work of a composer is very lonely. The need of conducting with live audiences really helps. Each side helps the other." Do this every time you produce a project plan.

Master of Understanding Anti patterns

Bruce Lee and the head of the secret services, Mr Braithwaite, watch a film about all the intelligence they have on the evil mastermind, Han. Bruce wants to know everything there is to know before going in for the fight. Defeating Han is the biggest and most riskiest challenge Bruce has ever faced. But he will win because Bruce Lee invented Jeet Kune Do. Jeet Kune Do was named for the Wing Chun concept of interception or attacking while one's opponent is about to attack. Jeet Kune Do students use minimal movements for maximum effect at extreme speed. Apply the same philosophy when you think about and apply risk management. The Jeet Kune Do system works by using different 'tools' for different situations. Bruce Lee invented Jeet Kune Do by understanding the 'anti patterns' in traditional martial arts. An anti pattern is a literary form that describes a commonly occurring solution to a problem that generates decidedly negative consequences. Bruce Lee removed the anti patterns. Potentially challenged IT projects consist of anti patterns waiting to happen. Study them, learn to spot the symptoms and defeat them.

Don't be Roper, an undisciplined financial manager

Out of the three heroes, Roper is the playboy. His ventures have run out of money and his lenders, the mob, are after him. Lucky, for him he is a martial artist when they come calling. Due to HR regulations, an IT Project Manager can go around using Kung Fu to fend off the accountants. These guys tend to appear from nowhere when they've been watching the burn of the budget and the IT project has not. Best not to get to that point. IT projects just don't suddenly overspend. Black holes appear when an IT project overspends by a couple of sheckles a day without anyone noticing. Shaolin monks disciplines themselves to do the regular mundane important exercises they need to do every day at the same time for as long as they need to do it. Keeping track of the finances effectively requires the same mindset. Become the Tai Chi master of budget vs actual vs forecast.

Williams Speaker of Truth to Power

Out of the 3 heroes, Williams is the idealist; but he is vane. His confrontations with the unacceptable face of authority has led to this point in his life. Williams is prepared to speak truth to power but there is fatal flaw in his approach- he has no back-out plan. IT projects fail when people fear speaking truth to power or lack the understanding to do so. Williams knows that confronting power may mean him having to start anew elsewhere. It is a price one may have to pay. Bureaucracies rely on fear of losing our job to keep us pliant and to influence managers into conforming. If you equate income with security, then you will be less inclined to speak truth to power and more inclined to tell power what they want to hear. IT projects fail because candour is not the norm in the culture around communication. The more wise-than-honest IT Project Manager will be more likely to fail, than the ulterior more-honest-than wise one. Have no fear when speaking truth to power by having a back out plan.

Do nothing : The Parsons Option

Parsons walks up to Bruce, gets in his face and showboats. Now Bruce being the toughest hombre on that boat could have round-housed Parsons into a well needed state of reflection. But he didn't. Why? Jeet Kune Do's core principle is minimum effort for maximum effect. Bruce tricks Parsons into a rowing boat. He'd beaten Parsons without throwing a punch. A day in the life of your average IT PM is dealing with a constant stream of risks and issues. Before going into risk-management-email-keyboard-process-game-of-phones mode because you think the acorns are going to fall from the sky. Just stop and ask yourself, 'What will happen if I do nothing?' Parsons made a lot of noise and threw some punches but he never actually hit Bruce. Bruce did nothing but anyone watching the film for the first time expected him to react in kind. And that is the expectation of someone who has never been an IT Project Manager; they expect you to always react. However, you don't have the time to react to everything. So learn to evaluate the do-nothing option before you react.

Han's philosophy

Because of: the failure rate; the coverage of the failure rate; and our own experiences; we may be inclined inadvertently to instantly assume from the outset that an IT project is going to be difficult and is likely to fail. Here is a mediation technique to get rid of that initial feeling. Imagine yourself at Han's opulent banquet and you are his guest. Now imagine him saying this to you:

"Gentlemen, welcome. You honor our island. I look forward to an IT project delivery of truly epic proportions. We are unique, gentlemen, in that we create ourselves... through long years of rigorous training, sacrifice, denial. We forge our technical and people skills in the fire of our will".

The morning ritual

Every morning, Han insists on his warriors attending the morning ritual. These rituals are energised. Participants know they are there to improve and be improved. There is absolute focus on why they are present. Successful IT projects are full of rituals with similar traits.

Let the tournament begin

The kick off for Han's tournament is a spectacle no one will ever forget. It's memorable for all the right reasons. The same can be said for successful IT projects - they always start with a memorable and exciting project kick-off. A kick-off is not a meeting; it is memorable event. Here are the ingredients:

You never get a second chance to make a first impression and you never get a second chance to successfully kick-off a project engagement. So this is your chance to get the project off to a perfect start. Your kick-off session, if well prepared and presented, is your chance to make sure that you are heading into the planning and design stages knowing exactly where you are going. You will make sure that everyone is singing from the same song sheet and ensure you have good sound knowledge.

From experience, the following steps have worked best for

me, in planning, preparing and then administering the formal project kick-off with the client.

Gather Information

The first step is to gather all the necessary information. Knowledge is power. This will involve meeting with Sales to go through the pricing of the project that they would have originally put to the customer. Fill out the project schedule with the details that Sales would not have included.

Engage the Customer

Next, you should have a face-to-face meeting with the client. This will help you get to know them and their team, and will allow you the opportunity to explain what is to be expected in the kick-off meeting i.e. some general rules and who should be in attendance.

Prepare to Present

Preparation, preparation, preparation - it's all in the preparation. You've gathered all your information and ensured it is all correct. You have the project schedule, the pricing from Sales, the statement of work. Assemble it together in the form of a formal presentation which will allow all the key points to be discussed with the client. I always include:

Statement of Work.

Draft project schedule.

Key dates - although they are in the schedule for all to peruse, they are so important that you should bring attention to them and discuss them.

Project pricing

Frequency of staus calls and reports

List of potential risks

How you intend handling risks

How you plan to manage the project

Change management & change order process practices

Conduct the Formal Kick-off Session

It's now time for the formal kick-off session. If you had the face-to-face meeting with the client (or their representative), you will already have agreed on a date and time for this session and its location. In my experience, the kick-off session is usually held at the client's premises.

Summary

Remember that your client is funding this project - it is their money you are spending. So they need to be confident that you, as Project Manager, will manage the project in order to deliver the end result successfully. Do not take this lightly.

O'Hara and His Useless Board

Bruce faces off to his opponent O'Hara, Han's number one warrior. O'Hara tries to intimidate Bruce by taking a thick wooden board and chopping it in two. The intimidation does not work. Bruce responds, "Boards don't hit back", and then proceeds to obliterate O'Hara. An IT project with a board as useless and as pointless as O'Hara's board, will fail to perform. Ineffective governance is the biggest risk to the delivery of any project. Learn how to spot one. Here are key indicators for a project board that will be as much use as O'Hara's bit of wood in a punch up with Bruce Lee.

1) Selective or incomplete information provided to the board about critical issues facing the project. 2) A board made up of the 'old boy network'. 3) Board members who sit on many other boards. They are unable to attend all the meetings because of double bookings. When the do finally turn up they are not in an informed position to contribute. 4) Board members who lack the skills, experience or understanding of the project to guide it. 5) Board members are close personal friends of the project sponsor. 6) The project board sessions are not well organised. 7) Board members who lack authority to make decisions.

As the Project Manager, you are a board member and being part of board is an honour. The IT Project Manager is an advisor who uses every bit of influence to get fellow board members to see themselves as a critical asset for the delivery of the project. You must demand and ensure all relevant information is sent to the board so everyone has time to prepare. Consensus is only successful when the tough questions are asked before it is built. When you come out of the board meeting, build relationships with everyone on the board. Best to be a leader on an effective project board than being led by an ineffective one.

Williams vs Han (the project sponsor)

Han accuses Williams of sneaking about the island being nosey and generally getting involved in things he should not be doing. The scene is a case study in how not to deal with a project sponsor when you've been naughty. When they threaten to get rid of you, best not to say, "When it comes, I won't even notice; I'll be too busy looking good." Williams does not like the tone of Han's questioning and responds, "Mr Han, suddenly I'd like to leave your island." This was kind of saying, "I do not agree with you and I want to leave the project." There will be many disagreements with the sponsor throughout a project. If your initial reaction is always wanting to leave, then your heart is not in the delivery. When a sponsor declines your request to disengage, take it as a complement. Do not say what Williams said to Han, "Bullshit, Mr Han-Man! Man, you've come right out of a comic book!" At that point, Han loses patience with Williams and proceeds to teach him a lesson.

Roper's Limit

Han shows Roper around his operation. He wants Roper to join his crime syndicate. Roper is tempted having seen the material rewards. To make a point about who is in charge, Han then shows Roper what he has done to Roper's friend Williams. Roper's ethics kick in and he turns Han down. Failed IT projects in the public sector have cost the tax payers billions, which is immoral considering all the good causes that could have been funded with that amount of money. It happened because of distinct lack of ethics during the decision-making process. When working for a supplier organisation as an IT Project Manager, one has a duty to provide services in a manner that is beyond moral approach. Roper's limit demonstrates behaviours that lead to ethical decision making. These behaviours are prevalent on IT projects that have beaten the plan.

Honour

Honesty

Professional adequacy

Fairness

Taking into account social cost

Being efficient

Clear Understanding

Bruce Lee once said, "Do not pray for an easy life; pray for the strength to endure a difficult one." This is the path an IT Project Manager must take. In the modern organisation all we have is the strength of our argument, our character and the will to succeed.

Cavern Combat : Low latency Risk Management

The final scenes start with Bruce Lee in the caverns, coming under attack from many of Hans guards. Every move Bruce Lee makes has purpose, defeating each assailant in one fluid action. Bruce uses every move he knows and every weapon at his disposal. He anticipates his assailant's move and responds instinctively. Bruce Lee manages the risk to his survival by anticipating before it happens. IT projects fail because of poor risk management, namely the inability to identify risk and an inability to deal with it before it becomes an issue. I am a fan of the Wikipedia definition for risk management i.e. *the identification, assessment, and prioritization of risks followed by coordinated and economical application of resources to minimize, monitor, and control the probability and/or impact of unfortunate events or to maximize the realization of opportunities.* There is no latency in the Bruce Lee thought process and subsequent physical action during cavern combat. An IT Project Manager with a Bruce Lee mindset thinks in the same manner when conducting risk management. There is no latency between the following steps in the risk management process:

Identification

Assessment

Prioritisation

Mitigation

Final scene : Han vs Lee

The dragon whips his tail and Han is no more.

"I wanted to do in boxing what Bruce Lee was able to do in the martial arts. Lee was an artist and, like him, I try to get beyond the fundamentals of my sport. I want my fights to be seen as plays."

Sugar Ray Leonard

HOLLYWOOD SCIENCE PART 2: DON'T LET CARL DENHAM'S BEAST KILLS THE BEAUTY OF AGILE

'When routine bites hard, And ambitions are low, Resentment rides high.'

Love Will Tear Us Apart

Joy Division

CAN ONLY RECALL 3 TIMES when I've been on the verge of tears because of extreme disappointment. The most recent episode was last year. I'm sitting in an empty bar on Wednesday evening with a pal when these two great looking women start talking to us. There is no way I'm going to admit I work in IT - so I lie. Off I go to the bar to fetch the drinks. When I come back they've gone. My pal has told them I am an IT Project Manager. There is a story in our family. Apparently, according to my sisters when I was 6, I cried with sadness as King Kong in the Merian C. Cooper and Ernest B. Schoedsack 1933 film, falls to his death in the final scene. Fay Wray is crying. King Kong did what he did for love, then paid the ultimate price. I think he died happy having gotten an eyeful of Fay Wray's boobs in the waterfall scene. King Kong is rated 43 in American Film Institute's greatest films of all time. The first programme for the film promises the audience it will be the greatest film they will ever see. My sisters normally remind me of this story when I've been winding them up. Fast forward to 2004 and my 3 year old son goes through a phase of making me watch King Kong every day for 6 months. As a result, I know everything there is to know about that film. In the same year my son was born, we saw the birth of the Agile Manifesto. It was not until 2009 that I had my first Agile experience. Up to that point, I'd read and heard a lot of good things about Agile; it all made perfect sense.

Individuals and interactions over processes and tools

Working software over comprehensive documentation

Customer collaboration over contract negotiation

Responding to change over following a plan

Unfortunately, the first Agile project I worked on did not live up to expectation. This was the third time I nearly cried. I learnt very quickly that for an Agile software development project to work, the team and stakeholders have to stick to all those principles. The allure of self organisation and right-first-time zero-defect code, is overwhelming when you've been brought up on a diet of micro management, big up-front, design crunch mode software project delivery. The reality is breaking one or more of those principles and Agile won't live to up expectation. It is a tall order when IT projects are conducted in organisational paradigm whose roots can be traced back to mechanistic command and control. Those cultural traits still permeate large organisations today. Command and control traits are a monster that can kill off the beauty of an Agile project when, in fact, the outcome of the battle needs be the other way around. My second observation is that Agile only works when the science behind it works. Right now we are seeing a body of knowledge emerging known as 'continuous delivery'. The scientific principles behind the Toyota Way that has given birth to lean and systems thinking, have found their way into the world of software development. Software development is probably the most risky type of IT project, given the stats. An Agile project conducted without the science of happiness or lean process design is a hot bed of risk. Agile is also becoming the norm so these hints and pointers will help you in the likely event that you find yourself working on an Agile project.

King Kong 1933 is rated 43 in American Film Institute's greatest films of all time. The first programme for the film promises the audience the film will be the greatest film they will ever see. At the time it was. Agile makes the same promise but after I had watched it for the first time it was no 1933 King Kong spectacle. Today, software projects have access to more money than the makers of King Kong had. Software projects have access to an incredible array of software and hardware technology that film makers, back in the 1930s, would never comprehend. The film King Kong and its history kind of reminds me of the challenges and gotchas on a software development project using an agile approach. So here is a chapter on some must-do and how-not-to. Your software development project need not become a monster consuming time and money; a late night terror source of constant frustration.

Carl Denham the ultimate scrum master

A central character in the King Kong film is Carl Denham. He is the famous big game filmmaker intent on visiting Skull Island to capture, on film, something enormous. He is driven, energetic, visionary and ambitious. He will let no barrier stand in the way of his team from being successful. These are the qualities of a great scrum master or agile PM.

We didn't check the chains

On the big night on a stage in New York, King Kong, the eighth wonder of the world is shown for the first time. Kong has other ideas and easily breaks the so-called unbreakable steel chains. The stage crew had not tested the chains holding Kong. Clearly, they were not designed for the show-off-a-big-monkey business. This kind of situation is a symptom of an unforeseen architectural breach. No one tested the let's-keep-the-big-monkey-secure part of the solution. Brian Marrick, an author in the production of the Agile Manifesto, has produced a framework called a 'testing quadrant'. Any complex software development that does not adhere to the principles in Marrick's framework, will become challenged. Marrick's testing quadrant de-risks the project in two ways; automation and showcasing. Manual testing is resource intensive and usually the first thing that gets squeezed when the time starts to run out. As a work centre on the critical path whose sole existence is to prove fitness for purpose, testing has to be uber efficient and effective-hence why automated testing is a must-have and not a luxury. Repeatable and iterative testing increases speed of feedback to the developers. Developers want and need constant feedback. Therefore, it is also a good idea to configure the automated tests so developers can run them without the testers. The other reason is that developers and testers tend to fight like cat and dog from time to time.

Unsustainable shake rattle and roll log moment

There is a scene in the film when the party, sent to rescue the damsel in distress, has to cross a ravine using a fallen tree as a bridge. They get half way across and Kong spots them. He picks up the log and starts to shake it. This scene reminds me of my first Agile project where the client, for some reason, had this perception that the development team sat around all day on bean bags smoking bongs. The indicator that reassured them this was not the case was presentism and knowing the team was burning the midnight oil. It is a perception I encounter regularly in organisations who don't really know anything about Agile and also have a history of challenged software project delivery. Working silly hours to catch up as a result of rework, is a sign all is not well in the development process. When organisational culture does not reward a decrease in cycle time, burning the midnight oil at an unsustainable pace becomes the norm. Like the Kong shaking-his-log-moment, those on it hang on for so long, then fall off. A little bit of a shake is fine; but constant shaking and then either the development team will burn out or the star players will leave. Organisations embarking on an Agile approach for the first time need coaching. The organisation has to be prepared and needs to understand the old way versus the new way. So when you set the Agile project up, have some communication and education activities in the plan to constantly educate everyone about why Agile has come about and why accepted behaviours in the traditional way of doing things don't work. Your goal as a Project Manager on an Agile project is to protect the team from anything that results in unsustainable pace. Measure what matters most i.e. the level of unsustainable pace and cycle time. Measuring and improving cycle time time (i.e. the time it takes to deliver a feature into production once it has been agreed to develop it), is as equally important as measuring time, budget, burn down, velocity and quality.

Legend of the Bugfest

The legend says there is a lost scene in the 1933 film. It is the scene after the log episode. The legend says there is a scene where the survivors fight off creatures at the bottom of the ravine. In the 2005 remake by Peter Jackson, the scene was recreated. Basically, armies of bugs come from nowhere to overpower the rescue team. It is kind of what happens on a challenged software development project where hidden bugs accumulate and accumulate into an infestation riot mode. The point where you don't want to discover these type of bugs is deployment. Deployment is a critical work centre in a software development project's critical chain. Central to achieving and improving velocity is a constant focus on optimising the deployment work centre. The creepy crawlies are the result of acquired schedule and quality risk i.e. risk as a result of doing something.

Creepy crawly generator number 1: technically risky development that offers little benefits. What I'm talking about here is modifying off-the-shelf (MOTS) software for no other reason than the customer is demanding a low value add feature and the customer is always right. If you have to do this, pay the vendor to do it or get the requirement fed into the vendor product development roadmap. The same applies to open source software for 2 reasons. Firstly, whoever built the application knows it better than anyone else. Secondly, there is a risk of invalidating the software's warranty.

Creepy crawly generator number 2: software being manual deployed. The approach is just prone to human error. It can also be a time stealer. Deploying software manually is a complex business. Developing and maintaining a run book describing such a process in a step-by-step manner, is very time consuming. Manual software deployment requires manual testing to check that the application is stable following a release. I've personally never seen a manual software deployment process that does not need constant correction. The impact of discovering the corrections normally means interrupting the development team to help root cause anything that has gone wrong with the release; resulting in fractional assignment of resources. Manual software deployments are more prone to rollback than software deployed using a repeatable and proven automated method.

Creepy crawly generator number 3: only deploying to production when all the development is complete. This risk of unforeseen bugs is a result of differences between: the environments used to develop and test the software; and the operational environment to run it. Unless the environments are carbon copies there is a likelihood something will come out of the wood work during release. The challenges are further exacerbated when the first time that Operations get to see it hang together, is at the point of release. In the event of problems, Operations have little knowledge of how the compute stack, common services, the applications stack and the network stack interact.

These creepy crawly generators result in latency and inefficiency in the development project's critical chain. The end result is schedule risk, quality risk and issues as a result of unforeseen rework. Now imagine a different scenario. In this scenario, the only actions required to release into production is picking from a list of builds, and pressing a big red command button that says 'build'. In practise, this means a plan for building a factory before building the software product. What would processes in this factory look like and feel like? There would be a turnkey and empirically repeatable process for releasing software products into any environment. Almost every testing and release management process would be automated. Everything needed to build, deploy, test and release any software product would be kept in version control. Anything that did not work would be checked into version control. In a Toyota factory, you will never see faulty products being stored. In the factory, operations and product development are unified in terms of management, process and culture. Processes in the old factory that hurt and caused difficulty at the last minute, were fixed at the last minute. In the new factory, opportunities are identified to experience problem processes more frequently but earlier. Culture, tooling and project organisation is such that a heuristic approach is the norm. According to Wikipedia *'a heuristic technique (/hjʉˈrɪstɪk/; Greek: "Εὑρίσκω", "find" or "discover"), sometimes called simply a heuristic, is any approach to problem solving, learning, or discovery that employs a practical methodology not guaranteed to be optimal or perfect, but sufficient for the immediate goals.'* This is the mindset of the contemporary software development Project Manager.

Stage Ops/Development Ops

Like all great films, King Kong to the onlooker revolved around a small number of actors: Fay Wray as Ann Darrow; Robert Armstrong as Carl Denham; Bruce Cabot as Jack Driscoll; Frank Reicher as Captain Englehorn; Noble Johnson as the Native Chief; Steve Clemente as the Witch Doctor; James Flavin as Briggs; Victor Wong as Charlie the Cook; and Sam Hardy as Charles Weston. But this was not the case. The acting team were unified with stage operations who operated the star of the show whilst laying out the multitude of props.

Height 50ft; face 7ft from hairline to chin; nose 2ft; lips 6ft from corner to corner; brows 4ft; mouth 6ft when smiling; eyes 10in; ears 1ft; legs 15ft; arms 23ft; reach 75ft.

The environment in which the actors performed needed to be prepared as and when the actors needed it. If there were no stage hands, the film stopped, which actors don't like. They tend to storm off set looking for another film to act in. It's the same on a software development project. Development teams need to be unified organisationally and culturally with operations teams. My first Agile project was problematic because operations did not engage until the point of release. They just did not understand the environment or how it was put together. Engaging them throughout the project was a constant challenge due to dealing with the support requests and incidents. From time to time, they'd dip in during the quieter moments but constant context switching between distinct operations setting and development setting is not sustainable. From the outset of the project and throughout its duration, the project's organisational strategy has to strive for unification of development and operations. This approach reduces latency when product gets moved into operational support. Latency is caused by time operations required to learn the environment. Latency is caused by time required by operations to set up configuration management and monitoring of the production environment. Unification of development and operations can result in zero latency caused by these activities at the point of release, thus increasing cycle time which increases beat-the-plan-loving agility.

Solomon Hykes Container Transportation Inc

How the hell did they get 1933 Kong off the boat into a cage before he went on stage? In the naff 1976 remake, they shipped Kong in a container. They put him in the container and moved him from one environment to another. Dockers and containers - guaranteed to speed up deployment from one environment to another. Docker is a container-based technology invented by Solomon Hykes. Docker-based applications run exactly the same on a laptop as they do in production. Because Docker encapsulates the entire state around an application, as a Project Manager I don't have to worry about the risk caused by missing dependencies, or bugs due to architectural differences in the underlying operating system. It is a Project Manager's dream come true. With products like Docker, preparing and executing a release goes from a long blue line on MS Project to a very thin blue line. Always have dock workers who love docker on your development team. If I docker type solution was used on the first agile project I worked then I don't think I'd be writing this chapter.

Eagled-Eyed Producers

It is hard to imagine Merian C. Cooper and Ernest B. Schoedsack tolerating on-going problems slowing down the production of the film. They'd look for the problems, then fix them. How would you quickly determine that you had been given a problem project? Here are some indicators you will find on a software project on a road to nowhere. Identifying them takes less than one working day. You just need to ask the questions.

Testers take a long time to close defects

Defects that were fixed a while back reappear

UAT of user stories seems to take a long time

The production environment inexplicably fails from time to time

Developers hardly ever get to show off what they have built

The project has a history of having to roll back releases

The overtime bill is high or overtime is the norm

No one can recall when the application could be demonstrated without lots of technical preparation

Very few people seem to understand the build and release processes

Email is the main form of communication between developers, testers and end-users

Average number of defects remains consistent on a monthly basis

The technical team are negative when a new feature is requested

Developers do not ask for work. They say, 'Tell me what to do'

The absence of commitment language

If Carl Denham was a software development Project Manager he'd probably say.......

"It's money and adventure and fame. It's the thrill of a lifetime and a long sea voyage that starts at six o'clock tomorrow morning."

Carl Denham, King Kong 1933

FLAVA YOUR IT PROJECT

'But you never know until you try. How things
just might be. If we came together so strongly'

Walls Come Tumbling Down

The Style Council

PUBLIC ENEMY WERE THE MOST emphatic rap group of the 20th Century. Their hard hitting lyrics provide great metaphors on what it takes to deliver, in a memorable and most excellent manner. Don Cornelius is a man who has seen many an interesting and strange site. Don Cornelius is a name not many of you may know. He was the presenter of Soul Train, a music programme from the USA that ran for 35 years showcasing music of black origin from 1971 to 2006. I have watched many episodes. Nothing ever shocked Don Cornelius, even the crazy dancing in the audience. Note the dancing can only be recreated if you've had 10 pints! Whatever the artist or the song, Don Cornelius always remained as cool as a cucumber - even when Johnny Taylor, for Stax Records, starting singing, 'Whose making love to your old lady?' in the 1972! Fifteen years later, a band called Public Enemy turned up on Soul Train, fronted by an excitable guy called Flava Fav with a big clock around his neck, jumping around shouting 'what time is it?' and 'your gonna get yours'. When Public Enemy finished their performance, Don Cornelius had an 'OMG that was special' kind of vibe about him. It's the kind of first impression a 'beat the plan' IT Project Manager needs to make. Public Enemy are known for their hard hitting political messages. Their tracks communicate the frustrations and concerns of the black American community. Public Enemy communicate clear and emphatic messages about how the system disempowered the community they represent. Their message is one of freedom from processes and systems that do not put the needs of people before compliance to the process. So what does a 'process before people' environment feel like? It feels like working on a challenged or impaired IT project.

Hierarchies

Risk aversion

Reports, reports, reports and more reports and pictures

Running to stand still

Lots of meetings with loads of managers who have little to offer to move the project forward

Over-planning

Fixed delivery dates over getting it right

Consensus instead of effective decision making

Paralysis of analysis

A small army of consultants and architects

Thou shalt not be flatulent in the workplace without cost centre approval

Personally speaking, I know when I have had a gutful of process. I have a reoccurring dream that leads me to conclude that I'm taking my job too seriously. In the dream, I am working away on MS Project when someone taps me on the shoulder. I swivel around on my sexy sleek 50 shades of black swivel chair. You know, the type you find in a skip. There standing in front of me is the most beautiful and alluring woman in the world ever, an absolute stunner sent from heaven. She speaks in the sexiest voice you can ever imagine. She wants me to stop working and follow her into a bedroom. She promises me the best 24 hours of nookie in the history of nookie. I say, 'I will be with you in an hour love. Just waiting for a WBS code so I can complete my timesheet.' Flava Flava jumps out waiving his big clock shouting, 'What time is it?! What time is it?!' I wake up thinking I must get a life. I ask my wife to make me a cup of tea and she says, 'Can I have a WBS code?'!

Public Enemy were the most emphatic rap band ever. Today's Project Manager has to be the most emphatic Project Manager in the history of project management. Public Enemy express themselves with emphasis. When they communicate, they are both forceful and positive. The band members are direct and all have emphatic personality. They are sharp and clean. They stress the emphatic points in their argument. So here are 10 emphatic metaphors to help you accelerate your delivery:

THE SONG…Don't Believe The Hype
THE LYRIC…You believe it's true, it blows me through the roof
THE LESSON…When your confidence is greater than your ability, your project will fail in the most spectacular fashion. Surround yourself with people who know their stuff and will tell you that you don't know when you think you know.

THE SONG…Rebel Without a Pause
THE LYRIC… I guess you know you guess I'm just a radical
THE LESSON…Always be a positive skeptic

THE SONG…You're Gonna Get Yours
THE LYRIC… Who is the one some think is great I'm that one
THE LESSON…exude certainty of delivery and certainty on cost without saying anything

THE SONG…Fight the Power
THE LYRIC… Yet our best trained, best educated, best equipped, best prepared, refuse to fight. Some might say they prefer to switch.
THE LESSON…The status quo will get in the way of your delivery. Empower your team

THE SONG…Shut 'em Down
THE LYRIC… Money in it, Corporations owe, Dey gotta give up the dough
THE LESSON…A project with no business case is not worth doing. An emphatic PM will shut it down

THE SONG…Harder Than You Think
THE LYRIC… You don't stand for something, you fall for anything, harder than you think It's a beautiful thing
THE LESSON…Obstacles are put in our way to help us become great

THE SONG…Can't Truss IT
THE LYRIC… 3 months pass, they brand a label on my ass
THE LESSON…Complex IT never works first time when used for the first time at the point your client needs IT most

THE SONG…He Got Game
THE LYRIC… There's something happening here. What it is aint exactly clear
THE LESSON…Listen to those who tell it like it is. They are the difference between project success and failure

THE SONG…Public Enemy Number One
THE LYRIC… A time for a crime that I can't find
THE LESSON…Risk is public enemy number one. The greatest risk is the risk you cannot see

THE SONG…Welcome to the Terrordome
THE LYRIC… I got so much trouble on my mind. Refuse to lose. Move as a team. Never move alone
THE LESSON….The lyric

Public Enemy are interesting and exciting. People gravitate towards things to do that interest and excite them. Therefore, the opposite has to be true. If the IT project is not exciting, fun or interesting, then people will be less inclined to spend time working on it. It is all well and good sticking a name against a blue bar but without an understanding of propensity to do the work, the project plan contains less certainty. Public Enemy are relevant in the eyes of their fans. There are millions of them. The IT project has to be relevant to everyone involved. Public Enemy preached a message of change to make a difference to people's lives. Everyone on the critical path needs to understand the difference they are making and why their contribution is relevant. How many IT project teams really get to see the true impact their efforts have on customers? The team needs to understand their importance and feel what they do is relevant. Public Enemy communicate their message with a sense of urgency with a 'time is running out' feel. Teams tend to perform better in a metaphorical do or die situation. There has to be a real incentive for doing well and a real 'kick in the balls' consequence for not doing well. At the start of the Public Enemy track Fight the Power, there is a speech, a quote from a 1967 Thomas TNT Todd speech about Vietnam deserters: 'Yet our best trained, best educated, best equipped, best prepared troops refuse to fight. As a matter of fact, it's safe to say that they would rather switch than fight.' The same thing happens in organisations that do not address inherent structural deficiency and rigidity that leads to poor IT project performance. The organisation leaks technical talent. What you've got to do is become the Soul Brother number 1 of the IT project management world.

It's 1989 and I am in the venue De-montefort Hall, Leicester, watching Public Enemy live. Their set kicks off with Rebel Without A Pause. I'm watching Flava Fav jump around on an 8ft Marshall speaker. He has a big clock around his neck. Behind him is Professor Griff with his team of enforcers marching in unison. You can disagree with their politics but what you cannot doubt is their sense of total unity about who they are, why they are there, their purpose and what they stand for. If Public Enemy were an IT project delivery team, they would beat the plan every time. Two decades later, Public Enemy is playing on the Holt Stage at Glastonbury. At the same time, I am fighting the 'process over people' to ensure a client's IT programme flourishes. I am looking to the future. That's where my head is at. Flava Flav once said exactly the same thing. IT Project Manager 2015+ is a clock watching rebel with a cause.

GAMIFICATION FUTURE SAVVY PART 2: LEARN THE ZX PROJECT DELIVERY EXPERIENCE

'I want to beat the....'

Space Invaders

The Piranhas

RALPH BAER WHO INVENTED THE game concept, Pong, and the first game console, Magnavox Odyssey, is quoted as saying, "There's a craftsmanship and art form to creating games." The same could be said of IT Project Management, given the myriad of different types of projects involving information technology. IT Project Management is generally linked to the corporate world, where the aim is to deliver some technology for processing transactions to improve the performance of a business process. Information technology has also spawned creative industries whose ways of working and digital inventions are crossing over. It is not beyond the realms of possibility that you may find yourself involved in this kind of project. Peter Drucker, a founder of modern management once said, "Today knowledge has power.

It controls access to opportunity and advancement." So here is a chapter on some useful meanderings you will find at the point where the creative industries that have emerged from the dawn of the digital, have crossed over into the corporate world. One such concept is called Gamification.

It is 2014, and not for the first time my wife is nagging me about the space that one of my magazine collections takes up - over twenty years worth of magazines, to be exact. Those magazines are an archive of the history of video games since 1994. How can I just throw them away? Something happened in 1994 in the home video entertainment market, namely, the release of the Sony Playstation. This was a giant leap in processing power from the 16bit dominance of Sega and Nintendo, to 32bit. So much for the Sega Megadrive and Super Nintendo consoles. Rewind 12 years back to 1982 and I'm programming in a game on ZX Sinclair Spectrum with 48k RAM and an 8bit central processing unit. 8 years later, Sega and Nintendo start to do the same damage to the European home computing market that Sony will do to them in 4 years time. When I got my 'speccy' for Christmas, I had no idea I'd be given something that led to the creation of the billionaire dollar industry we see today. I found that out when I watched a documentary called Bedroom to Billions, a documentary about how the early Sinclair, Commodore, Atari and BBC computers, to name a few, created the home video entertainment industry. OK back to the magazine conundrum. I couldn't just throw them away; all that history about the consoles and the games just discarded for some shredding machine to digest. Every year, a company called Retro Revival Events (RRE) runs an expo where you can play on all the antiquated computers and consoles. So there I am like a kid in a candy shop and I see this section run by the Retro Gaming Museum. I think that's interesting - I would love to visit a museum like that. Then I see their address; they are based in Leicester where I live! In fact, they are 20 minutes from my house. Small world or what. Then it hits me - I will donate my magazine collection to a museum. Problem solved and I will have made my contribution to preserving a piece of history. Earlier that same week, I'm having lunch with my favourite entrepreneur. One day, he will be a millionaire but today I'm going to argue with him again. He shows me a prototype Citizen Centric smartphone app hooked into social media, where you can photograph a street scene problem and off it goes into a cloud SaaS CRM application for the local council to access. The data gets fed into some open source big data app flux capacitor for sentiment analysis type shenanigans. It is all very clever with the potential to save Local Government a few sheckles to keep George Osborne happy. Then I ask him a question all digital entrepreneurs fear: Given all the apps that one could download and use, why would anyone want to use yours? He responds, "I'm going to use gamification." For those who don't know what gamification is, it is the use of game mechanics to engage a customer, keep their attention and drive desired behaviours. Basically, these companies want to neuro-linguistic-programme you to buy their products and services. It is all a bit too Stepford Wiveseque but an effective digital marketing technique nonetheless. So being very knowledgable about how computer games have been produced and published since 1981, I ask my good friend, "Do you know how to make a computer game?" He looked at me perplexed along the lines of why do I need to know how to do that uber geeky stuff? He gave me a woolly mammoth answer about using Agile. True, those great games from the 8 bit days were the product of an Agile process in its purest form where products were developed in bedrooms and garages. However, making a game or even elements of a game does require the delivery of processes, organisations and products that would be very alien to a business software development team. What subsequently followed was a conversation whereby I told my friend about the stories behind some of the greatest games ever made. He kind of pretended to be interested just to keep me happy! Then I told him that the game mechanics we see in gamification evolved from video games. These mechanics include points, leaderboards, avatars, levels, missions, challenges, quests, avatars, rewards, naming badges and experience points to name a few. I say evolved because before video games, there were board and card games that used similar systems.

Back to Retro Revival Event. At these events, they hold seminars from some of the greatest game designers and producers from days gone by. They can talk about the game development process from an informed perspective because they invented it. I tell my good friend that at the weekend I'm going to meet John Romero, the guy who gave us the first person shooter. Again, he looked at me perplexed along the lines of, why are you telling me this? Now I have two choices:give up on him; or tell him that if he does not employ the process that a guy like John Romero employed to make a game, the gamification in his app will be (to coin a phrase) 'pants'. Fortunately for him, I took the sensei schifu asharifa choice. So what followed was a conversation about taking a business software development team following the principles of Agile then slightly reorienting it to deliver gamification. I've kind of come up with the basics of organising and managing the gamification requirements in a business type application development. This chapter is my attempt to demystify the process of managing and delivering gamification scope. Why have I done this? I've done this because gamification is becoming more and more prevalent in the development of digital products for interacting with suppliers, customers and employees. Gamification is all around us: in politics; retail; e-commerce; healthcare; human resource management; and the not-for-profit sector. It is not beyond the realms of possibility that you may be asked to deliver an IT project or programme, whose scope includes gamification. So here the key stages in a gamification project that a Project Manager needs to shape. Oops, I mean producer.

Central Cavern

Inception Deck Game on

A project will be more susceptible to failure when the team believes there is consensus when, in fact, there is none. Successful game developments do two things very well before pressing ahead: the team makes sure they are all 'on the same page'; and they ask the tough questions up front. An inception deck consists of 9 exercises, the first being the 'Commanders Intent'. A Commanders Intent is a mission statement. Mission statements help govern every decision in a creative project. In a creative project, lots of ideas are possible candidates for transition into features within the game. But you can't do everything, and lots of time can be wasted arguing the toss about whether or not the feature should move into production. A Commanders Intent helps answer the question by asking another question: Will the development of a feature help us achieve the Commanders Intent?

Next up is the elevator pitch. The elevator pitch is a kind of mini business case. It's a couple of lines that state what the gamification project is doing, why and for whom. The theory goes that if you cannot differentiate the digital product using the gamification solution, the project is not worth doing.

For [target customer]—Explains who the gamification solution is for or who would benefit from playing our game.

Who [statement of need or opportunity]—Elaborates the problem the player has and why we are using gamification to encourage the player to solve it.

The [product name]—Gives life to our digital product by naming it. Names are vital because a great name communicates intent.

Is a [product category]—Explains what the gamification solution actually is or does.

That [key benefit, compelling reason to buy]—Explains why our player would want to purchase the gamified digital product.

Unlike [primary competitive alternative]—Covers why a customer wouldn't already use what's out there.

Our product [statement of primary differentiation] — Articulates why our digital product is awesome and beats the competition. This is the reason that's the difference between moving into production and not moving into production.

If a gamer could buy the gamification element of the digital product off the retail shelf, what would the game box look like? Would a gamer buy it and why? That is essentially the point behind the 'product box' exercise. What the team are doing here is converting what they think could be gamification features, into benefits. This allows the team to envisage at a very high-level what the gamification product could be, and what is so compelling about it. This process helps sets the team's production goals and again elaborates the hard questions. Why would gamification be a benefit? Why would our customer consider gamification of the digital product to be a benefit? Why would gamification increase customer propensity or inclination to use the underlying digital product?

Hindsight is a wonderful thing but there is also a problem with hindsight; it is useless at preventing the failure in the first place. A more valuable exercise is the post-production pre-mortem. The pre-mortem is like a post-mortem but done before we have started the project. The key trigger for the post-production pre-mortem is to ask the the question, "What keeps the gamification development team up at night?"

The aim is a future memory exercise to gain valuable insight upfront namely, the doings that the team don't want to happen. These matters need to be out in the open, so the development team can start to think about how to stop them happening.

Creative projects are at risk of trying to do too much with not enough time. So the team need to think about what is going to give i.e. scope, time, budget or quality. And more importantly, think about the risk to customer experience and related objectives gamification is designed to achieve. These objectives are fostering engagement, inspiring customer loyalty and retaining customers.

Definition of done (DOD) is exactly what it means. How will you know your gamification project is done? Definition of done is a bullet point list describing what 'done' looks like and feels like.

Working out what exactly is out of scope and what the project team are not going to do, can save lots of time and arguments. We've all done projects where the stakeholders have asked, 'Can we do this?' or 'Why aren't we doing that?' and then the team have to come up with detailed explanations or proof that it was previously discussed. To avoid this, it is prudent to communicate what the project team are not doing.

The last part of the inception deck is working out the production's neighbours – people in the organisation who would most likely have a vested interest in our gamification project. Having completed the inception deck the cold room beckons....

The Cold Room

3 Stage Urban Legend

There is a level in a famous ZX Spectrum game (that will remain nameless) that has wasted more hours than any other game I know. When the game came out, there was a rumour it could be done in 3 moves. Of course, it was completes lies and impossible but some people believed it. Gamification projects broadly follow the 3 stages found in a traditional game development. Understanding these stages will help you shape the project plan. Game development has evolved by using movie production as a reference model. In a gamification centric project the title of Project Manager is not the norm. The job title becomes Producer.

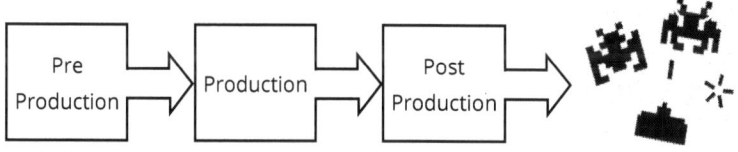

In the pre-production stage, the designs are drawn up. Evolutionary proto-types for demo purposes are produced. In the pre-production stage, the technology and tools are stood up. Gamification and game development requires art. So art direction i.e. the way the art needs to be produced, is understood and planned for. Production is the stage where the team is scaled up to full size. Your role is to oversee the scheduling and logistics. In the production stage, the programmers finalise the tools and technology. Artists focus on creating the digital art, animate characters and assets. Gamification involves a lot of designing and building levels within the gamification element of digital product. Sound engineers do all the work to make the experience aurally engaging. As the development proceeds, testers engage in software quality assurance. Post production primarily involves all the activities to localise the game experience for the foreign territories where the customers live. The last stage of post production is about distributing and launching the digital product which includes the gamification element.

The Menagerie

Level Up & Power Up

Depending on the extent of the gamification, a variety of roles and specialist resources are needed. These resources fall into 8 families: design; development; art; sound; testing; behavioural SME; localisation; and marketing.

Design	Lead designer
	Writer
	Level designer
	Mission designer
Development	Lead programmer
	Tools programmer
	Engine programmer
	Artificial intelligence programmer
	Graphic programmer
	Content developer
	Technical Support
	Network Support
Artists	Character artist
	Animator
	Texture artist
	Background artist
Sound	Musician
	Sound engineer
Testing	Test Manager
	Game tester
Behavioural	Psychologist
	Loyalty expert
Localisation & Marketing	Localisation Manager
	Brand Manager

Abandoned Uranium Workings

Don't go to Ravensholme

Ravensholme is a place you don't want to go to. In the world of gamification and game development, Ravensholme represents the graveyard of failed projects. Quite a few are in there because they chose to build a gamification engine in-house. Coding gaming applications is a complex business nowadays fraught with risk. Running with a gamification provider mitigates these risks. Basically, your team gets a turnkey proven gamification toolset offering the analytics, processing power, flexibility and scalability. Your team also gets a team of experts on-hand to support the development team. Acquiring this capability leaves the project to focus on what really delivers the value:

1. Homing in on behaviours to reward
2. Level definition and point scoring mechanism
3. Thinking through rules for achievement and rewards.

The Processing Plant
Watch your stats

Delivering gamification is more than just making the game bit. On your plan, there needs to work packages which deliver the analytics engine. The project paymasters will want to see how gamification is driving the behaviours to achieve the business objectives. This means the project will need to design, build, test and deploy an analytics solution into the organisation, that is, a solution to help the organisation understand customer engagement and retention metrics. Such a project has all the hallmarks of a big data type of implementation. But I will leave the detail for another chapter.

The Final Barrier
A Suspension of Disbelief

In the world of digitisation, gamification is about encouraging customer loyalty towards the use of a digital channel. It is about encouraging the masses or converting one-time customers tobecome repeat visitors. It is about rewarding them for visiting, sharing, buying, contributing and offering feedback etc. IT projects become challenging when those asking for the project or benefiting from the project, are no longer engaged. They've become loyal to something else going on in the organisation. To beat the plan, you have to keep them loyal. Understanding gamification will lead to a greater understanding of social loyalty. Loyalty to your project is priceless and needs to be nurtured. Everyone you need to get the project delivered, has a basic need to be recognised for achievement. When recognised for achieving actions that directly linked to making the project a success, they will keep engaging. Visualisation of progress is central to the success of any IT project. Take two highlight reports. The first will tell the world what has been achieved and what needs to be achieved. The second will tell the reader what they achieved to help the project achieve. Now ask yourself this question: Which type of highlight report will they be more inclined to read the following week? Which type of highlight report will make them more inclined to phone you up and offer help?

The secret of a good game is it has to make you want to play it, and keep playing it. It just has to avoid — the first five minutes sometimes — it has to avoid annoying you so much that you don't want to play it again. And... er, a really good game that's fun to play, even if you're not very good at it. And also it must carry on being fun to play when you are very good at it.

Matthew Smith 2005

Manic Miner and Jet Set Willy

Swap the word 'game' for IT Project

```
                ####
                ####
            #########
            #########
            #########
            #########
             ##   ####
             ##   ####
            #########
             ########
              ########
              ########
                ####
                #####
              #######
              #######
            ###########
            ###########
          ################
          ################
        ####################
        ####################
        ####   ########   ####
        ####   ########   ####
              ##########
              ##########
           ##   ####   ######
           ##   ####   ######
          ######        ####
          ######        ####
           ##          ######
           ##          ######
```

WHAT NOT TO HAVE ON THE CRITICAL PATH

"Come into my parlour," said the spider to the
fly... "I have something... "

Lullaby

The Cure

A CRITICAL PATH IS THE MINIMUM amount of time needed
for the completion of the project. Moving at the pace
necessary to achieve the critical path invariably means
keeping off the path, those things that will slow you down.
Popular culture is filled with many tales of straying from the
path when you were told not to, or embarking on a path only
to encounter the unexpected. Impaired and challenged IT
projects suffer from the same fate. Either someone points out
very early on in the project that it would be ill advised to follow
a certain path only, to be ignored; or the team encounters a 'we
did not expect that' moment. There are many names for these
scenarios. We hear the terminology everyday e.g. curveball,
sucker punch and pear-shaped, to name a few. This chapter is
not about clairvoyance but there are indicators and behaviours

you can watch for, that may mean your IT project is on a road to nowhere or you are the Piper of Hamlet taking the team to a storm of the century Croatoan destination. Your critical path could be a yellow brick road full of scary surprises.

Scarecrows

Scarecrows are creepy old things. Never really warmed to them as a kid; they tended to freak me out. In the 1939 film, Wizard of Oz, Dorothy encounters one, quite a friendly type of character but definitely in a decrepit old state on the verge of falling to bits. More than anything the Scarecrow wishes he had a brain. A scarecrow represents two things. Firstly, poorly performing IT tools and equipment. You know the type - equipment on the verge of falling to bits because the organisation skimped on funding. Equipment whose performance is akin to the physical state of a scarecrow results in the IT project's critical chain becoming inefficient. Time and money are wasted on fixing things instead of building things. To beat the plan, an understanding of the IT project's critical chain is necessary. Greater focus should be placed on how the tools influence the performance of the project's critical chain. Traditional IT project management tends to focus its teachings on understanding critical path. The second metaphor for the scarecrow is inexperience. According to Wizard of Oz folklore, the scarecrow is only two days old. IT projects are either impaired or challenged because inexperienced resources are placed on the critical path. Without sufficient slack to accommodate learning from mistakes or support for coaching, poor quality and a subsequent need for rework are the likely outcomes.

Tin Folk

The Tin Man in the Wizard of Oz had no heart. He also looked like a prototype Cyberman for the BBC series, Dr Who.

The last thing you need on a critical path are people who won't do anything without a prescriptive set of painting-by-numbers instructions. Now I am not talking about documented and repeatable method statements. The theory goes that clever technical people are at their best when empowered, delivering a stretched goal on the cusp of their comfort zone and given an outcome to work towards. So watch for the technical person who asks you for a list of things to do and documentation about how to do it. When a technical step snags, the work stops until the PM or a technical manager they report into, sorts it out. After all its your list not theirs. The rate of technical SME ranges from £350 – £900 per day. For that amount of money, you'd think they would have standard documentation describing how they should go about delivering technical works.

A Sheep in a Lion's Clothing

My black cat looks like a mean lean slick ninja hunting machine. However, when faced with a floppy fluffy pet rabbit for the first time, it ran and hid in the shed. The last member of Dorothy's party to slow her down on her travels was a lion with no courage. Successful IT projects have strong teams who have the necessary courage to change what can be changed, and to endure what cannot. An IT Project Manager or team that lacks courage won't beat the plan.

Awkwardly Tense Locals Who Won't Be Heard

1981 saw the release of the John Landis horror film, An American Werewolf in London. As a result of the special effects, John Landis went on to direct Michael Jackson's Thriller video. Two American students, Jack Goodman and David Kessler backpack across the Yorkshire moors and then visit a pub called 'The Slaughtered Lamb'. The locals are very suspicious. After Jack asks a question about a pentagram, the pub falls silent. A local played by Brian Glover warns Jack and David, "Beware the moon, lads. Keep to the road." Unfortunately, they do not heed the advice and end up as a werewolf's supper. Jack ends up in purgatory because he died an unnatural death. David becomes the next werewolf. They should have listened to the locals. Impaired and challenged IT projects can start with a similar 'Slaughtered Lamb' moment. For the avoidance of doubt, I am in no way implying poorly performing IT projects contain hairy people with big teeth. But they may contain awkwardly tense locals who are ignored. There is always a senior end user or technical person who, as a result of 5+ years experience, knows the current architecture inside out. They will start to make subtle comments about the viability of the new solution. The comments become less subtle if they are ignored. Addressing these concerns before moving out of design and into a build stage could be the difference between project success or project failure.

Mythical Shortcuts

Stephen King is an author of horror and suspense. According to Wikipedia, his books have sold over 350 million copies worldwide. September 2013 sees the release of Dr Sleep, the follow up to The Shining. I've read most of his books. There are two stories from a Stephen King anthology: Skeleton Crew published in 1985 that reminds me of experiences on impaired or challenged IT project deliveries; and The Mist, which sees an American town engulfed in a strange mist. A crowd of people are trapped in a Supermarket. In the face of incontrovertible proof that the mist contains a bunch of creepy viscous creatures, a group leaves the supermarket and heads straight into the mist. Needless to say they end up as lunch. The group suffered from hubris. Hubris can be defined as extreme arrogance. Hubris indicates a loss of contact with what is really going on. Hubris is an overestimation of one's own competence. Poorly performing

IT projects can be the result of pressing full steam ahead, without any appreciation of the challenges ahead or learning from what happened the last time the team headed off into the fog. In the story called Mrs Todd's Shortcut, a busy lady who is always pressed for time constantly seeks ways to save time. Mrs Todd discovers a worm hole through a distorted reality to cut the journey time down on a regular trip. Her driver experiences the jaunt. On the trip, he notices strange looking and ugly wildlife. He warns Mrs Todd not to use the shortcut. Mrs Todd does not listen. The following day Mrs Todd does not return. The story represents those one-off risky short cuts that IT projects take in the belief that they will save time or make time. Classic examples include: skimping on testing; plugging a network in on the day it is needed and expecting it to work first time; or not rehearsing a complex data migration.

Murphy's IT Law

IT will never work first time when you need it to.

LEARN SIEM PROJECT BASICS: LOCKING OUT GUS GORMAN & DAVID LIGHTMAN

'Intruder Alert'

Stakker Humanoid

NORAD MID 80s - THE American military are watching the screens for Russians launching ICBMs. NATO is on DEFCON 3. Films like 'Threads' and 'The Day After' are constantly on the TV. CND are protesting daily across the UK. David Lightman, an American teenager, gets home from high school. He has invited a girlfriend around; they go into his bedroom. He shows off his computer equipment and hacking skills to impress. The TCL prompts, 'Do you want to play a game?' and gives David a list. He opts for Thermonuclear War. The screens in NORAD suddenly show vectors coming from the east and all hell breaks loose. Of course, this did not really happen. It is a scene from the 1983 film 'Wargames', starring Matthew Broderick playing a hacker who accidently logs into WOPR (War Operation Plan Response). The computer plays out a simulation of a first nuclear strike by Russia. However, the

American military do not know that that it is merely a computer game. In the same year, a chap called Gus Gorman, gets a job on minimal wage as a data processor for a multi-national. Gus discovers he has an aptitude for computer programming. He works out how to transfer minute fractions of digital cash into a single back account from hundreds of thousands of daily transactions. Within days he becomes very rich. The only way the company knows is when he turns up to work in an expensive sports car. Again this did not really happen. It is a scene from the 1983 film 'Superman III' starring Richard Pryor, who plays Gus Gorman.

These stories are the urban myths and fables that have led to the creation of the IT Security industry (along with some great games). Now known as the cyber security industry, analysts predict the industry will be worth $155 billion by the year 2019. There was a time when IT security was a tick in the box afterthought on an IT project. It was a bit of a nice-to-have to keep the internal auditors happy. Today, every IT project's mandatory requirement set will involve demonstrating, and continuing to demonstrate, compliance against a mandated security standard e.g. ISO 27001 and PCI to name a few. Robbing a bank with a gun is too hard nowadays; all that surveillance and physical security. Only stupid people rob banks like that. The best way to score nowadays is cybercrime. The techniques are easy to learn and easy to get away with if you know what you are doing. Unlike criminals of yesteryear, the hacker does not have to be a hard man. In fact, when you see these guys in court you feel sorry for them. You do not want the judge to send them to prison. So given the rise in cybercrime, along with its coverage in the news, we have seen the emergence of security incident and event management (SIEM) applications. It is now not uncommon to have to deal with IT security specialists and consultants on a daily basis. The good ones always recommend a password policy of 8 characters long. They eat their own dog food you know. Most will set their password to 'snow white and the seven dwarves'. Just ask one, next time you get to work with one. Anyway, what follows is a guide to implementing an SIEM application, with some hints and tips on working with IT security folk. Cybersecurity has become an intrinsic part of IT project delivery. Learning about implementing SIEM will provide you with some basic tools and knowledge to deliver robust cybersecurity in any IT project.

There are some key terms used in cybersecurity project language that are useful to understand, the first being controls.

Controls either prevent, detect or deter hackers like David Lightman and the inside man, Gus Gorman. There are also virtual versions of David Lightman and Gus Gorman trying to infiltrate corporate systems i.e. viruses, worms and Trojans. Controls come in two flavours: physical e.g. door locks and security guards; and logical e.g. firewalls, password systems, encryption, intrusion detection systems and authentication etc. A SIEM solution is a logical control that integrates with network devices and hosts i.e. servers, virtual appliances to monitor and analyse activity. Around the SIEM solution is a process that acts on any incidents or suspicious activity reported by the SIEM application.

The attack space is a term used to describe the total area of a computer system that could be attacked. An attack vector is a point on the attack space. Network devices are hosts are potential attack vectors in the attack space.

The attack life-cycle describes the stages in a security event. You may hear the attack life-cycle referred to as a cyber kill chain.

A SIEM project is not just about implementing the SIEM solution; there is much more to it than that. It is about understanding the risks faced by the organisation, then implementing a SIEM solution as capability to mitigate the risk. In Wargames, no one thought that some teenager hacking into WOPR accidentally was a possibility. In Superman III, no one thought those fractions of a dollar could be converted into cash. It's our old friend, the Douglas Adams quote holding true here: 'A common mistake that people make when trying to design something completely fool proof is to underestimate the ingenuity of complete fools.' SIEM solution, process and organisation combines to become the organisation's eyes and ears across the attack space, looking for ingenious fools trying their luck and eliminating vulnerabilities.

Leading a SIEM implementation project starts with a Lord of the 7 Rings mindset. Gandalf comes to you and asks you to build helms deep. The design and build will very much depend on understanding the attackers. So for each type of attacker, the SIEM project executes the following stages:

Discovery

Scoping

Solution design

Deployment

Optimisation

In the discovery stage, the aim is to identify why an organisation needs a SIEM solution. There are generally 4 reasons driving the requirements:

Getting rid of the threats and vulnerabilities before anyone uses them.

Understanding the current level of threat and risk. Speeding up the time it takes to minimise the impact of an event from the point it is identified to the point it is dealt with.

Complying to regulatory or contractual requirements.

Protecting the organisation's reputation and assets.

Protect the organisation's customers' reputation and assets.

The most effective way to elaborate the requirements is through the use of business use cases in a workshop format. You need some key people to play the following roles. Note some roles lend themselves to being combined.

A security consultant

These wise guys understand the methodology that needs to be followed to achieve and sustain compliance.

A workshop facilitator

Cyber security is an emotive, subjective and quite boring topic. Excellent facilitation is required to ensure everyone remains focused and interested.

A business analyst

Analysis in the cyber security domain generates lots of needs, questions and desires. A BA is needed to ensure requirements are properly documented, understood, version controlled and effectively prioritised.

Whoever is paying for the project

Unless the project is delivering the next best security as a service solution (SECaaS), solution SIEM does not make money. It is an investment to reduce the risk of materially high financial consequences in the event of a major security breach. The potential loss in the event of breach will be astronomically higher than the investment. Discovery reminds the budget holder why the investment is necessary. Without an understanding of the potentially catastrophic consequences, the project is unlikely to secure the budget it needs to deliver an effective solution.

Whoever gets in trouble because of a lack of cyber security

These are the people who are accountable for the consequences in the event of incident. A SIEM project needs c-level advocates to ensure the wider organisation gives it the attention it deserves.

Those with knowledge of the risks faced by the organisation

A SIEM solution needs to be designed to mitigate, or ideally avoid, the riskiest nearest proximity threats and vulnerabilities. You need people in the workshop with this knowledge and insight.

Technical experts with in-depth knowledge of the attack vectors

SIEM solutions log and monitor events from many many different types of technologies, physical and virtual, the latest being software defined network (SDN). Each of the technologies' devices have their own unique way of capturing data on who or what is doing what.

A SIEM expert

Implementing SIEM is a complex business for the

uninitiated. There are many opportunities to solve the wrong problem in the right way - which will waste time. Having a consultant or coach on hand to help the team through the process on implementing SIEM, will pay off.

Scoping is a stage involving the usual activities you would expect to find on any IT project. There is one difference, though, in a SIEM project. The emphasis on scoping is bounding the scope of the events to be monitored, logged and correlated. It's about determining ease of access to the log data generated on the attack vectors, then making a decision on the viability of going after it. This is the stage when the project team needs to assess whether or not the operational data source contains the content to meet the requirements. The principle here is only collect what you need to collect. The effort and complexity involved in the delivery of SIEM project is sensitive to volume of data and the structure of data being fed into the SIEM solution. Bounding the scope effectively reduces the level of unforeseen project activity to filter out the white noise. During the scoping stage, there will always be someone who says, "Let's just log everything, then filter out what we don't need." That's OK if the project team consists of technicians with privileges, and the time to reconfigure the configuration of the devices being monitored. However, in today's organisation, anything in production cannot be touched without formal change management. A non-emergency change normally has a lead time of 5-10 working days, which results in latency being introduced onto the SIEM project's critical path.

When it comes to solution design there are 3 options; buy, build or use a managed service. Nobody builds their own SIEM solution anymore for obvious reasons. 'Buy' involves the procurement of COTS software, either hosted on premise or in the cloud i.e. security as a service (SECaaS). Using a managed service involves procuring a service from a third party to provide an end-to-end SIEM solution. Either way, all you need to do is follow standard practice for being cloud solutions or COTS software. Just pay special attention to what the provider needs the customer to do so that the data gets generated with the content and in the format required by the SIEM solution. Otherwise, when the end user first tries to run the reports, the project runs the risk of lots of white space. The £150-200 per hour supplier consultant will offer some totally brilliant and insightful advice. 'The reports are blank because there are no events being generated. Please pay us as we have proven the solution works.' Really? To get value for money, consider making payment to the supplier conditional on supplying the attack vector configuration, along with method statement for generating events for consumption by the reports. Part of the solution is the solution that will prove the reports; alerting, correlation, dashboards, aggregation and data archiving functionality all do what they say on the tin.

Deployment involves the installation of the SIEM solution. Do not deploy a SIEM solution until first configuring the event sources to provide the data into the SIEM solution. Otherwise, when the SIEM solution gets deployed it just won't do anything. What will follow is a period of turning on the event sources in a piecemeal manner. This will elongate the testing stage. In effect, the testing stage becomes a bit stop start. To effectively test the SIEM solution, its functionality needs multiple data sources with technical resources on hand to optimise the configuration of the devices and hosts being monitored. Testing a SIEM should follow the ISEB V-model approach. Primary focus should be placed on service validation testing because it's the processes for managing the possible impact of an event of interest, that ultimately mitigates the risk. Just testing and proving that the SIEM application provides the necessary functionality, is half the picture. A best-in-class SIEM project acceptance criteria will include proving the process design to mitigate the risks, driving the need for a SIEM solution.

Optimisation is a tuning process. Firstly, tune the data feeds. Secondly, tune the business processes that are triggered as a result of identifying an event of interest, which may be an indicator that a kill chain has started. The most pragmatic point to close the SIEM project is at the point it moves from deployment into optimisation. Optimisation is an iterative process. So an aim of the project is really to deliver capacity and capability so that SIEM can be sustained on an ongoing basis. This means delivering people, process and technology outputs so that SIEM just becomes a matter-of-fact ongoing BAU process. A SIEM project increments the organisations cyber security capability and adherence to regulation.

The SIEM project sets the precedents for the performance of the ongoing process once the project has been delivered. If there are any deficits in the product from the problem, then there is a risk they will become inculcated into the daily way of working. In that situation, two things happen post-project closure. Either the SIEM process becomes defunct; or it just gets lip services. When this happens, the project cannot be classed as a successful project. There are several gotchas the team need to watch for during the delivery. Otherwise the project is at risk of churning out a solution that will fail. The first scenario is called constantly and continuously looking for a needle in a haystack. This happens when the project delivers solution that monitors and logs masses and masses of non value add information. Solutions that are boring or inefficient to use don't get used. The second scenario is called 'no training no use'. To the uninitiated,SIEM solutions are not intuitive to use. Vendors believe they are; but that is because they live and breath the solution on a daily basis. On-going training is a must and not a nice-to-have. The project must lead on delivering, learning and development for the SIEM solution. Otherwise, the SIEM solution won't get used or even worse, misused. The effectiveness and longevity of a SIEM solution depends on what risks were focused on during discovery. There is a tendency to focus on current threats only. A pragmatic eye on the future leads to a project delivering a better quality solution.

So there you have it - the basics of a SIEM project. Experiencing the delivery of a SIEM project is great way of moving up the cyber security learning curve very quickly. Every IT project you will ever do will need to have an element of cyber security in its scope.

'Computers rule the world today. And the fellow that can fool the computers, can rule the world himself.'

Ross Webster Played by Robert Vaughn
Superman III 1983

PERSPECTIVES PART 1: BREAKING BAD GOVERNANCE IN AN AGILE WORLD

By Saul Cozens

I wanted the book to contain a few chapters that would provide an external perspective on the world of IT project management. I've known Saul for several years and he sees the world of IT project delivery from a less mechanistic point of view. This is why I approached Saul Cozens an agile coach and digital strategist. So here is a piece on how governance needs to change because the corporate world needs to be agile. As always he gave me food for thought. Saul is currently supporting the CTO and the Technology Team at Comic Relief as they continue their Agile transformation programme. Every organisation embarking on a transition to Agile needs a Saul Cozens otherwise suppliers and customers end up calling the other Saul from the series Breaking Bad. DP.

FOR THE PAST 20 YEARS or so, since Bill Gates realised his dream of a computer on every desk, the provision of IT systems within businesses and organisations has been driven by the desire to reduce costs. IT managers have been striving to make every desktop, every application, every system, the same in order to better manage them. This is why, in many large corporate environments, the PC is locked down in order to prevent those pesky staff changing things, putting photos on their desktop, making the mouse pointer larger, installing some useful piece of software. All of those changes make each PC different, individual, personal and of course, more difficult to manage. If the PC goes wrong someone will have to think about how to fix it rather than simply replacing it with another identical black box. This standardisation of the desktop makes it a commodity and allows the cost to be driven down by both in-house IT teams and external outsourced providers However, the push to commoditise software has gone beyond desktop PCs and extended into the provision of business systems and applications. It is normal now for an 'Enterprise Architecture' to define the technology that a business application will be

- implemented on before anything else about the application is known. This

- commoditisation of business applications means that the costs of building and

- maintaining that application can be reduced.

However cost isn't only thing that organisations look to reduce through standardisation. They also look to commoditisation to reduce risks. The thinking goes - if the solution to a business system is standard, then it must be more easily defined and therefore delivered by an external provider. Traditionally any project can be defined by just three attributes
- scope (what it is), time (when it will be delivered) and cost (the money). These three attributes act in tension with each other - the project management triangle – where changing any one will have an impact on the other two. If you want it delivered sooner, it will cost more or it won't do all the things it

was supposed to. If you want a new feature, it will be delivered later and cost more, etc. External providers seek to fix the three corners of the project management triangle to give you the confidence in their ability to deliver. They set out a contract to deliver the defined solution to a fixed time and budget no matter what happens, whether flood, plague or meteorite strike, the provider will deliver the solution. This is seen by the customers as a good thing as it appears to take away their risk. However, when a project needs to change, even a little, the deadline shifts or perhaps a new essential feature is identified the provider has three options, they either:

1. pass the impact (the additional cost, time delay) on to the customer. This makes them look bad

2. absorb the impact themselves, effectively taking it out of their profit on the project. They really don't like doing this

3. Try and squeeze the change in without it impacting the project cost, time or scope putting pressure on the delivery team to work faster and cut corners

As you can imagine, this third option is where most end up. However, it is not without consequences. Most of these consequences fall on the fourth corner of the project management triangle. The one that is most often not considered as it is more difficult to define - that is quality. It is because it is difficult to define that is so often sacrificed. It is commonly considered to be whether the solution passes a number of tests, but a binary pass/fail approach doesn't help fit the real world analogue better/worse understanding of quality. An 'I'll know it when I see it' quality assessment is just as unhelpful. So we need a expression of quality that we can measure. One way is to consider the quality of a solution to be a measure of how well it does its job. That isn't perhaps all that much more helpful until we note that most solutions have quite well defined benefits, the things that the solution is intended to enable. They are not generally about the solution but about the business drivers for the solution. Things like: Reduce the operating cost of our customer contact centre by £2.4M by making 80% of customer detail updates self service. Or increase our fraud detection rates by 20% by allowing our fraud investigators to access case notes and communicate with colleagues while in the field. In each of these examples, the realisation of the benefits is directly related to the quality of the solution, not just its scope, cost and delivery date. The benefits of such solutions are not about cost saving by reducing the IT management costs, they are about doing things differently to make potentially huge differences to the business bottom line. They are strategic. I have heard of or seen many solutions to business problems fail to deliver the benefits they set out to simply because they don't work well enough. The effort required to use them outweighs the savings they were going to give, they miss fundamental steps in a process that required human involvement, they are simply confusing or cumbersome to use. All in all, they don't work well enough. The delivery of the technical solution of a business application is rarely the biggest risk to the success (the realisation of its benefits) of a project. It is more often that adoption of the solution that poses the biggest threat. And yet most projects focus on the risks of delivery, the scope, time and cost and mostly ignore the quality. User Centred Design and Agile project processes are seen as the remedy to this problem. They work from user needs, defining a minimum viable product and iterating based on user testing and, where possible, real usage data. Agile teams are designed to have an inverted authority structure to traditional teams. It is the people who do the work who tell the 'managers' what needs to be done, how long it will take and when it can be done. The managers are there to make decisions about priorities and to ensure that the 'doers' are able to get on and do. The team is empowered to make all the decisions about how things are implemented, where system components are standard enough to be commodities and where they should be custom built. They are expected to work with other teams to identify where there is commonality of technology and to see the 'bigger picture'. Project governance in this environment changes too. In traditional projects governance is about checking that delivery milestones and deadlines are hit (to the three project criteria of cost, time and scope) and making decisions about change. But now the important issues to govern are whether the quality will be good enough, will the benefits be realised. The Project Board's role is to ensure that there is sufficient rigour to reduce the risk that the project will fail because the quality of the project is not good enough. The Project Board must focus on ensuring that enough evidence is gathered to be confident that the system will work effectively, is usable and will be used. It should be reviewing the user data, obtained from data or direct user testing, that shows what impact design and scope changes on the ability of the project to deliver the intended benefits. They are then able to make informed decisions on whether to change the other constraints on the project, the cost and time. For example, when the project team report that a set of features will not make it into the initial delivery, the Project Board should ask how the lack of those features will impact on the take up of the system, the working practices of the users and the decommissioning of any systems that are currently in use. Changing the scope of a project will likely be because:

- the features were found to be unnecessary to the success of the project (they did not impact the benefits)
- the features are not achievable within the current constraints of the project

Of course, because projects are developed in iterations, a change in scope may simply be a temporary thing - pushing features back into a later iteration, or simply delivering a cut down version of the feature until a later iteration. The Project Board can then give the Project Team direction on any additional evidence. They would like to support their assessment of the impact of the scope change, the relative priority of the remaining features and if necessary allocate more time or money to the project. Quite often projects are undertaken within the wider context of a programme of related projects. Managing a group of interdependent projects is traditionally done with a Programme Manager, reporting to a Programme Board. A group of suitably authorised people who have the job of ensuring that the multiple projects all join up. When we commoditised and outsourced system provision Programme Management was about keeping track of various projects and ensuring that the delivery milestones (that are often aligned to inter-project dependencies) are met. This is an essentially a top down approach - attempting to simplify the problem of interdependency by setting firm contracts. The Agile way is to not to retry and simplify the interdependency problem and solve it from above, but rather to tackle it using open communication allowing them to be solved within the project teams. This approach means that compromises and work-arounds can be reached between the project teams rather than imposed from above. Because they would be worked out by the teams they are more likely to be both workable and sensible utilising the detailed knowledge of the projects and their features. This changes Programme Management from a process of interdependency to one that ensures that communication between teams happens and is effective. And the role of the Programme Board is no longer about checking that various projects are delivering to milestones, but is concerned with making sure that the right projects are being progressed. The identification, prioritisation and 'green lighting' of the most important projects is a far more useful use of a Programme Board than trying to resolve interdependency issues. The selection of projects for progression will be affected by many factors from pragmatic to political, but the primary driver for deciding which projects to work on should be their contribution to the strategic goals of the organisation itself. This approach draws straight lines from the organisation's goals and objectives through to what actually gets delivered, while still enabling design and scoping decisions to be made from the bottom up. So, we can see that as technology has become of strategic importance to organisations again (just as it was 30 years ago), we must change the way we manage and govern technology projects. We must move away from techniques driven by top down, manage-to-the-contract, approaches to ones that enable adaptability and embrace change. Luckily, the principles are simple and clear:

- allow the people closest to the problems to make the decisions on how to fix them
- provide those people with all the relevant information
- make sure that they talk to each other and work to solve the same problems
- focus on the real risks to project success, not just the delivery problems
- use direction rather than instruction to ensure that the right things are being done

PERSPECTIVES PART 2: THE WAY OF THE PUBLIC SECTOR IT PROJECT LEADER

By Martin Webster MBA IEng MIET MBCS CITP

Martin and I met over 12 years ago when we worked together at Leicestershire County Council in the hey day of e-government. Delivering an IT project in the public sector was tough back then. It is even tougher now given the climate of austerity. The truth is delivering change in the public sector has always been tough because the problems the sector is trying to solve are complex and multi-faceted. In 2014 Martin become the Head of Oracle Applications at Arriva. Arriva is one of the largest providers of passenger transport in Europe, employing more than 55,000 people and delivering more than 2.2 billion passenger journeys across 14 European countries each year. Before he left Leicestershire County Council I asked him for some thoughts on the qualities required in a project manager delivering solutions for wicked problems faced by the public sector. Martin has more than 20 years' experience in project delivery and business change. He writes regularly about project management, leadership and business change on his website http://www.leadershipthoughts.com, which has about 30000 subscribers. Including me. DP

WHILST THE BASIC TENETS OF project management are simple managing projects is not straightforward. Indeed project management today goes beyond the complicated and needs a new breed of project leader. One who successfully solves *complex* problems because they are *aware* of the environment in which they operate. The state of public finances means we have a finite level of economic resource to deliver our services. And when budgets are severely cut service reduction inevitably follows. But we must continue to enable business change and remain competitive. How is this possible? Can the problem be solved? In truth we cannot solve this problem. It is too complex! It is a **wicked problem**. Rather *we* must learn to operate in a different world and make the best of it we can.

My team's job was to solve problems. However, many business managers come to us with solutions in mind. For instance, implementing a new business application or developing a website. Whilst the manager may not completely comprehend the problem they do have an answer. The problem is resolvable since there is little uncertainty. In contrast, some business leaders have much difficulty articulating what needs to be done. The problem is complex and often intractable. Invariably these are wicked problems and characterised by uncertainty, the absence of an answer, and no clear relationship between cause and effect. An example of a wicked problem is delivering a response to antisocial behaviour. For instance, the government's "troubled families" project aims to reduce public spending by helping households who have financial and social problems. This includes the challenges of worklessness, antisocial behaviour, and truancy. In a nutshell the troubled families project is about preventing problems not fixing them. The great challenge for business leaders and project managers who carry out the vision is enormous. We cannot facilitate such change using traditional approaches. Since uncertainty and ambiguity are the way of the world today we must break from the norm and learn to manage uncertainty rather than attempt to remove it. I suspect most project managers will be uncomfortable with this.

What's more, I venture that many project managers would wish to start their projects from a clean sheet of paper. That's to be expected if the problem were *tame*. For example, the new website I spoke of earlier or introducing a storage area network into the IT infrastructure. However, a wicked problem has no known solution. Multiple partial solutions are always needed. Therefore we must put aside our inclination for elegance and opt for **clumsy solutions**.

Troubled families is about doing something very different. Something that hasn't been done before and where there is no perfect solution. You may ask, "What has this got to do with project management?" And I will say, "Everything!" But first I must briefly introduce a model of cultural theory. Cultural theory offers a way of thinking about change in organisations. Simply put it provides four ways of organising social life in groups

- Hierarchists – those who see successful change relying on leadership, rules, expertise, and regulation

- Individualists – people who see successful change as a result of individual initiative or competition

- Egalitarians – see successful change driven from the bottom up through collective action and shared values

- Fatalists – think successful change is unlikely

The important point for project managers is that these are cultural preferences. Much of the time they matter little. However, in times of change and uncertainty—where project managers operate—each of these characteristics come into to play. Indeed there is often tension between each group. Clumsy solutions consider each perspective. For instance, the hierarchists may insist that data are stored in an electronic document and records management system whereas the individualist may advocate the use of a line-of-business system. In contrast, the egalitarian takes the collective view. But a clumsy approach does what is needed to make some progress. Leading imperfect change can propel an organisation forward. And in developing these new clumsy solutions we need to have an understanding of how people work.

In 2012 I attended a very entertaining presentation on leadership by Professor Keith Grint. He spoke of three forms of authority and three different approaches to power

1. Command (physical power)

2. Management (rational power)

3. Leadership (emotional power)

Coercive or physical power is needed in crises. For example, when a problem or situation threatens the viability of a project. Decisive action is needed and people respond to a call to action. Project managers use rational power to deal with problems of compliance. For instance, when a service provider isn't performing. The project manager's role is to solve puzzles for which there are always answers. Wicked problems are different because they cannot be solved by the individual. Solving wicked problems is about engaging people and working together in a common purpose. Wicked problems and their clumsy solutions demand a different kind of project manager. It seems to me that the project manager and most literature has focused too much on managing projects—focusing on the rational—whilst neglecting the human side of business and technological change. Today's project manager needs to be cognisant of the role of leadership in project management. Indeed today's project manager needs a better understanding of their social setting.

Some maintain that a project manager must instil regulation and provide stability in an uncertain and changing world. Accordingly it is reasonable to think that an awareness of task complexity concerns planning, monitoring and controlling time, cost, and quality expectations. However, this is only part of the picture. The project manager must develop an awareness for complexity and context to make sense of a problem and to construct a plan of worthy tasks. This cannot be done in isolation since there is only so much a person notices, expects or can handle. For the IT project manager this is crucial. You may be expert in your domain. However, you cannot influence outcomes when you have no knowledge of a situation or fact.

A strong stakeholder awareness is an essential competence of the project manager. Use it to understand those who have a stake in your project, to create productive relationships, and influence their views. However, your job is not simply to influence stakeholders' focus and priorities but to help them to contribute to increased knowledge, understanding and skills, and to build relationships between stakeholders.

Self-awareness is vital to the development of a leader. It's about how we are perceived by others. It's about understanding how our behaviours affect people. The self-important project manager can't see how they sabotage themselves and their project because they focus on their needs and feelings and not those of stakeholders. They don't encourage feedback because it never seems relevant. It is in the character of wise leaders to have a great appetite for feedback. And this is still the best way to gain an awareness of yourself.

Perspective awareness is inextricably related to self-awareness. However, it's not limited to an awareness of your own perspective—point of view—or even those of stakeholders. Rather it is recognising that your actions are interpreted through the filters of different perspectives. Only when you are aware of these differences may you begin to deal with the tensions associated with differing perspectives and construct goals in which everyone is reasonably comfortable. Indeed it may be possible to accomplish something! Moreover, exploring different angles and asking people with very different perspectives for their views on things makes much sense and is essential when dealing with complexity.

We are part way through a long period of public spending cuts with no end of austerity in sight. Whilst there may still be opportunity to cut costs in administration and back office or for re-engineering services this will not see us through. We need to rethink what we do and we need solutions that work in the difficult world we are now moving. In developing solutions the IT project manager will need to understand how people work. Knowledge of systems and processes is no longer sufficient. My expectations of the IT project leader are a self-awareness and a recognition of the part everyone plays in solving complex problems. Moreover, they must know how to create propitious conditions and how to influence people.

LEARN TO ASCEND BIG DATA'S WUTHERING HEIGHTS

'I read all sorts of things. There's so much
to learn.'

Christian

China Crisis

N IT PROJECT MANAGER IS flying across the desert in a hot air balloon when he realizes he is lost. He calls down to a man below him riding a camel and asks where he is. The man replies, "You're 40 degrees and 10 minutes, 19.3 seconds north, 115 degrees, 9 minutes west, 165 metres above sea level, heading due west by north west."

"Thanks," replies the balloonist. "By the way, are you a data analyst?"

"Yes," replies the man, "how did you know?"

"Everything you told me was totally accurate, you gave me way more information than I needed and I still have no idea what I need to do."

"I'm sorry," replied the camel-riding analyst. "By the way, are you a Project Manager?" "Yes," said the balloonist, "how did you know?"

"Well," replied the analyst, "you've got no idea where you are, no idea what direction you're heading in, you got yourself into this fix by blowing a load of hot air, and now you expect me to get you out of it."

This is an old joke from the days when data warehousing was all the rage. Nowadays, big data is all the rage.

You can't read anything technology business related nowadays without coming across an article on big data. Data is the new natural resource and the Klondyke gold rush fever is taking place right now in the digital world. We live in two worlds; the physical one and the digital one. Our actions and body language in the digital world generates data. The government and big business are using it to understand what we need and what we will come to need so they can offer it to us. According to Forbes, the Big Data analytics market is worth a massive $125 billion! Why? Any organisation that can figure out what you need or desire before you know it and before a competitor knows it, will put themselves in a position where they will dominate the market. Anyone who can walk into an organisation and deliver a big data capability, is a valued asset. Big data has only come about because of development in the underlying information technology. This makes whoever is providing and delivering the ICT just as important as R&D, sales and marketing; business functions that traditionally viewed the IT organisation as a bunch of geeks wearing Iron Maiden tee shirts who play Dungeons and Dragons. Those days are gone. Big data technical SME are the Lionel Messi's of the digital games that are being played out between organisations competing in the digital space. These guys and gals are becoming participants in the multi level marketing game. They create the means to sell to anyone and, when combined with gamification, create the means to achieve 'sticky marketing'. But before any of that good stuff can happen, someone has to deliver the big data capability. Given the popularity of big data, it could be you one day.

Delivering a big data capability is not a project - it is a

programme consisting of many different types of IT projects, namely: networking; storage; hosting; integration; and applications development. You can't buy a piece of software called Big Data and then install it to do big data stuff. Big data is a combination of many different types of solutions converged together to create the capability. Each project in a big data transformation programme increments an organisation's capability to achieve the promises of big data. It requires many different methodologies to make it happen. From a managerial perspective, nothing short of best-in-class programme management, portfolio management and project management is required.

Big data is many things solution-wise. It has constantly evolved from the days of data warehousing. Because of the constant evolution, the management methodologies have to evolve too. So whatever I write now for the challenges facing anyone implementing big data scope, may not be relevant tomorrow. The evolution of big data reminds me of the career for Kate Bush. Kate Bush was tutored by Lindsey Kemp, the renowned mime artist and choreographer. Kate Bush has a soprano vocal range. Her songs are eclectic. They span the genres of rock, pop, and art rock. She has woven together many diverse influences, combining classical music and a wide range of folk sources. If ever there was a metaphor for a big data capability it would be the Kate Bush collection. The evolution of Kate Bush's musical career is free flowing, creative, flexible but thought through and disciplined at the same time. That is exactly how one should go about delivering a project within a tranche in a big data programme. The closest and most proven methodology I can think of is DSDM (Dynamic Systems Development Methodology). It's a method that has been around since the 90s. More than likely, it will be superceded by PRINCE2 Agile being launched by Axelos Q2 2015. What this chapter will do is take the DSDM framework, then contextualise it with the delivery of a big data capability in mind.

At the heart of the philosophy is a focus on early delivery of the benefits that big data can bring to the organisation. For the approach to work, there are some principles that the organisation needs to buy into.

WOWWOWWOW unbelievable

A focus on the needs of the organisation driving the demand for big data capability.

Always deliver on time

Empower the big data delivery team to take decisions. Big data delivery requires multi disciplinary and multi-skilled teams. Organisations that try to deliver big data using distinct functional teams organised into silos, will move slower on their journey than those who pull together as one team.

Active involvement of the right stakeholders from across organisation.

Big data delivery needs stakeholders from marketing, operations, ICT, finance, logistics, partners and customer services. Big data can involve integration into data sources from external organisations so they should be considered a key stakeholder.

No compromise on quality

If the storage holding the data is a poor solution, the programme will fail. If data quality is poor, the programme will fail. If the network is slow and flaky, the programme will fail. If the analytics software is buggy, the programme will fail.

Running up the big data hill incrementally and iteratively.

An increment is a step change in capability to deliver benefits to the organisation early. Essentially there are 4 increments in capability: ICT capability; exploration; codification; and incorporation. The chapter will focus on delivering the ICT capability. Run these increments sequentially and it could take years to deliver. Run them in parallel and you've got potential for chaos. Create the steps and you've got a stairway to the benefits. Successful big data delivery requires the organisation implementing it, to run up the stairs every time there is a need to increment big data capability. Each increment may consist of one or more projects. A set of these increments can be viewed as a tranche as per description in classical programme management. In a programme as complex as big data, the detail emerges later rather than sooner.

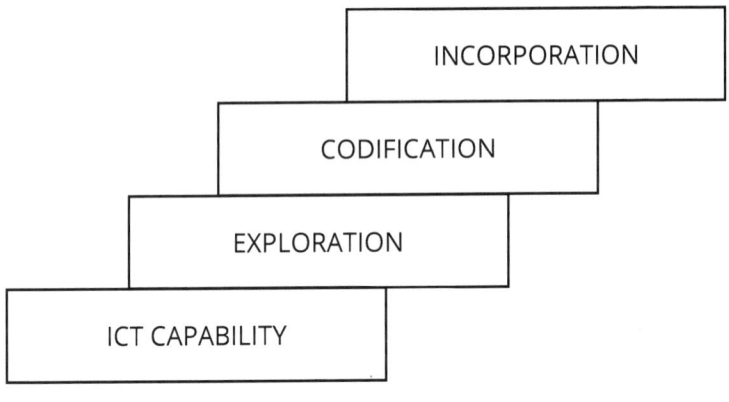

Showcase Control

Implementing big data is a costly and complex business. What makes it complex and costly? Big data projects deliver solutions that deal with a high volume of data, a wide variety of data, and high velocity of data. So the organisation must make plans and progression, that are visible to all. The viability of each project needs to be continually evaluated. You can use the DSDM project assessment questionnaire to quickly assess project viability. The PAQ is available from http://www.dsdm.org/product/project-approach-questionaire-paq.

Moving Through the Life-cycle

The DSDM method consists of the following phases. Each phase has a series of objectives and number of outputs. This chapter aims to contextualise the method for a big data programme. A detailed description of the roles that must be filled can be found athttp://www.dsdm.org/content/7-roles-and-responsibilities.

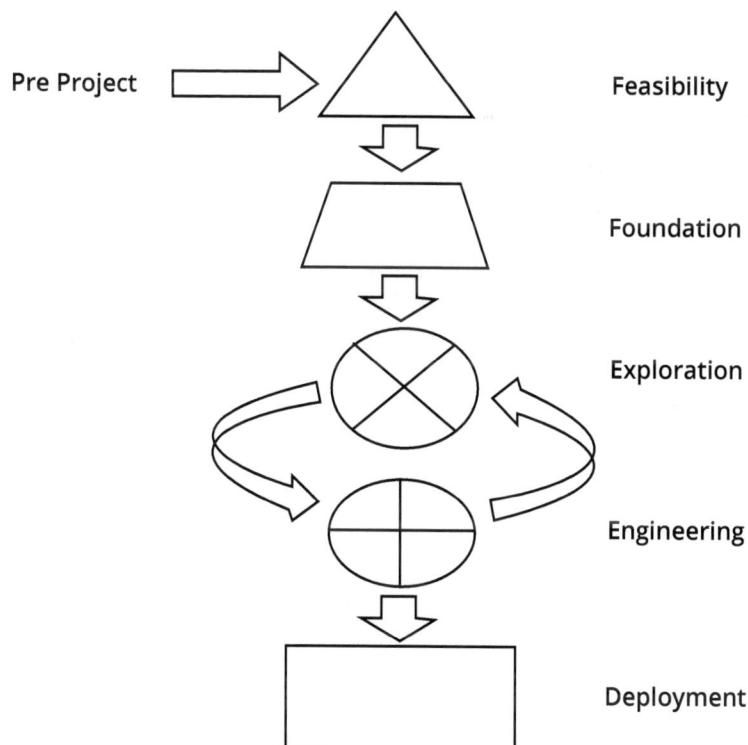

As the organisation moves through the life-cycle, the end result is an increment in big data capability. The deployment of these 4 capabilities, delivered by a big data programme, provides the organisation with the means to operationalise the use of big data. There are some ways of working, organisation and tooling that will further increase the speed and reduce risk. The subject matter would warrant chapters of their own to show benefits from a project and programme management perspective. However, it is important to make you aware of them as a potential accelerant. These capabilities are devops, continuous delivery and customer insight driven business process management. Using them on your big data creates efficient and effective work centres. To build a big data solution, imagine a virtual factory turning out virtual products. The products are big data ICT capability increments; the programme builds the factory; and the factory only remains opens when there is finance to run it.

Capability Delivered by the Programme	Description
ICT Capability	The compute, network, storage, software and services that form what is known as the big data tech stack.
Data exploration	People, organisation, tools and process to search for patterns in the data.
Codification	People, organisation, tools and process to take the learning from the pattern and codify into the business operations to act on the insight.
Integration	Integration of the output from codification into operational systems and process.

Pre Project Hounds of Love

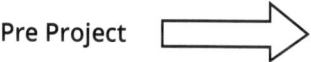

Pre Project

In today's organisation, a big data programme will form part of a portfolio of other programmes. They should all be aligned to achieve the organisation's strategic vision and outcomes. The aim of the pre-project phase is to formalise a proposal for a project within big data programme tranche. It needs to be placed in the context of future work or work currently being done by the organisation. For example, a big data solution nowadays will require cloud hosting. There may be a programme introducing cloud capability into the organisation. There may be a programme seeking to exploit the power of social media for permission marketing. Both of these programmes deliver capabilities symbiotic with implementing big data capability. So you can see a primary aim of the pre-project stage is to confirm the big data project in line with business strategy. If not, Frankie says, "Relax don't do it." Delivering big data capability requires an understanding of the problem that the organisation is trying to solve. Quite rightly, DSDM insists on identifying a business sponsor and business visionary who can make it happen. If not, listen to Frankie. Big data is a journey. Therefore, one of the first things to do is to sketch out a big data roadmap, based on: known business urgency that drives the demand for big data capability; known capacity; available budgets; known skill sets; and the organisation's appetite for risk.

Feasibility, A Deeper Data Driven Understanding

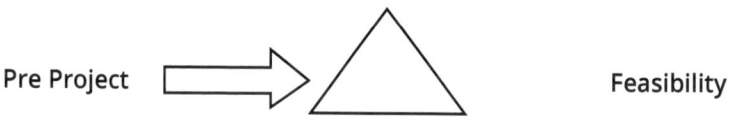

Pre Project   Feasibility

A big data project is a risky proposition. To the uninitiated, there is a belief that once all the data is fed into a database for complex event processing (CEP), the rules engineer will magically tell the organisation what it needs to know but does not know in plain English. It takes a lot of effort to get to that point. The feasibility stage is the point where the question asked is, 'Is the project that's delivering the ICT increment worth the effort?' Big data is a complex business so there may not be a solution. If this is the case, then stop. Big data is all about data management. A feasibility study needs to assess the organisation's current position on the maturity model or data management in a big data context. If exploration, codification or integration maturity is low, then just implementing the ICT capability alone won't fix that. The outputs from the ICT portfolio will be a white elephant. Feasibility is the stage where organisation costs and governance are described.

One Last Look Around the Foundations House

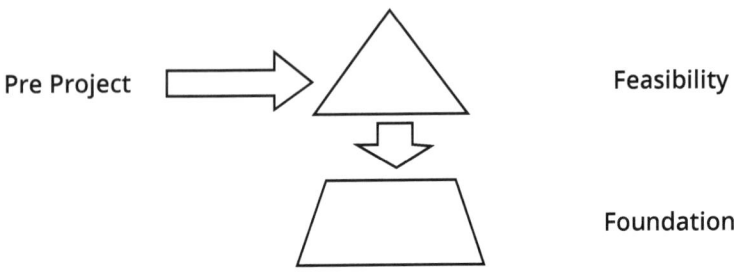

Pre Project   Feasibility

Foundation

During foundation stage, requirements are base lined. The quality of these requirements depends on how they are elicited. The most effective analysis exercise seeks to understand the problems the organisation is trying to solve with big data. That means having analysts and designers that have an excellent understanding of how big data solves problems for specific industries. This analysis helps identify the business processes involved in the capability increments, and information required by those increments to solve the problem. This in turn points the organisation in the right direction towards the data it needs to answer the questions it wants answers to. Foundation contains the activities to define the solution's technical reference model and solution architecture. Governance is established during the foundation phase. A schedule for exploration and engineering is baselined.

Experiment IV Exploration

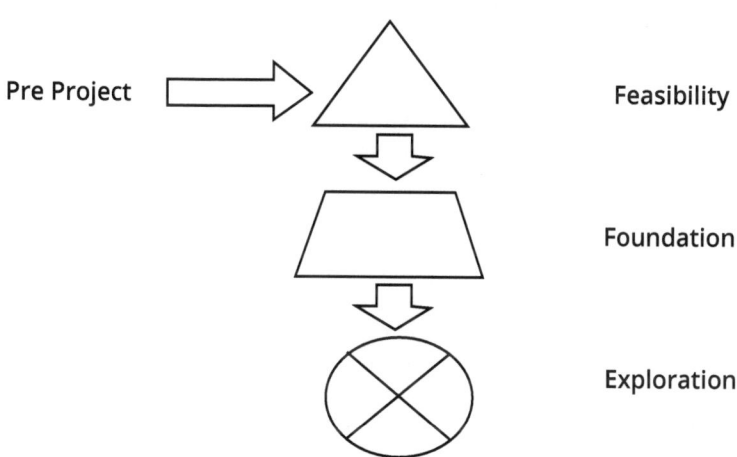

Exploration is a constantly rolling assembly line to cyclically deep dive the detailed business requirements then turn the art of the possible into the possible. Exploration results in just enough built ICT capability to demonstrate that the ICT capability increment will deliver what is needed. Logical outputs from this stage are outlined below.

Data streams	This is the data that needs to flow into the big data solution. They can come from social media, operational data stores, ERP applications, data sensors from the internet of things, smart phones, digital body language, to name a few.
Events	A big data solution contains lots of hardware and software that needs to run like clockwork. The solution needs to be configured to tell the people looking after it how the machinery is doing. These events come from infrastructure, network, security and applications.
Input Handlers	An input handler is a solution component that takes events and data streams, then feeds into the big data processing plant.
Adapters	Data streams and events come in many different formats and protocols. Adapters provide a pipe with translation so the input handlers can do their thing.
Databases	Databases hold all the data and rules to process and store streams and events.
Rules Engine	The rules engine takes the data streams and business, then correlates into information the organisation can use.
Event Router	The event router is the nerve centre which takes the interesting stuff produced by the rules engine and sends it to an output handler.
Output handler	The output handler is the mechanism for work flowing the interesting stuff into the wider organisation.

Rolling the Engineering Ball

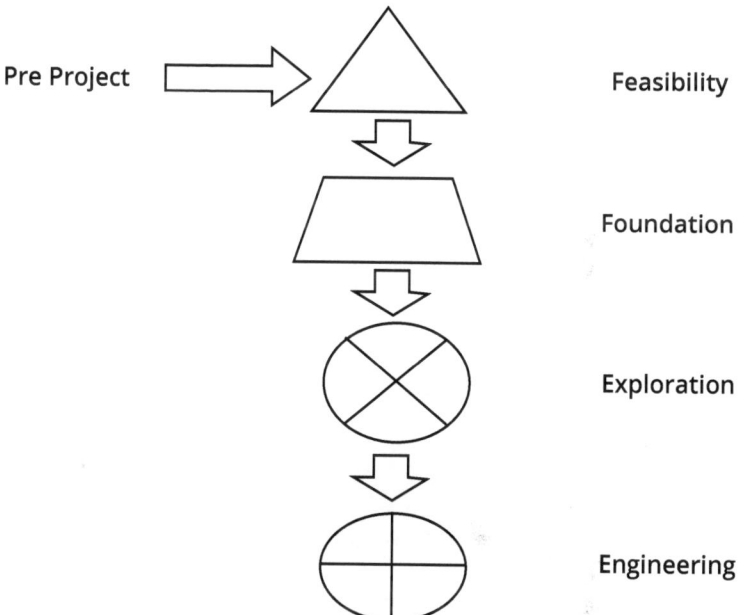

The engineering phase takes the build from exploration and makes it production capable; it makes it supportable and useable. Engineering ensures the build has the necessary level of performance, capacity, security, supportability and maintainability. If the programme delivery architecture exhibits a high level of performance against devops and continuous delivery maturity model, then transition into deployment will be slick. Otherwise, it won't be and should be considered an intolerable risk.

Warm and Soothing Deployment

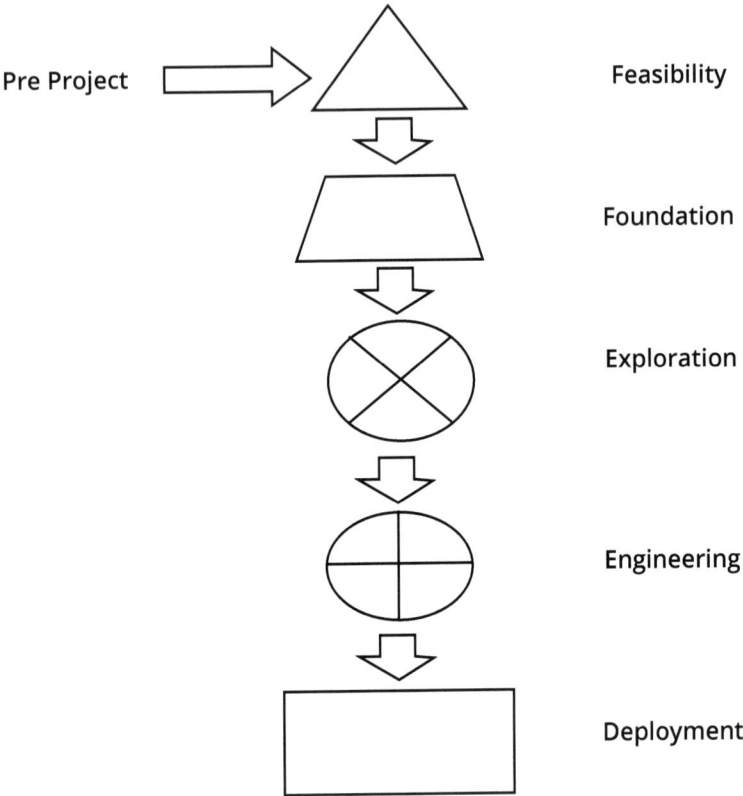

Deployment sees the project deliver a build of a big data ICT capability increment into live use. It is all the activities you tend to find on any major change involving lots of complicated ICT. Kind of begs the question, 'So what exactly is being deployed ICT capability-wise?'

Network	The network infrastructure and configuration.
Interfaces	Interfaces into the digitalsphere. Interfaces into the internet of things Interfaces into everything as a service (Xaas) Interfaces into internal systems
Applications	Big data application stack
Reporting	Reporting tools Visualisation tools
Analytics	Analytical tools for quantitative and qualitative analysis Analytical tools for sentiment and predictive analysis Analytical tools for protecting security and stability
Databases	Databases for holding data and business rules. Database for holding structured and unstructured data
Infrastructure	Security and physical infrastructure

The aim of the game is to increment capability in the above after completing one cycle of the method. To accelerate, run multiple exploration and engineering stages in parallel. It all depends on the boundaries - unless, that is, you think like Kate Bush.

'That's what all art's about - a sense of moving away from boundaries that you can't in real life. Like a dancer is always trying to fly, really - to do something that's just not possible. But you try to do as much as you can within those physical boundaries.'

Kate Bush

ABOUT THE AUTHOR

Donato Piccinno is a MBA graduate and accredited project manager with 20 years cumulative experience in FTSE 500 companies delivering focused business change, applications and infrastructure projects. He delivers a broad spectrum of technology propositions managed within client expectation alongside management of organisational change. He lives in Leicester with his wife Catherine and three children Luca, Rosa and Nico. Beyond family, his loves are food, film, football, 20th century popular music and retro video games.

COMING SOON

The Ultimate IT Project Manager II : Master of Projects

On the day an IT project goes live the project manager will be pacing the floor like an expectant father outside a delivery room. Except one guy I know Scott Mason. Scott Mason is the only project manager I know out of the hundreds I know that went on holiday the day one of his IT projects went live. It was planned so meticulously and so perfectly he'd done himself out of a job. Enter Scott Mason, Master of Projects. Learn the secret in The Ultimate IT Project Manager II : Master of Projects by the man himself, Scott 'Master of Projects' Mason.

'I'd rather regret doing something than not doing something.'

James Hetfield Metallica

Printed in Great Britain
by Amazon